MW00783614

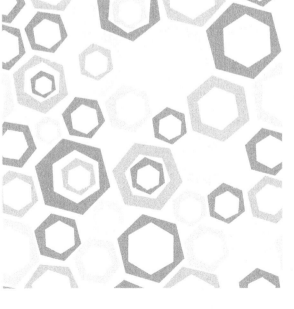

Beyond Repeat After Me

Marla Tritch Yoshida

Teaching Pronunciation to English Learners

tesol press

This book has a
companion website. Go to
www.tesol.org/BeyondRepeatAfterMe
for additional resources.

R
online
resources

www.tesol.org/bookstore

TESOL International Association
1925 Ballenger Avenue
Alexandria, Virginia, 22314 USA
www.tesol.org

Director of Publishing: Myrna Jacobs
Copy Editor: Elizabeth Pontiff
Production Editor: Kari S. Dalton
Cover Design: Citrine Sky Design
Design and Layout: Capitol Communications, LLC
Printing: Gasch Printing, LLC

Copyright © 2016 by TESOL International Association
All rights reserved. Copying or further publication of the contents of this work are not permitted
without permission of TESOL International Association, except for limited "fair use" for
educational, scholarly, and similar purposes as authorized by U.S. Copyright Law, in which case
appropriate notice of the source of the work should be given. Permission to reproduce material
from this book must be obtained from www.copyright.com, or contact Copyright Clearance
Center, Inc., 222 Rosewood Drive, Danvers, MA 01923, 978-750-8400.

Every effort has been made to contact copyright holders for permission to reprint borrowed
material. We regret any oversights that may have occurred and will rectify them in future printings of
this work.

ISBN 9781942799467
Library of Congress Control Number 2016945358

Contents

Preface

Welcome! Teaching English pronunciation can be a challenge. It requires some technical knowledge about phonology; an ability to predict the problems students may have; plus a good supply of strategies, tools, and activities to help students understand and practice. Teaching pronunciation implies that the teacher can provide a good pronunciation model for students to follow, give explanations and demonstrations of things the students need to know, and lead them through a series of practice activities to help them make their new pronunciation automatic.

There are many good books about teaching pronunciation. So why do we need another one? First, all the existing books are simply *books*. They are written on paper, representing sounds only through written symbols and descriptions. They may come with a CD with recordings of exercises, but sound is not an integral part of the "story." Pronunciation is a unique topic that really needs sound as part of the presentation. With recent innovations, authors can now provide explanations that combine words and sounds.

Second, books and articles about teaching pronunciation have almost always been written with an audience of mainly native speakers of English in mind. Besides assuming that readers have an instinctive knowledge of the sounds and "music" of English, most books don't touch on many issues that teachers who have learned English as a second language want and need to know about—questions that may not occur to native-speaker teachers. This book has been written with special consideration of the needs and interests of nonnative speakers of English, who are, after all, the majority of English teachers worldwide. (Canagarajah, 1999). I assume that most of these teachers are working in **English as a foreign language** (EFL) situations, that is, in countries where English is not a commonly spoken language and students have few chances to hear English in everyday life.

Of course, native speakers also need the same types of information and can benefit from an introduction to the system behind the sounds, the problems their students might have, and ideas about how to help students overcome these problems. After all, the details of pronunciation are an aspect of language that most native speakers are not consciously aware of.

What's in This Book?

I've tried to choose the topics related to pronunciation, phonology, and pedagogy that are most necessary for EFL or **English as a second language** (ESL) teachers to know about and to explain them simply and clearly. In this book, you will read about

- the pronunciation of American English: Both individual sounds and the musical aspects of pronunciation, such as **intonation**, **rhythm**, and **word stress**;
- typical problems that students may have in learning the pronunciation of English;
- some ways to teach pronunciation to your students in an interesting and meaningful way, including suggestions for teaching tools and types of activities.

The explanations and examples in this book are based on the pronunciation of **standard American English**. This is because it's the variety of English that I speak and the kind I've always taught, not because I think it has any superiority over other varieties of English. When it seems helpful, we'll also look at differences between standard American English and other varieties.

This book contains basic information about the pronunciation of English and suggestions for ways to introduce and practice sounds and other aspects of pronunciation. The accompanying website also contains sound recordings and video tutorials to supplement the text. When you see ▇ 🔊, go to www.tesol.org/beyondrepeatafterme to hear the audio recordings. There are also videos to accompany many of the chapters in this book. These videos repeat some of the basic information from the chapter, but with sound. By reading the text and watching the videos, I hope you'll be able to increase your understanding of how the English sound system works and get ideas for ways to help your students develop good pronunciation habits.

At the end of the book is a selection of resources that you might find interesting and helpful, as well as a glossary. The terms in the glossary are bolded the first time they appear in a chapter.

My Background

I'm a teacher. I've taught all aspects of English, including many, many pronunciation classes, for more than 25 years. I have a master's degree in **linguistics** from California State University, Fresno, where my coursework gave me a foundation in phonology, along with linguistics in general. For the past 14 years I've been teaching in the ESL and **Teaching English as a Foreign Language** (TEFL) programs at the University of California, Irvine Extension (UCI). I've taught the Teaching Pronunciation Skills course that is part of UCI Extension's TEFL Accelerated Certificate Program for more than a decade to students from many countries. The topic choices in this book are based in part on my TEFL students' insightful questions, comments, and stories about their teaching situations and experiences. Thank you, TEFL students!

I'm a native speaker of English, but I've also been a learner of other languages, including German, Japanese, Spanish, French, Latin, Russian, and Sanskrit. This is not to say that I speak all those languages well, but I've studied them. I know what it's like not to be able to hear the difference between unfamiliar new sounds, to struggle to pronounce them, and to feel satisfaction when I finally can (if that ever happens). I've experienced language classes where the teacher valued pronunciation and taught it well and others where pronunciation was basically ignored.

I know that the thought of teaching pronunciation can be intimidating, whether English is your native language or not, but it will be much less scary if you equip yourself with some basic knowledge and ideas for teaching techniques and activities. I hope you find this book helpful in reaching that goal.

CHAPTER 1

Introduction to Teaching Pronunciation

There are many things that English teachers need to fit into their limited class time—grammar, vocabulary, speaking, listening, reading, and writing. Pronunciation often gets pushed to the bottom of the list. Many teachers say there's just not enough time to teach pronunciation. Students often think it isn't that important—after all, it won't be tested on their college entrance exams!

But if students need or want to speak English understandably, pronunciation *is* important. The days when learners only needed reading and writing skills in English are past. Depending on where you teach, many or all of your students will need to speak and understand English in real life to communicate with both native speakers of English and speakers of other languages. Even if students' grammar and vocabulary are strong, if their pronunciation isn't easy to understand, their communication will fail. We owe it to our students to give them the tools they'll need to be able to communicate successfully in English.

What Are Your Goals?

Most teachers agree that they want their students to be able to speak English with good pronunciation. But what does that mean? What *is* good pronunciation?

One answer might be "sounding like a native speaker." However, this answer is problematic for a couple of reasons. First, it's hard to define what "a native speaker" sounds like. There are so many varieties of English and so much variation within each type that it's almost impossible to define that elusive "ideal" pronunciation. Trying to sound like a native speaker is like throwing a ball at a moving target—difficult, frustrating, and likely to fail.

Another problem is that very few learners will ever be able to sound exactly like their preferred pronunciation model, no matter how hard or how long they try. This is especially true for adult learners and for those who don't constantly hear English in their daily lives. Whatever the definition, speaking with nativelike pronunciation is not an easy goal to reach.

A more realistic goal, and one that more and more teachers and researchers recommend, is *intelligible* pronunciation—speaking in a way that most listeners, both native and nonnative speakers, can understand without too much effort or confusion. It's not a bad thing if you can still tell that the speaker comes from a particular country or region, as long as the speaker can be easily understood by others (Celce-Murcia, Brinton, & Goodwin, 2010).

Still, while it's not practical to set our goal impossibly high, we also can't afford to set it too low. It's not helpful for students to become too complacent and to believe that their pronunciation is fine when, in fact, it may not be easily understood by anyone other than their own teacher and classmates. To be truly intelligible to a wide range of listeners, and not just to willing listeners of their own language background, speakers need to come fairly close to some kind of a recognized standard, whether it's one of the major native-speaker varieties or a nonnative variety of pronunciation that is easily understood by listeners from many backgrounds. As responsible teachers, we must make sure we don't set the bar too low.

We should also realize that English teachers, both native and nonnative speakers, are often *not* the best judges of whether someone's pronunciation is intelligible. Many **English as a second language** (ESL) or **English as a foreign language** (EFL) teachers can understand their students' speech when people in the wider world can't; in fact, it sometimes seems that we teachers can understand practically anything. We're used to inaccurate pronunciation. We know what students are going through and how hard they're trying. We're on their side and *want* to understand them, while a future employer or a cashier at Starbucks might not try so hard. Nonteachers are a tough audience (Lane, 2010).

Accuracy and Fluency

We often think of pronunciation teaching in terms of helping students achieve accurate pronunciation so that their production of sounds, stress, rhythm, and intonation begins to match an ideal pattern. But **accuracy** is only one part of good pronunciation. **Fluency** in producing sounds and other aspects of pronunciation is equally important. The two don't always go together. For example, many students learn to produce a new sound correctly when they're concentrating carefully and saying it alone or in a single word. When they need to use that same sound in conversation, however, it's much more difficult to keep producing it correctly—they can't pronounce the sound *fluently*. After all, in real-world speaking, pronunciation is just one among many things that students have to think about. Vocabulary, grammar, the ideas they want to express, and the appropriate degree of politeness and formality also occupy their attention.

It's hard to use pronunciation accurately and fluently at the same time. Because of this, when we're practicing pronunciation, we should include some activities that emphasize pronunciation fluency—speaking smoothly and easily, even if not all the sounds are perfect—along with activities that emphasize accuracy—producing sounds correctly. Both accuracy and fluency are important in pronunciation, just as they are in speaking in general, and both deserve attention and practice.

Trends in Teaching Pronunciation: The Pendulum Swings

Over the years, styles of language teaching have changed greatly, and the same is true of teaching pronunciation. In some time periods, teaching pronunciation has been considered extremely important, while at other times it hasn't been given much attention at all. Trends in teaching pronunciation are like a swinging pendulum—the emphasis goes from one extreme to the other.

Until recently, the focus in pronunciation teaching was almost entirely on producing individual sounds and words correctly; not much attention was given to features such as **intonation** and **rhythm**. (You'll read about these things in Chapters 8 to 12.) In the last 20 years or so, however, teachers and researchers have begun to realize the importance of these

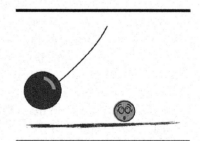

Figure 1.1. Pendulum.

"musical" aspects of pronunciation and to emphasize them more strongly in teaching (Celce-Murcia et al., 2010; Goodwin, 2001). Some scholars have gone so far as to claim that teaching individual sounds is not so important, and intonation, stress, prominence, and rhythm should be emphasized above all (Lane, 2010; Celce-Murcia et al., 2010; Gilbert, 2008).

It seems more practical, though, to realize that no single aspect of pronunciation can stand on its own. Our students can benefit from learning about both individual sounds and the musical aspects of pronunciation, and we need to find a balance between these two areas. The pendulum of teaching trends might keep swinging, but we don't have to let it knock us down. Choose methods and activities that combine both aspects of pronunciation so that the combination works best for you and your students. (For a more complete discussion of the history of pronunciation teaching methods, see Celce-Murcia et al., 2010, Chapter 1.)

What Affects Pronunciation Learning?

Many things contribute to learning pronunciation, from students' ages, motivation, and personality—which depend on the learners themselves—to the quality of the teaching and the students' first language—which are outside factors.

The Age of the Learner

We've all observed how easily babies and very young children learn languages. They just seem to absorb the sounds and words they hear around them and, little by little, learn to imitate them accurately. **Linguists** call this time in a child's life, lasting up to the age of about 12 to 14 years, the **critical period for language acquisition**. Children can learn the sounds of language more naturally than adults and can approach native speaker pronunciation, but only if they are surrounded by the language and have many chances to hear its pronunciation. Young children who hear English only a couple of hours a week lose much of their learning advantage.

Effective pronunciation learning is not limited to young children, however. Older children and adults have their own strengths and can also learn pronunciation well, even if they never sound quite like native speakers. Adults are better able to set goals and to practice purposefully. They can understand more abstract explanations and analyze how sounds are produced and how the melody and rhythm of a language sound. Adults should not give up the hope of having easily intelligible pronunciation; they just have to reach their goal in a different way than children.

Motivation

Learners in any subject area tend to make more progress if they *want* to learn. No teacher can force students to learn if they're not motivated. A proverb says, "You can lead a horse to water, but you can't make him drink." This also applies to teaching pronunciation. We can provide information and many chances to practice, but we don't have the power to change our students' pronunciation for them. They have to want to do it and be willing to do the work themselves.

Three general sets of goals or desires have been suggested that can motivate students in language learning (Celce-Murcia et al., 2010, p. 21):

- Learners want to be accepted into a group that uses the language. The group might still recognize the learners as "outsiders," but they can function well in the group. This is sometimes called **integrative motivation**.
- They want to be accepted as real members of the group. They don't want to be thought of as "outsiders." This is called **assimilative motivation**.
- They want to be able to use the language to reach a goal: To get a job, to conduct business, to pass a test, or to travel easily in a foreign country. This is called **instrumental motivation**.

If we recognize our students' goals in learning English, we can help motivate them by showing them how improving their pronunciation will help them reach their goals.

Personality and Aptitude

No two people are alike. We each have our own personality, talents, strengths, and weaknesses. These factors can affect how people learn pronunciation.

Teachers sometimes assume that more outgoing learners will be able to learn pronunciation better than shyer students, and there may be some truth to this. Confident students might speak more and be more willing to try new sounds, and this extra practice could help them improve their pronunciation. However, this improvement is certainly not guaranteed. Some outgoing students may be producing a lot of language, but they may also be jumping ahead without paying attention to the accuracy of their pronunciation. If listeners are impressed by their fluency and accept their imperfect pronunciation, they have no way to know that they need to improve.

Some more introverted students might actually be thinking carefully about sounds and practicing "within themselves," even if they don't speak much in class. Don't underestimate the quiet students. Appreciate the strengths and possibilities of all your students, and encourage everyone. All students can learn and improve in their own way.

Another aspect of personality that can affect pronunciation is the degree to which a person is willing or able to change the way he or she sounds. Most of us have been speaking and listening to language in the same, familiar way since we learned to talk. Our voice and our pronunciation are a central part of the way we see ourselves. It can be uncomfortable, and possibly even frightening, to try out unfamiliar sounds and melodies of language. For some people this process seems like a small bump in the road, but for others, it's a serious roadblock.

Finally, some people seem to have more of an aptitude or talent for learning language or imitating pronunciation than others. We say that some people "have a good ear" for language. Of course, this is something that is almost impossible to define or measure. What seems like a natural talent may be partly due to special motivation, encouragement from parents or teachers, or growing up in an environment where there are many opportunities to hear and learn other languages. In fact, there's no magical ability possessed by some people but not others that determines whether someone can be a successful language learner. As teachers, we need to believe that everyone has an ability to learn pronunciation. Then we need to give all our students the help they need to do it well.

Methods and Quality of Teaching

So far I've discussed factors that depend on the learners themselves, but there are also outside factors that affect pronunciation learning. The kind of teaching students have experienced, both in amount and quality, has a strong influence on their learning. Have they received a lot of training in pronunciation, only a little, or perhaps almost none at all? How much practice have they had? Was it effective practice using a variety of activities or entirely "repeat after me" without effective feedback from the teacher? Were the teachers interested in pronunciation, or did they consider it to be only unnecessary fluff? Is it even possible that their past teachers have given them false information or provided an extremely inaccurate model? The quality of teaching that students receive certainly affects the quality of their learning.

Exposure to the Target Language

Students' pronunciation learning is also affected by how much English they have a chance to hear in their daily lives. Learners who live in an English-speaking country where they are constantly surrounded by the language will be more familiar with the sounds and melodies they're trying to imitate than those who have few chances to hear spoken English—perhaps only during English classes for a few hours each week.

The Influence of the Learner's Language

A learner's first language (often referred to as the **L1**) has a strong influence on the way he or she learns the pronunciation of a second language (referred to as the **L2**). Often this influence is helpful, such as when some sounds are very similar in the two languages. For example, knowing how to pronounce /m/ in one language makes it easy for a learner to pronounce /m/ in another language.

However, learners' pronunciation habits in their first language can also make it more difficult for them to pronounce sounds in the new language that don't exist in their L1 or that are used in a different way. This influence is called **native language interference** or **language transfer**.

Effects of Differences Between First Language and Second Language

What happens when learners hear and try to pronounce strange, new sounds in a new language? These types of problems often occur:

Merging. When learners hear unfamiliar sounds in a new language, they tend to interpret the sounds of the new language in terms of the categories of their original language. The learner's brain may hear two sounds as being the same when they're actually considered separate sounds in the new language. This is called merging and leads to pronunciation errors. When our brains and ears can't tell the difference between two similar sounds, we tend to pronounce both of them in the same way. For example, many languages don't have separate vowel sounds like the ones in *reach* (/iy/) and *rich* (/ɪ/). Speakers of these languages may merge the two sounds and pronounce them both in the same way.

Substitution. When learners hear a new sound that doesn't match any of the sounds they know, they often substitute a familiar sound that is somewhat similar and easier for them to produce. For example, the first sound in *think* and *three* is found in relatively few languages in the world. Speakers of languages that don't have this sound often substitute /s/, /f/, or /t/ so that *think* sounds like *sink, fink,* or *tink*.

The effect on intelligibility. The processes of substitution and merging can cause serious problems for learners' intelligibility. When listeners expect to hear one sound but actually hear a different one, communication can break down. Even when teachers make learners aware of what's happening, it's difficult not to fall into one of these traps.

Problems with Individual Words

So far we've been thinking about pronunciation problems that are very general—they affect all the words with a particular sound or combination of sounds. However, sometimes specific words can cause pronunciation problems. Two causes of this are described here.

Spelling. English has many words with irregular or unpredictable spellings, and this can lead students to mispronounce those words. For example, if students learn the words *rain, plain,* and *maintain,* they will naturally assume that the letters *ain* must represent /eyn/. Then if they see the written word *mountain,* they may mistakenly pronounce it /mawnteyn/. Since students often meet words first in their written form, this can lead to incorrect pronunciation of many words.

Borrowed words. Many languages have borrowed words from English, adapting their pronunciation to fit the sound system of the borrowing language. (Sometimes the meanings of the words have also changed, but that's a separate issue.) For example, Table 1.1 shows some Japanese words borrowed from English and the sound changes they've undergone in the process.

We might think that knowing words that have been borrowed from English into the student's native language would make it easier to learn those words in English, and this is often true with word meanings. However, familiarity with these borrowed words can actually make it harder for learners to pronounce the words correctly in English if they assume that the pronunciation is the

Table 1.1. Japanese words borrowed from English.

Japanese word	Comes from this English word	Main sound changes
ジュース /ʤuusu/	juice /ʤuws/	Extra vowel is added after final consonant.
ガラス /garasu/	glass (the material) /glæs/	Extra vowel is added to split up consonant cluster. Extra vowel is added after final consonant. /l/ is replaced by /r/. Main vowel sound becomes /a/ instead of /æ/.
ハンバーガー /hambaagaa/	hamburger /ˈhæmbɚgɚ/	First vowel becomes /a/ instead of /æ/. In second and third syllables /ɚ/ becomes /aa/.

same in English as it is in their native language. This can cause misunderstandings. In an ESL class that I observed recently, the teacher asked a Japanese student about his favorite food. The student answered: /karee/. (The last vowel is similar to the vowel in *bed,* not *need.*) The teacher had no idea what the student meant, and it took several tries by the student and his classmates until the teacher recognized the word as *curry,* which in American English sounds like /ˈkəriy/. Teachers need to take special care to point out and practice words that are pronounced differently in English than their borrowed counterparts.

Fossilization

One of the most stubborn problems that we face in teaching pronunciation is **fossilization**. Fossilization is a process that occurs when a language learner progresses to a certain point but then has a hard time making further progress. For example, a student who has been studying English for many years might still not be able to differentiate /v/ as in *very* and /b/ as in *berry*; this error just seems to have become a permanent part of the person's English.

When students begin to learn a new language, they usually feel like they're making progress fairly quickly. Since they're starting from zero, any new knowledge feels like a great step forward. But after a while, students may find that their teacher and classmates understand them when they say /b/ instead of /v/, and so they lose their incentive for trying to say /v/ accurately. Their habit of saying /b/ for /v/ seems frozen in time, like a fossil of an ancient animal. Their mistake has become fossilized, and at this point, it becomes very hard to change.

Most students who have been learning English for a while have some fossilized pronunciations that are very hard to change or improve. So what can the teacher do to help crack up those fossils?

First, we have to recognize the fossilized forms and help students realize what error they're making and why it's causing a problem in understanding. Next, the learner has to be willing to put lots of effort into changing his or her pronunciation. It won't happen easily, and it won't happen at all if the student doesn't work at it. We need to provide information, opportunities for focused practice, and feedback to the learner on how well his or her pronunciation is reaching the goal. It's difficult to change fossilized pronunciation, but it's not impossible.

A more effective strategy in the long run is to try to prevent fossilization in the first place. Emphasize pronunciation at all levels of teaching, *especially for beginners*. It's easier to get learners started on the right path than to try to change their fossilized pronunciation later.

Hypercorrection

A less common pronunciation problem is **hypercorrection**, which means "too much correction." This happens when a student has learned a rule and tries to apply it, but applies it in too many cases. For example, a common error among Korean learners is to substitute /p/ for /f/, since /f/

doesn't exist in the Korean language. The predictable error is to say *pan* instead of *fan* or *punny* instead of *funny*. But sometimes a learner has been concentrating so hard on not saying /p/—on saying /f/ instead—that he or she sometimes says /f/ even when the correct sound actually should have been /p/. The speaker might say *fan* instead of *pan*.

Hypercorrection is a much less frequent and less serious source of error than fossilization—more like an occasional slip of the tongue than a long-term problem.

Learning to Hear

Being able to hear the difference between sounds in a new language is as important as being able to produce the sounds. However, hearing new sounds is not always easy. How we as adults hear sounds is a result of the way we've become used to hearing and classifying them in our own language. We don't "hear" and pay attention to all the speech sounds that come into our ears—only the ones that we're used to hearing.

When we were babies just learning our first language, our brains were ready to hear and accept the sounds of any language. Babies are talented that way. But as we grew up and became more firmly anchored in our own language, we got used to paying attention only to the sounds we needed to hear—the sounds of our own language that we heard around us every day. We didn't need to understand any other sounds, so our brains never built up the ability to identify and produce them. Our brains developed a **phonological filter** that lets us hear the sounds of our own language very efficiently but "filters out" and ignores unfamiliar, unnecessary sounds. As adults, when we hear new sounds, it's difficult to identify or understand them—we're still hearing through the filter of our first language.

To pronounce a new language well, we need to learn to hear again. We have to remove the filter that's hiding some of those new sounds so that our brains can hear, accept, analyze, and get ready to imitate them. The first step in doing this is to be aware of the filter and deliberately try to get past it. The next, ongoing step is to build up our awareness of new sounds, to pay close attention to what we hear, and to imitate the new sounds until we can do it accurately. We need to practice hearing sounds well, just as we need to practice pronouncing them well.

I sometimes tell students that to learn pronunciation well, they need to hear with their mouths and speak with their ears. That is, when they listen, they think to themselves, "How would I move my mouth to make that same sound? Where would I put my tongue and lips?" According to **phonologist** Peter Ladefoged (2006, p. 110), "It seems as if listeners sometimes perceive an utterance by reference to their own motor activities. When we listen to speech, we may be considering, in some way, what we would have to do in order to make similar sounds" (p. 110). The other side of this idea is that when we speak, we should constantly listen to what we're saying and compare it to what we know it should sound like. We monitor and self-correct our own pronunciation, using our ears to give feedback to our mouths about what we're doing right or wrong and what needs to be changed.

Feelings That Can Stand in the Way

Learners' feelings about language and pronunciation sometimes make it harder for them to develop accurate pronunciation, especially for students who don't have a choice about learning English. For example, junior high or high school students in EFL settings are sometimes reluctant to seem different from their peers by using new, "foreign-sounding" pronunciation. It's easier and more comfortable to pronounce words in a way that fits their own, familiar language patterns. They also may not see the point in concentrating on pronunciation. After all, English is just one school subject among many, and depending on their country and culture, they may not foresee a need to speak English in their future lives. If pronunciation isn't tested and doesn't count for part of their grade, why try?

For all of us, our voice is an important part of ourselves, and our customary pronunciation is a vital part of our voice. Throughout our lives, we've become used to hearing certain sounds come out of our mouths and not others. Our pronunciation has always marked us as members of a certain language or dialect group. Changing our pronunciation can seem threatening, as if it will cause us to lose our identity as a member of our own group. It seems safer and easier not to change (Gilbert, 2008). However, if students can look at their attempts to change pronunciation as a way of adding a new skill or a new, temporary language identity rather than replacing their original selves, it can seem less threatening.

In addition, sometimes learners can feel uncomfortable if they imitate a speaker or other model too exactly. They might have the feeling that the speaker will think they're mocking them if they try to sound *too* similar. (After all, young children sometimes make fun of a friend by imitating his or her way of talking, and they might be scolded for this.) But in pronunciation practice, learners have to get over that feeling and realize that imitating someone exactly helps lead them toward their goal. It's a valuable skill in pronunciation learning.

Learning Pronunciation Takes Time

Pronouncing sounds involves both our minds and our bodies. When you learn new sounds, you need to learn to move the muscles of your mouth in new ways and change the pronunciation habits you've built up all through your life. This isn't easy, and like learning any other muscular activity, it takes a long time. Most people can't learn to dance or to play a musical instrument immediately; they have to start out slowly, practice a lot, and gradually build up speed and skill. Your mouth also needs to build up **muscle memory**—the ability to do something more easily after practicing it many times. Your muscles begin to "remember" how to move in a certain way because they've done it so often.

Teaching pronunciation also takes time. As teachers, we can't just teach something once and expect our students to master it right away. We need to come back to the same point again and again, giving students lots of review and continued practice.

What Do Teachers Need to Know?

To teach pronunciation effectively, you need several types of knowledge:

- You need to know the facts about pronunciation: How speakers' mouths move when they produce the sounds of language, and how word stress, rhythm, connected speech, and intonation work.
- You need to understand and be able to predict the kinds of problems your students might have with pronunciation and why they happen.
- You need to know many ways to teach pronunciation to your students, adapting your methods to fit them and their needs, and helping them practice effectively to overcome any problems they might have (Celce-Murcia et al., 2010).

You also need to know these basic principles of teaching pronunciation:

- Include more than just "repeat after me." Having students listen to a recording or to the teacher's voice and then repeat is a useful part of a pronunciation lesson, but by itself it is not enough.
- Encourage students to use more than one of their senses, which is more effective anyway. We can use many different ways of learning—through sight, sound, and movement—to help students understand and remember better.
- Keep lessons practical. For most students, even adults, theory and technical explanations are hard to understand and are easily forgotten. Simple, concrete demonstrations fol-

lowed by lots of practice produce better results. Lessons need to fit our students' level of understanding.

- Include communicative practice whenever possible. Students need to work toward using their new pronunciation in real speech. During class, we can help them practice in activities that are similar to real communication.

- Train students to become independent and autonomous learners. Our students won't be with us forever. Someday they'll be facing pronunciation puzzles on their own. If we can help them build up their own skills in listening, imitating, and monitoring their own pronunciation, it will be a big help to them in their future learning.

In the rest of this book, we'll talk about all of these things and how they can make your teaching of pronunciation more engaging and effective.

CHAPTER 2

Some Basic Concepts of Phonology

Phonology is the study of speech sounds in language—the sounds themselves, how they are produced, and how they work together as a system in a particular language. Phonology can be an incredibly detailed and complex subject. As a teacher, you don't have to know everything about it, but there are some basic concepts that are very useful to know. In this chapter, you'll learn about some of them.

Letters Are Not Sounds

First, it's important to remember that sounds and letters are two separate things. Letters are written symbols. We can see them, but we can't hear them. Sounds are vibrations that our ears can hear and our brains can interpret. We can hear sounds, but we can't see them. Even though people sometimes talk about "the *g* sound" or "the *a* sound," *g* and *a* are letters, not sounds. In the English spelling system, a letter can often represent more than one sound, depending on the word it's used in. For example, the letter *g* represents two completely different sounds in the words *go* /gow/ and *gentle* /dʒɛntəl/. Also, a written letter sometimes represents no sound at all, like the *k* in *knee* or the *e* in *bake.*

Be careful not to confuse letters with the sounds they represent. When we talk about pronunciation, we're talking about *sounds,* not written letters.

Phonemes and Allophones

Phonemes are the distinctive sounds of a language, the sounds that a native speaker of the language considers to be separate sounds. Every language has its own set of phonemes; no two languages have exactly the same set.

In reality, no two spoken sounds are precisely the same. After all, speech sounds are produced by human beings, not machines. Each time we say a sound, it might be slightly different. Sometimes the differences are tiny and random, and sometimes they can be pretty substantial. When we listen to someone talk, we don't usually notice all these differences. We don't realize that we're really hearing many different variations of sounds. Our minds only recognize a limited number of sounds—in English, about 42. These basic sounds of a language are its phonemes.

If sounds can have so many variations, how can we know if two sounds are the same phoneme or different phonemes? That is, how can we tell which variations of sounds that we hear count as the same sound in a particular language?

We can use this test: If we change one sound to another in a word and the meaning of the word changes or the word becomes meaningless, those two sounds are different phonemes. We say they are **in contrast**. For example, if we say *talk* (/tɔk/), it means "to speak," but if we say *walk* (/wɔk/), then it means "to move around on foot." Because changing /t/ to /w/ changed one word into a different word, we know that /t/ and /w/ are separate phonemes in English. They function as different sounds. If we start with the same word *talk* and change /t/ to /z/, the word becomes meaningless—*zalk* isn't a real word in English. So we can be sure that /t/ and /z/ are also different phonemes.

On the other hand, if we change one sound to another and the meaning of the word does not change, those sounds belong to the same phoneme.

For example, in the word *butter* (/bʌtɚ/), we can say the /t/ sound in different ways (**sound 2.1**). We might say it the way most Americans do in words like this—like a quick, voiced /d/—and the word will still be *butter*. We could also say /t/ in *butter* as a "normal," voiceless /t/, or even say a very puffy, breathy /t/, and it will still be the same word, *butter*. Because saying /t/ in these different ways did not change the meaning of the word *butter*, we can tell that these sounds are *not* separate phonemes in English. They're just three variations of the same phoneme, /t/. These variations of a phoneme that are still heard to be the same sound are called **allophones** of the same phoneme. Although they're physically different from each other, they *function* as the same sound in English.

A phoneme is an abstract concept. It's related not so much to the physical sounds themselves but to the way our minds perceive and categorize sounds. And the way our minds categorize sounds is different for each language. That is, each language has a different set of phonemes.

To illustrate how phonemes and allophones work, let's compare sounds to colors. Look around and find several things that are blue—for example, I can see the pale blue sky, a bright blue notebook, a dark blue pencil, a purplish blue flower, and a greenish-blue book cover. No two of these things are exactly the same color. Some are lighter or darker, more greenish or more purplish. So why do we call them all by the same name, "blue"? It's because the English language has a category of meaning called "blue" that includes all these colors, not because they're really physically identical. (In fact, in another language, the color categories might be divided differently, and these shades might not all have the same color name.) We could say that in English, all these shades of blue are "allocolors" of the same "coloreme." (These are not real words, so you don't have to remember them.) We understand them as all being "blue," even though they're really slightly different. They all *function* as the same color.

In the same way, allophones are groups of (usually) similar sounds that native speakers of a language recognize as being "shades" of the same sound. Speakers don't usually even notice that the sounds are different. They just assume that they're the same.

Types of Variation Among Allophones

Sometimes we have a free choice of which allophone we'll use. For example, we usually say the phoneme /p/ in this way: Our lips come together, air pressure builds up behind our lips, and then we release the air with a little "pop." But when /p/ comes at the end of a word, we might say /p/ in a different way: Our lips come together, air pressure builds up behind our lips, and that's all—no release. We have a free choice of which kind of /p/ to use at the end of a word. Either one is all right, although one may be more common than the other. In this example, we say the sounds are in **free variation**—we can use either one without sounding odd.

In other cases, the **environment** of a phoneme—the sounds around it—determines which allophone we'll use. For example, the words *car* and *key* both start with the same sound: /k/. But if you listen carefully and feel the position of your tongue when you say these words, you'll notice that the /k/ sounds are not exactly the same (**sound 2.2**). When you say /k/ in *car*, your tongue touches much farther back in your mouth than when you say *key*. (Try whispering the two words to hear the difference better. One /k/ will be higher in pitch than the other.) The /k/ sound changes because it's affected by the vowel that comes after it. The two vowel sounds are pronounced with the tongue in a different part of the mouth, and they pull the /k/ sound into a different position, too. These two allophones are in **complementary distribution**. That means you can predict which allophone you'll hear based on its environment—the other sounds around it. This is very common in many languages.

Complementary distribution among allophones is a lot like the comic book hero Superman and his day-to-day identity, Clark Kent. They're really both the same person, but you never see them at the same time. When things are calm, you see mild-mannered reporter Clark Kent. When there's trouble, he turns into Superman. The environment—a normal day or an emergency—determines who you'll see.

Every Language Is Different

As I've said before, every language has its own set of phonemes. Two sounds that are different phonemes in one language might be allophones of the same phoneme in another language. For example, in English, /s/ and /ʃ/ are separate phonemes. (*See* and *she* are different words; changing /s/ to /ʃ/ changes the meaning of the word.)

However, this is not the case in all languages. For example, in Japanese these two sounds are allophones of the same phoneme. They *function* as the same sound. If /s/ comes before the vowel /i/, it sounds something like [ʃ]. If it comes before any other vowel, it sounds like [s]. For example, the phoneme /s/ in a word like /simbun/ (newspaper) is pronounced [ʃ] because there's an /i/ after it: [ʃimbun]. If someone pronounced it [simbun], the word would sound odd, but it would still be understandable, and it wouldn't become some other word. On the other hand, when /s/ is followed by a vowel other than /i/, it sounds like [s], for example, in words like /soko/ (there) or /sakura/ (cherry blossom).

I sometimes hear teachers equate sounds in a new language with sounds in the learner's language. For example, a teacher might say, "The English sound /t/ is pronounced like the Spanish sound /t/ in *tener* (to have) or *tienda* (shop)." However, these sounds are actually *not* the same; the tongue is farther forward for the Spanish sound, right up against the teeth, and farther back for the English /t/, on the ridge just behind the teeth. In addition, the English sound is **aspirated**, or pronounced with a small puff of air, when it's at the beginning of a word, and the Spanish sound doesn't have this puff of air. The written letters may be the same, but the sounds aren't.

We teachers need to be very careful to avoid teaching students that a sound in a new language is "the same as" a sound in their own language. Often the two sounds are similar, but *not* exactly the same. We also need to be very careful about **transliterating** English words into the writing system of another language as a pronunciation aid. This often gives students a very inaccurate idea of what the words really sound like. It's important to encourage students to hear and produce the sounds of a new language as they really are, as accurately as possible.

Consonants and Vowels

We can divide the phonemes of any language into two types of sounds: **consonants** and **vowels**. Consonants are sounds in which the airstream meets some obstacles in the mouth on its way up from the lungs. The airstream might be bumped, squeezed, or completely blocked. Words like *big*, *map*, and *see* begin with consonants. Most words contain at least one consonant, and some contain many more. For example, *saw* contains one consonant sound, *play* contains two, and *split* contains four. But a word doesn't have to have any consonants at all. For example, the words *eye*, *a*, and *oh* don't have any consonant sounds—only vowels.

Vowels are sounds in which the airstream moves out of the mouth very smoothly because there's nothing blocking or constricting it—it doesn't meet any obstacles on the way. Vowels are the "**heart**" of words and **syllables**. Words like *apple, east, open,* and *out* begin with vowels.

We sometimes think of consonants and vowels in terms of stationary positions of the tongue, lips, and teeth, especially when we look at diagrams of the vocal tract like the one shown in Figure 2.1. (This one might represent /t/, /d/, or /l/.) However, phonemes are actually produced by *movements* of parts of the vocal tract, not static positions. The tongue doesn't pause in one position—it keeps moving smoothly from one sound to the next. The diagrams show just one instant in the whole movement of a sound.

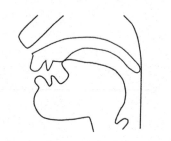

Figure 2.1. Sagittal section diagram.

Minimal Pairs

A **minimal pair** is a set of two words whose pronunciations are exactly the same except for one sound. Here are some examples of minimal pairs (**sound 2.3**):

- *b̲oat* and *v̲ote*
- *sat̲* and *sad̲*
- *p̲aper* and *p̲epper*

Minimal pairs are very useful in teaching pronunciation, especially when students confuse two similar sounds. We'll hear more about using minimal pairs in pronunciation practice in Chapter 7, "Teaching Consonants and Vowels."

The Phonemic Alphabet

A **phonemic alphabet** is a set of symbols that represent the sounds of a language. One symbol represents exactly one phoneme.

Why do we need a phonemic alphabet? It's necessary because languages generally don't have perfect spelling systems, with exactly one symbol for each phoneme. Sometimes the same symbol can stand for more than one sound. For example, in English the letter *c* can represent at least three different phonemes (**sound 2.4**):

- /k/ as in *cat*
- /s/ as in *city*
- /ʧ/ as in *cello*

In other cases, the same sound can be represented by more than one spelling. For example, the /f/ sound in English can be spelled in these ways (**sound 2.5**):

- *f* in *fun*
- *ph* in *phone*
- *gh* in *laugh*

Because of this, it's useful to have a special set of symbols that can represent sounds more consistently. These **phonemic symbols** can help both teachers and learners record and interpret the pronunciation of new words accurately.

Some of the symbols in the phonemic alphabet of English, such as /g/ and /ɑ/, look like letters used in ordinary spelling. However, they don't always represent the same sounds that they do in normal spelling, and when they're used as phonemic symbols, they can each represent only *one* sound. For example, the phonemic symbol /g/ can represent *only* the first sound in *good*, not the first sound in *gentle;* /ɑ/ can represent *only* the vowel sound in *car,* not the vowels in *cat, cake,* or *care.* Those have their own symbols.

Other phonemic symbols, like /ə/, /θ/, and /ŋ/, are not found in ordinary English spelling. They've been added to represent sounds that didn't have satisfactory spellings in the regular alphabet. Lists of all the phonemic symbols for American English are in Chapter 4 (consonants) and Chapter 5 (vowels). Click on the symbols in the chart on the accompanying website to hear the sounds they represent.

There are actually several different versions of the phonemic alphabet that are used to represent the sounds of English. They're all variations of the **International Phonetic Alphabet**, or **IPA**, a system of symbols developed in the late 1800s to try to represent all the sounds that are used in human languages. Variations of IPA are used in many textbooks and dictionaries to represent pronunciation. Although these alphabets are often referred to as "IPA," most of them are not exactly like "real" IPA. They've been changed a little to make them better fit the needs of language learners and teachers. The symbols used in this book are like those used in many American **English as a second language** (ESL) textbooks.

Should you use a phonemic alphabet in teaching pronunciation? Maybe, or maybe not. For some students it's valuable, but for others it's confusing and scary. You'll need to think about your students—their age, expectations, and learning styles—before making this decision. We'll look at this question in more detail in Chapter 14, "Different Places, Different Learners."

Segmental and Suprasegmental Features

When you hear the word "pronunciation," the first thing that usually comes to mind is the individual sounds of a language—the vowels and consonants. But the sounds themselves are not the only important parts of pronunciation. There are also more "musical" aspects of pronunciation, such as **rhythm**, **intonation**, and **word stress**. You also need to know how sounds affect each other and how they change in **connected speech**. (You'll read about all these things in Chapters 8 to 12.) These aspects of pronunciation, which affect more than just a single sound, are called **suprasegmental features of pronunciation**, or **suprasegmentals**. The individual phonemes of a language—the consonants and vowels—are called **segmental features of pronunciation** or **segmentals** because they affect only one small segment of sound. It's important to know about and practice both segmental and suprasegmental features. Both of these work together to make pronunciation understandable to listeners.

Syllables

A syllable is a rhythmic unit in speech—a unit of sound that gets one "beat" in a word. A syllable must have a vowel (or a **syllabic consonant**, which you'll read about in Chapter 4). It might also have one or more consonants before the vowel and one or more consonants after it. For example, the word *potato* has three syllables: *po•ta•to.* Each syllable in this

---

Phonemic Symbols and Phonetic Symbols

Symbols that represent the phonemes of a language are called **phonemic symbols**. We write phonemic symbols with slash marks around them: /p/. Phonemic symbols represent only the basic phonemes of the language, not all the slight variations of them that are possible.

Symbols that represent the allophones of the phonemes of a language are called **phonetic symbols**. We write phonetic symbols with square brackets around them: [p]. Phonetic symbols are intended to represent smaller, more precise variations of sound than phonemic symbols.

When we want symbols to represent actual letters of the alphabet, we can put them in italics: *p* or quotation marks: "p."

When you write phonemic or phonetic symbols, be careful to write them exactly as they are. You can't change from a lower case to an upper case letter or make other changes in form. For example, /R/ is a totally different symbol than /r/. Different letter shapes might also be different symbols; /e/ does not represent the same sound as /ɛ/; /a/ is not the same symbol as /ɑ/.

Typing Phonetic and Phonemic Symbols

Some common fonts, like Times New Roman and Arial, actually include many of the IPA symbols, like æ, ŋ, and θ. It's just not easy to find them or know how to type them.

You can download free IPA fonts for Windows and Mac at the website of SIL International (formerly called Summer Institute of Linguistics): http://scripts.sil .org/FontDownloadsIPA. Their Charis SIL font is a good one.

Both Mac and Windows computers have utilities that let you see what keys to press to type unusual characters. I also recommend an inexpensive program for Mac called PopChar, available from Ergonis Software: http://www.ergonis .com/products/popcharx/. If you often type IPA symbols or any other unusual font characters, it's worth the €19.99 price (around $25 USD at the time of writing).

Type It (http://ipa.typeit.org/) is a website that lets you type IPA symbols or letters from languages that don't use the Latin alphabet, then copy and paste them into a document.

word has one consonant sound followed by one vowel. The word *strong* has just one syllable: *strong,* with three consonants, then one vowel, then one consonant. (The end of the word has two letters: *ng,* but these stand for just one sound: /ŋ/.)

Varieties of English

The English language is not the same everywhere. There are many different **varieties,** or **dialects**, of English that are spoken in many countries around the world. A dialect is a form of a language that is associated with a particular country, region, or social group. When **linguists** use the term "dialect," it does *not* mean an unusual or inferior way of speaking; the word "dialect" does not have a negative meaning. A language can have both standard and nonstandard dialects, and some dialects may have more prestige than others. *Everyone* speaks a dialect of some kind. However, since many people have come to associate the term "dialect" with types of language that are not considered standard or desirable, it may be safer to use the term "variety" of a language instead of "dialect."

These two varieties of English are most often used as models in pronunciation teaching:

- **Standard American English** is the form of English spoken widely in the United States and Canada by educated speakers and most TV or radio announcers. (There are only slight differences between the pronunciation of standard U.S. and Canadian English.) It can also be called North American English, General American English, or just American English. Many people in the United States and Canada speak Standard American English, often with slight regional variations.
- **Received Pronunciation (RP)** has long been considered the standard form of British English pronunciation, and it is based on educated speech in southern England. It is sometimes also called the Queen's or King's English or BBC English (since announcers on broadcasts of the BBC—the British Broadcasting Corporation—have traditionally been expected to speak in this way). Actually, only a small percentage of people in the United Kingdom speak RP, and these days, even some BBC presenters speak different varieties of British English.

Of course, there are also many other varieties of English besides these—Australian English, New Zealand English, Scottish English, Irish English, Indian English, and many others—each with its own regional variations. There are also varieties of English that are spoken in countries where English is not the main language but is used as a common language of business or education. In fact, there are many, many "Englishes."

We'll look again at varieties of English and the question of choosing a pronunciation model in Chapter 14, "Different Places, Different Learners."

What Are Pronunciation Rules?

When we describe the pronunciation of English, we often talk about pronunciation rules, or we say that certain combinations of sounds are or aren't allowed in English. It's important to understand what we mean when we say this and to think about where language rules come from. They're not like the rules that tell you that you can't touch the ball with your hands when you're playing soccer, or that you have to drive on the right or the left side of the road. Those rules were consciously made by people. Someone had to decide the rules first, and now people are required to follow them when they play soccer or drive a car. If someone breaks a rule, there are negative consequences.

Rules in language don't work that way. They were *not* artificially created for people to follow; instead, they're a description or summary of what people already do naturally when they speak. Language rules exist primarily in speakers' minds; the speakers are usually not even aware of them. Linguists and teachers try to discover the rules, not to create them. They observe how people talk and make generalizations about what they hear. The rules don't tell what a language *should* be like; they're a summary of what it *is* like. (In other words, they're **descriptive rules**, not **prescriptive rules**.)

There are many varieties of English, and not all speakers sound the same. Because of this, we shouldn't be surprised if we find that some speakers don't follow all the rules that we've read in a textbook—this one or any other. This is pretty normal.

Language Is Messy

Finally, here's a basic truth to remember: Language is like a living thing—messy, inconsistent, and constantly changing. In fact, it's often said that the only thing that's constant in language is the fact that it's always changing. New words are invented, grammar rules change gradually, and sounds come and go. If we listen to what English sounded like hundreds of years ago, it's almost impossible to understand—it's changed that much (**sound 2.6**).

In the same way, the sound system of English is changing even now. We can't always be sure what direction the change will take or what the accepted forms will be like in the future. We just have to stay calm and accept the fact that change is inevitable.

When we see diagrams, rules, and lists describing a language, they look neat, exact, and permanent, but the reality is that sounds and other aspects of language vary a lot from speaker to speaker, and they're always in a state of change. Linguists do their best to analyze this amazing mess, but we know that rules often have exceptions, and what is true today might not be true 50 years from now.

Even the experts often disagree on the details of what's happening and why. Language and its sounds are not as neat and tidy as we sometimes imagine, but that just makes them more interesting.

CHAPTER 3

The Articulatory System

Think for a minute about what happens when you talk. Say a few words and concentrate on what's happening inside your mouth. The movements of your tongue, lips, and jaw are incredibly quick, delicate, and complex—just as complex as the movements of an Olympic gymnast or a surgeon's hands. When you think about it, it's a miracle that anybody can talk at all. So how do we produce speech sounds?

When we speak, we push air out of our **lungs**, up through our throat, and out our mouth or nose. The vibration of our **vocal cords**, along with movements of our tongue and lips, changes the airflow and produces different sounds. Even a slight change in the position and movement of these parts can make a perceptible change in the sound that is produced (Figure 3.1).

The Articulatory System

The group of body parts that we use to produce speech sounds are called the **articulatory system**. Teachers need to understand how the articulatory system works so they can help students learn how to produce sounds accurately. The most important parts of the articulatory system are in Figure 3.2.

The lungs are where sound production begins. When we breathe, air moves in and out of these two bag-like organs in our chest. When we speak, our lungs push air up past the vocal cords and through the rest of the **vocal tract**, the space in the throat, mouth, and nose where sound is produced.

The vocal cords or vocal folds are two small membranes

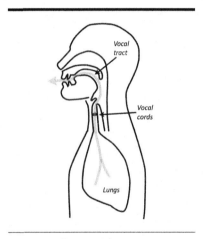

Figure 3.1. The articulatory system (less detailed drawing).

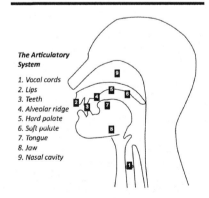

The Articulatory System

1. Vocal cords
2. Lips
3. Teeth
4. Alveolar ridge
5. Hard palate
6. Soft palate
7. Tongue
8. Jaw
9. Nasal cavity

Figure 3.2. The articulatory system (more details).

in the throat that produce the sound of the voice. When the vocal cords are stretched tight and come closer together, air passing through them makes them vibrate rapidly—more than 100 times per second—and the sound that comes out is louder. When the vocal cords are more relaxed, the sound that comes out is quieter, like a whisper. The vocal cords also affect the **pitch** of the sounds we produce. Pitch is a measure of how high or low the voice is at a particular point in time; that is, high or low in the sense that a musical note is high or low; it doesn't mean a high or low volume or loudness. When the vocal cords are longer, the sound has a lower pitch; when they are shorter, the sound has a higher pitch. The empty space between the vocal cords is called the **glottis**.

Above the vocal cords, in the vocal tract itself, are several parts that move in various ways to change the size and shape of the open part of the vocal tract and produce all the sounds of English, or any other language. These moving parts are called the **articulators**.

The **lips** are used in the production of several consonant sounds: /p/, /b/, /m/, /w/, /f/, and /v/. The way we move our lips—making them rounded, relaxed, or stretched a bit wide—also affects the sounds of vowels.

The **teeth** are used when we say the consonant sounds /f/ and /v/, with the upper teeth touching the lower lip, and also /θ/ and /ð/, with the tip of the tongue touching the upper teeth.

The **alveolar ridge** is the slightly rough area just behind the top teeth. It can also be called the *tooth ridge* or the *gum ridge*. The tongue touches or almost touches the alveolar ridge when we say the sounds /t/, /d/, /s/, /z/, /l/, and /n/.

The **hard palate** is the hard part at the top of the mouth, beginning just behind the alveolar ridge. It can also be called the *roof of the mouth*. When you close your mouth, your tongue is probably touching your hard palate. The tongue touches or almost touches the hard palate when we say the sounds /ʃ/, /ʒ/, /tʃ/, /dʒ/, and /y/.

The **soft palate** is the softer part of the roof of the mouth, farther back than the hard palate. It is also called the **velum**. If you touch the roof of your mouth with your tongue and then keep moving your tongue farther back, you'll find that softer area. The back of the tongue touches the soft palate when we say the sounds /k/, /g/, and /ŋ/.

The **tongue** is involved in producing almost all the sounds of English, both consonants and vowels. We'll sometimes need to refer to different parts of the tongue: *the tip of the tongue, the blade of the tongue,* and *the back of the tongue* (Figure 3.3).

The lower **jaw** moves up and down to allow the mouth to open and close. Raising or lowering the jaw also helps the tongue move to higher or lower positions and makes the open space inside the mouth bigger or smaller. All these movements have a great influence on the sounds we produce.

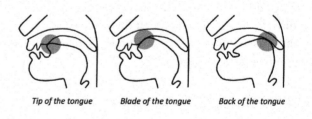

Tip of the tongue   Blade of the tongue   Back of the tongue

Figure 3.3. Parts of the tongue.

The **nasal cavity** is the space inside the nose where air passes in and out when we breathe through our nose. It can also be called the *nasal passage*. This area is important in producing the nasal sounds /m/, /n/, and /ŋ/. For these sounds, the airstream moves up and out through the nose instead of the mouth.

Teaching About the Articulatory System and the Articulation of Sounds

It's important for students of all ages to become aware of the parts of their mouths and how they move when they produce sounds. It's much less important for them to memorize the names of the parts of the articulatory system, either in English or in their native language.

We can use tools, models, and illustrations to help students of all ages understand the articulatory system:

- Have students look in a mirror to see how their mouths move, whether their lips are rounded or not, and how wide open their mouths are so they can compare these things with an illustration or the teacher's example.
- Have students touch their throats to feel the vibration of their vocal cords.
- Use a dental model (a set of giant teeth like dentists use to show children how to brush their teeth) to show students what's happening inside their mouths (Figure 3.4). It's much easier to show students where the alveolar ridge is on a model, for example, than to try to get them to look inside the teacher's mouth. (It's dark in there!) We'll talk more about using a dental model in Chapter 7, "Teaching Consonants and Vowels."
- Diagrams of the vocal tract, like the ones we've seen in this chapter, also give students a visual image of the position of the articulators during speech. This type of diagram is called a **sagittal section diagram** or a **Sammy diagram**. However, these diagrams are sometimes hard for students to understand and connect to reality, especially for younger students (see Figures 3.2 and 3.3).

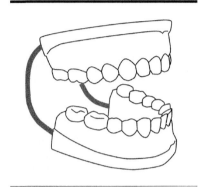

Figure 3.4. Dental model.

- Many websites, apps, and software programs offer videos or interactive diagrams showing the articulation of sounds. One of the best-known is the Phonetics Flash Animation Project of the University of Iowa (Figure 3.5; see the Resources section for further details). A related app called Sounds of English is now also available for iPhone, iPad, or Android devices. For each of the phonemes of American English, you can see an animated sagittal section diagram, a video of a speaker pronouncing the sound, and recorded example words. The site also illustrates the phonemes of Spanish and German.

For young learners, *show* students what to do and keep explanations especially simple. Children are already aware of the more visible parts of the articulatory system—the tongue, teeth, and lips—and this is usually enough to help them understand what they need to do to say a sound.

Think of images or actions to help children understand how to pronounce new sounds, and keep them within the realm of children's experience. For example, when practicing the /θ/ sound, you might say, "Pretend you're licking a lollipop" to make it easier for them to stick their tongues out just a bit. To get them to round their lips for sounds like /w/ and /uw/, have them pretend they're blowing soap bubbles. (Or if it's allowed by your school, bring in actual lollipops and bubbles for them to practice with.) Sounds or names of familiar animals can also be helpful. For example, for the /s/ sound, ask students to make a sound like a hissing snake.

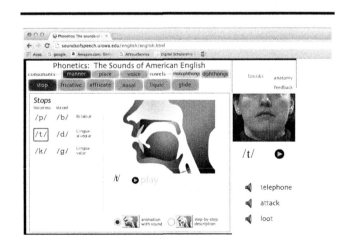

Figure 3.5. Screenshot of Phonetics Flash Animation Project.

CHAPTER 4

The Consonants of American English

Consonants are sounds in which the airstream meets some obstacles in the mouth on its way up from the lungs, as we learned earlier. Most consonants are not as smooth-sounding as vowels; they pop, hiss, snap, or hum. Table 4.1 shows the phonemic symbols for American English consonants. There are alternate symbols for a few of these sounds, but overall, the consonant symbols are very consistent across different versions of the phonemic alphabet, and they are basically the same for American English and British English.

Most words in English contain at least one consonant, and some contain many more. For example, _do_ and _am_ each contain one consonant sound, _play_ contains two, and _spring_ contains four. (Remember that we're counting the consonant sounds, not the consonant letters. The letters ng together spell one sound: /ŋ/.) But words don't have to have any consonants at all. For example, the words _eye_, _a_, and _oh_ have no consonant sounds—only vowels.

Phonologists describe consonants using these three criteria (see Table 4.2 for a **consonant chart** of American English):

- **Voicing**
- **Place of articulation**
- **Manner of articulation**

Voicing

When the vocal cords are stretched tight so that they vibrate during the pronunciation of a sound, we say that the sound is **voiced**. Sounds that are produced without vibration of the vocal cords are called **voiceless**. To tell if a sound is voiced or voiceless, touch the front of your throat gently as you say it. When you say a voiced sound, you can feel a vibration or buzzing in your throat. For a voiceless sound, you can't. You can also feel the voicing of sounds by putting your hands over your ears. When you say a voiced sound, it will seem louder. When you say a voiceless sound, it won't.

When you name sounds when you're talking about voicing with students, try to say only the sound you're talking about, without a vowel after it. For example, when practicing /t/, say only /t/, not /tə/ or /tiy/. If you pronounce a vowel after /t/, the voiced vowel will cause vibration and students might be confused and mistakenly think that /t/ is voiced.

Table 4.1. Consonants of American English (sound 4.1).

Example	Symbol	Example	Symbol
<u>p</u>ot	/p/	<u>sh</u>op	/ʃ/ or /š/
<u>b</u>ook	/b/	bei<u>ge</u>	/ʒ/ or /ž/
<u>t</u>ake	/t/	<u>h</u>ouse	/h/
<u>d</u>og	/d/	<u>ch</u>ip	/ʧ/ or /č/
<u>c</u>at	/k/	<u>j</u>ump	/ʤ/ or /ǰ/
<u>g</u>ood	/g/	<u>m</u>an	/m/
<u>f</u>un	/f/	<u>n</u>ow	/n/
<u>v</u>ery	/v/	si<u>ng</u>	/ŋ/
<u>th</u>ick	/θ/	<u>l</u>amp	/l/
<u>th</u>en	/ð/	<u>r</u>oad	/r/
<u>s</u>un	/s/	<u>w</u>in	/w/
<u>z</u>oo	/z/	<u>y</u>ou	/y/ or /j/
(<u>wh</u>y)	(/hw/★)		

★ Most speakers of English don't use /hw/ as a separate phoneme. They use /w/ instead.

Many of the consonants of English form pairs—a voiced and a voiceless sound that are the same except for voicing. For example, /b/ and /p/ are identical except that /b/ is voiced and /p/ is voiceless. (Notice that one of these pairs—the voiceless sound /θ/and the voiced sound /ð/—are both spelled with the same two letters in normal spelling: *th*.)

The voiced sounds /m/, /n/, /ŋ/, /l/, /r/, /w/, and /y/ have no voiceless counterparts, and the voiceless sound /h/ has no voiced counterpart.

Table 4.2. Classification of American English consonant phonemes (sound 4.2).

Manner of articulation	Place of articulation						
	Bilabial	Labiodental	Dental	Alveolar	Palatal	Velar	Glottal
Stop Voiceless Voiced	/p/ <u>p</u>ig /b/ <u>b</u>y			/t/ <u>t</u>wo /d/ <u>d</u>id		/k/ <u>c</u>at /g/ <u>g</u>o	
Fricative Voiceless Voiced		/f/ <u>f</u>our /v/ <u>v</u>an	/θ/ <u>th</u>in /ð/ <u>th</u>e	/s/ <u>s</u>un /z/ <u>z</u>oo	/ʃ/ <u>sh</u>y /ʒ/ <u>beige</u>		/h/ <u>h</u>it
Affricate Voiceless Voiced					/ʧ/ <u>ch</u>ip /ʤ/ <u>j</u>og		
Nasal Voiced	/m/ <u>m</u>an			/n/ <u>n</u>o		/ŋ/ si<u>ng</u>	
Liquid Voiced				/l/ <u>l</u>ie	/r/ <u>r</u>at		
Glide Voiced	/w/ <u>w</u>ith				/y/ <u>y</u>es		

Table 4.3. Voiced and voiceless consonants (sound 4.3).

Voiced consonants		Voiceless consonants	
/b/	big	/p/	pen
/d/	dog	/t/	top
/g/	give	/k/	cat
/v/	vote	/f/	food
/ð/	this	/θ/	thick
/z/	zoo	/s/	sun
/ʒ/	beige	/ʃ/	ship
		/h/	house
/dʒ/	juice	/tʃ/	chip
/m/	man		
/n/	now		
/ŋ/	sing		
/l/	love		
/r/	run		
/w/	wet		
/y/	yes		

Table 4.3 shows the voiced and voiceless consonant sounds of English. Paired sounds are in boxes next to each other. If a sound has a gray box next to it, it has no paired sound.

Place of Articulation (Where?)

We can also classify consonants by referring to the parts of the articulatory system that are active when we produce each sound. This is called the **place of articulation**. As you can see in the list below, some of these terms are similar to the names of the parts of the articulatory system that are used in making those sounds. The same information is summarized in Table 4.4.

Table 4.4. Place of articulation.

Name	Meaning	English sounds
Bilabial	Both lips come together	/p/, /b/, /m/, /w/
Labiodental	Lower lip and upper teeth touch	/f/, /v/
Dental (or interdental)	Tongue tip and inner edge of upper teeth	/θ/, /ð/
Alveolar	Tongue tip and alveolar ridge	/t/, /d/, /s/, /z/, /n/, /l/
Palatal (or alveopalatal)	Blade of tongue and hard palate	/ʃ/, /ʒ/, /tʃ/, /dʒ/, /r/, /y/
Velar	Back of tongue and soft palate	/k/, /g/, /ŋ/
Glottal	Friction is created by constricting the throat passage	/h/

- **Bilabial**. Both lips touch or almost touch. The sounds in this group are /p/, /b/, /m/, and /w/.
- **Labiodental**. The upper teeth softly touch the lower lip. The sounds in this group are /f/ and /v/.
- **Dental** (also called interdental). The tip of the tongue touches the bottom edge of the top teeth or slightly between the teeth. The sounds in this group are /θ/ and /ð/.
- **Alveolar**. The tip of the tongue touches or almost touches the alveolar ridge (the tooth ridge). The sounds in this group are /t/, /d/, /s/, /z/, /n/, and /l/.
- **Palatal** (also called alveopalatal). The blade of the tongue touches or almost touches the hard palate. The sounds in this group are /ʃ/, /ʒ/, /ʧ/, /ʤ/, /r/, and /y/.
- **Velar**. The back of the tongue touches the soft palate. The sounds in this group are /k/, /g/, and /ŋ/.
- **Glottal**. There is friction in the **glottis** (the space between the vocal cords). The only phoneme in this group is /h/.

Manner of Articulation (How?)

More than one sound can be pronounced in the same part of the mouth, that is, with the same place of articulation. To distinguish between these similar sounds, phonologists describe their **manner of articulation**. This tells how a particular consonant sound is produced—whether it comes out smoothly or roughly, whether it's like a pop or a hiss or a hum. The manners of articulation for English consonants are listed below and tips for demonstrating them can be found in the sidebar "Tips for Demonstrating Manner of Articulation." The same information is summarized in Table 4.5.

- **Stops** (also called plosives). The air stream is blocked completely somewhere in the mouth, air pressure builds up, and then it's released, like a pop or a tiny explosion. The stops in English are /p/, /b/, /t/, /d/, /k/, and /g/.
- **Fricatives**. The air stream is compressed and passes through a small opening in the mouth, creating friction—a hissing sound. The airstream is never completely blocked, so the sound can continue. The fricatives in English are /f/, /v/, /θ/, /ð/, /s/, /z/, /ʃ/, /ʒ/, and /h/.
- **Affricates**. A combination of a stop followed by a fricative—an explosion with a slow release. The affricates in English are /ʧ/ and /ʤ/. Each of these symbols is made up of two parts—a stop symbol and a fricative symbol. This reminds us that the sounds also have two parts.
- **Nasals**. In these sounds, the tongue or lips block off the vocal tract so air can't go out through the mouth. Instead, the passage leading up into the nose opens so that the airstream can go out through the nose. The sounds in the nasal group are /m/, /n/, and /ŋ/.
- **Liquids**. These are sounds that are pronounced very smoothly, like water flowing in a river. The airstream moves around the tongue in a relatively unobstructed manner. The liquid sounds in English are /l/ and /r/.

Tips for Demonstrating Manner of Articulation

Stops. A stop works like a toy pop gun. The tube is like the vocal tract. The cork plugs the tube, then when you push the handle, air builds up and pushes the cork out, just as air builds up behind a blockage in the mouth and is released in a stop sound.

Fricatives. When you push air out of a balloon pump, it passes through a small opening, making a hissing sound like a fricative. The sound is never completely blocked.

Stops and affricates. Stops "explode" suddenly, like a balloon popping. Affricates also "explode," but they end more gradually. Think of a flat tire—it pops, but the air hisses out slowly.

Nasals. To show that air comes out the nose rather than the mouth, have students hold a mirror under their noses and say /m/. The mirror should fog up because air is coming out through the nose. Or have them hold their noses closed. If no sound can come out, the sound is a nasal.

Liquids. Think of the image of water (a liquid) flowing smoothly in a calm river to illustrate these sounds. Contrast them with the "rougher" types of sounds, such as fricatives and affricates, which are more like a roughly flowing river with lots of rocks and rapids.

Table 4.5. Manner of articulation.

Name	Meaning	English sounds
Stop	The airstream is blocked completely before it is released, like a small explosion.	/p/, /b/, /t/, /d/, /k/, /g/
Fricative	The airstream passes through a small opening, creating friction—a hissing sound.	/f/, /v/, /θ/, /ð/, /s/, /z/, /ʃ/, /ʒ/, /h/
Affricate	The sound is a combination of a stop and a fricative—an explosion with a slow release.	/ʧ/, /ʤ/
Nasal	Air passes through the nose instead of the mouth.	/m/, /n/, /ŋ/
Liquid	The airstream moves around the tongue in a smooth, unobstructed way.	/l/, /r/
Glide	The sound is like a very quick vowel.	/w/, /y/

- **Glides** (also called semivowels). A glide is like a very quick vowel. This is why they're sometimes called semivowels, which means "half-vowels." They sound like vowels, but they can function as consonants. The glides in English are /w/ (which sounds like a quick /uw/) and /y/ (which sounds like a quick /iy/).

An Almost Extinct Consonant Sound: /hw/

Most speakers of English today pronounce the first sounds in *wear* and *where* in the same way: as the voiced glide /w/. However, until fairly recently, these were two separate sounds (Table 4.6). Words like *weather, woman,* and *wish* started with a voiced /w/, and most words spelled with "wh,"

like *whether, which,* and *what,* started with a different sound, a voiceless glide that can be represented by the symbol /hw/. Gradually the /hw/ sound has been going out of use, and it's been replaced by /w/. Today the main areas where people commonly distinguish these two sounds are Scotland, parts of

Table 4.6. Words with /w/ and /hw/ (sound 4.4).

/w/	/hw/
witch	which
weather	whether
Wales	whales

Ireland, and some parts of the Southern United States. In other areas, some speakers may differentiate /w/ and /hw/, but most people don't. For pronunciation teaching purposes, it's not necessary to teach students to use the /hw/ sound unless your textbook teaches it.

Restrictions on Where Some Consonants Can Occur

Most consonant sounds can appear in all positions in words: at the beginning, in the middle, or at the end; however, a few cannot:

/ŋ/: The consonant /ŋ/ cannot begin a word in English, but there are many words that have it in the middle or at the end: *singer, think, song, tongue* (**sound 4.5**).

/ʒ/: English has only a few **borrowed words** that begin with the consonant /ʒ/ (*Genre* may be the only common one) and only a small number that end in this sound (*beige, garage, prestige*—and even these may be pronounced with /ʤ/ instead of /ʒ/). It is more often found in the middle of words: *usual, measure, leisure, vision.*

/h/: The sound /h/ cannot occur at the end of a word. When we see the letter *h* at the end of a word, it is either silent (*oh, hurrah*) or part of a two-letter combination that spells a different sound (*rich, fish, tooth*).

Syllabic Consonants

I've said before that every syllable needs a vowel. However, this is not 100% true. Sometimes we can have a syllable with no vowel if a consonant stretches out longer to replace the vowel. Only a few consonants are able to do this in English: /n/, /l/, and /r/.

The phonemes /n/ and /l/ most often become syllabic after a stressed syllable that ends in an alveolar consonant: 'Kitten, 'button, 'didn't, 'shouldn't, 'kettle, 'little, 'ladle, 'tunnel (**sound 4.6**). Keep reading to find out how the /t/ sound can change when a syllabic /n/ comes after it.

In American English, /r/ often acts like a vowel sound in words like her, learn, word, water, and butterfly. (**sound 4.7**) In the underlined syllables in these words, we only hear the /r/ sound with no separate vowel before it. This is different from words like wear, wore, here, or tired, where we can clearly hear a separate vowel before /r/. Many textbooks use the symbol /ɚ/ or /ɝ/ to represent this "syllabic /r/," while others use a double symbol like /ər/ or /ɜr/. (Notice that /ɚ/ is not the same symbol as /ə/.)

Allophones of Some Consonant Phonemes

Some consonants are pronounced differently depending on where they are in a word and what sounds are around them. (That is, some consonant phonemes have more than one allophone, depending on their phonetic environment.) Let's look at the consonant variations in American English that are most important for you to know about as a teacher.

Allophones of Voiceless Stops

In English, the three voiceless stops, /p/, /t/, and /k/, have allophones that follow the same pattern. (The phoneme /t/ also has some additional allophones; see Table 4.7.)

When /p/, /t/, and /k/ come at the beginning of a word or at the beginning of a stressed syllable, they are **aspirated**. That is, they are pronounced with a small puff of air. When we want to be very exact, we can represent these sounds by adding a small superscript "h" to the phonemic symbol (**sound 4.8**):

> [pʰ] pan, price, po'tato, a'ppear
> [tʰ] top, 'table, to'gether, a'ttend
> [kʰ] can, 'kettle, com'puter, a'ccuse

When /p/, /t/, or /k/ are in a **consonant cluster** after /s/ at the beginning of a word, they are **unaspirated**. There is no puff of air when we say them. To represent these sounds, we don't add anything to their phonemic symbols (**sound 4.9**):

> [p] span, 'special, spring
> [t] stop, 'staple, string
> [k] scan, 'scatter, screen

When /p/, /t/, or /k/ comes at the end of a word, it is often (but not always) **unreleased**. This means that we start to say the sound by blocking off the air flow in our mouth, but we don't release the air. We add a small superscript circle to the phonemic symbol to represent stops that are pronounced this way (**sound 4.10**):

> [p°] stop, hope, de'velop
> [t°] coat, late, 'basket
> [k°] back, lake, 'stomach

(The rules we have just looked at only apply to voiceless stops (/p/, /t/, /k/). Voiced stops in English (/b/, /d/, /g/) are never aspirated. They don't have a puff of air in any position.)

In addition to these sound variations that work the same way for all voiceless stops, in American English /t/ has two more allophones that /p/ and /k/ don't have.

First additional allophone of /t/. The first additional allophone of /t/ is the sound that we usually hear in American English in the middle of words like *water, city,* and *bottle.* This is a voiced sound called an **alveolar flap** or **tap**. The tongue taps the alveolar ridge very quickly so that it sounds like a quick /d/. The flap is represented by this symbol: [ɾ]. It's very much like the sound represented by the letter "r" in Spanish and many other languages, but it's different from an English /r/. (When we say an English /r/, the tongue doesn't touch the alveolar ridge. For the flap, it does.) The symbol also looks similar to the letter *r,* but the left part is slightly different.

When words are pronounced with the alveolar flap [ɾ], some words with /t/ sound just like words with /d/ (**sound 4.11**):

ˈlatter and ˈladder sound the same: [ˈlæɾɚ]
ˈwriting and ˈriding sound the same: [ˈrayɾɪŋ]
ˈmetal and ˈmedal sound the same: [ˈmɛɾəl]

When do we pronounce /t/ as a flap? We say it this way only when two things happen:

1. When /t/ comes between two vowels (*wri<u>t</u>ing, da<u>t</u>a*) or if the vowel before or after /t/ is followed by /r/: (*star<u>t</u>ed, wa<u>t</u>er, shor<u>t</u>er*)
2. When the syllable before /t/ is stressed, and the syllable after /t/ is unstressed.

Look at the examples in Table 4.8. When the stress is before the /t/ sound, it's a flap. When the stress is after /t/, /t/ is not a flap.

Table 4.7. Allophones of voiceless stops (sound 4.12).

Phoneme	Allophone	Example words	Description
/p/	pʰ	<u>p</u>an aˈ<u>pp</u>ear	When /p/ comes at the beginning of a word or the beginning of a stressed syllable, it's aspirated.
	p	s<u>p</u>ot s<u>p</u>ring	When /p/ comes after /s/ or at the beginning of an unstressed syllable, it's unaspirated.
	p°	sto<u>p</u> li<u>p</u>	When /p/ is at the end of a word, it's often unreleased. The lips come together, but they don't open.
/t/	tʰ	<u>t</u>op aˈ<u>tt</u>end	When /t/ comes at the beginning of a word or the beginning of a stressed syllable, it's aspirated.
	t	s<u>t</u>and s<u>t</u>ring	When /t/ comes after /s/, it's unaspirated.
	t°	ca<u>t</u> pas<u>t</u>	When /t/ is at the end of a word, it's often unreleased. The tongue blocks the air, but it doesn't open.
	ɾ	ˈci<u>t</u>y ˈwa<u>t</u>er	When /t/ comes between vowels or vowels followed by /r/, before an unstressed syllable, it's a voiced flap. It sounds like a quick /d/.
	ʔ	ˈbu<u>tt</u>on ˈsen<u>t</u>ence	When /t/ comes before an unstressed syllable /ən/, it can become a **glottal stop**—a sound like the beginning of a cough.
/k/	kʰ	<u>k</u>ite <u>c</u>ry	When /k/ comes at the beginning of a word or the beginning of a stressed syllable, it's aspirated.
	k	s<u>k</u>y s<u>c</u>ream	When /k/ comes after /s/ or at the beginning of an unstressed syllable, it's unaspirated.
	k°	sic<u>k</u> mar<u>k</u>	When /k/ comes at the end of a word, it's often unreleased. The back of the tongue closes, but it doesn't open.

Table 4.8. Examples of flaps and glottal stops (sound 4.13).

"Normal" /t/	/t/ is a flap	/t/ is a glottal stop
be'tween	'butter	'button
a'tomic	'atom	'satin
four'teen	'forty	im'portant
re'turn	'reticent	'retina
pa'ternal	'pattern	'patent
'master	'matter	Man'hattan

Second additional allophone of /t/. The second additional allophone of /t/ is a **glottal stop**, represented by this symbol: [ʔ]. To produce this sound, the vocal cords close tightly, air builds up behind them, and then they open quickly. It's like the beginning of a small cough, or the middle sound when we say *huh-uh* to mean "no."

In American English, the phoneme /t/ can be pronounced as a glottal stop when two things happen:

- When the syllable before it is stressed and the syllable after it is unstressed.
- When the syllable after it is /ən/ or syllabic /n/. (That is, /ə/ disappears and /n/ is lengthened and becomes a whole syllable. The symbol for syllabic /n/ is [n̩].)

Table 4.8 also has examples of words pronounced with the glottal stop [ʔ]. It's not absolutely necessary for learners to pronounce the flap [ɾ] or the glottal stop [ʔ] allophones of /t/, but they need to understand them when they hear them. And in normal American English speech, they will hear them often.

Light and Dark /l/

The consonant /l/ is traditionally said to have two allophones: "light" or alveolar /l/ (with the symbol [l]) and "dark," or **velarized** /l/ (with the symbol [ł]), each occurring in different positions:

- [l] (light /l/) is found at the beginning of a syllable, especially before front vowels, in words like *lip, left,* and *believe.* It is pronounced with the tongue touching the alveolar ridge and the sides of the tongue open.
- [ł] (dark /l/) is found at the end of syllables and before back vowels, in words like *ball, pool, look,* and *low.* It is also pronounced with the sides of the tongue open, but with the tongue higher at the back of the mouth. The tip of the tongue might or might not touch the alveolar ridge. In some dialects, particularly some types of British English, dark /l/ sounds almost like /ow/ or /uw/.

However, in the speech of most Americans, the difference between these two types of /l/ is small, and some Americans don't make this distinction at all. Instead, they pronounce a sound that's similar to a dark /l/, with the tongue touching the alveolar ridge and the back of the tongue raised, in all positions (Ladefoged, 2006). Because of this, if your pronunciation model is American English, the distinction between dark and light /l/ does not need to be a high priority. You and your students have more important things to think about.

Consonant Clusters

Consonant clusters are groups of two or more consonant sounds in a row, as in *spot, strong, desk, desks,* or *sister.* It's important to remember that we're talking about groups of consonant *sounds,* not consonant *letters.* These are not always the same thing. For example, *ship* and *sing* each have groups of two consonant letters, but each group represents only one sound (*sh* = /ʃ/ and *ng* = /ŋ/). On the other hand, the letter *x* as in *six* represents a consonant cluster of two sounds: /ks/.

Consonant clusters in English can occur at the beginning, middle, or end of words. There are restrictions on how many consonants can occur in a particular position and which consonants can occur together. For example, /sk/ as in *sky,* /pl/ as in *play,* and /spr/ as in *spring* are all possible consonant combinations at the beginning of a word in English, but /sd/, /fp/, and /zpr/ are not. There just aren't any words that start with those combinations of sounds in English.

Consonant Clusters at the Beginning of Words

In English, we can find words that begin with one, two, or three consonant sounds, but never more than three.

Two consonants. In initial clusters with two consonants, we can find the combinations listed in Table 4.9. Notice that while some of the example words begin with only one consonant *letter,* they actually have two consonant *sounds.* For example, *cute, beauty, pure, few,* and *huge* all begin with one written consonant, followed by the glide /y/ and the vowel sound /uw/. We hear a /y/ sound, which counts as a consonant, even though there's no letter *y.* (For example, *cute* is pronounced /kyuwt/, not /kuwt/. There's more about this invisible /y/ in Chapter 5, "The Vowels of American English.") In words like *quick, quiet,* and *question,* the letters *qu* stand for the consonant cluster /kw/.

Three consonants. When three consonants come together at the beginning of a syllable, we find fewer possible combinations. The first consonant is always /s/, the second is a voiceless stop, and the third is a liquid or a glide. However, not all of these combinations actually occur, and some are very uncommon. Table 4.10 lists possible three-consonant combinations at the beginning of syllables.

Table 4.9. Initial two-consonant clusters (sound 4.14).

First sound	Second sound	Examples
/p/	/l/, /r/, /y/	play, pray, pure
/b/	/l/, /r/, /y/	blue, brown, beauty
/t/	/r/, /w/, /y/	true, twin, (tune)
/d/	/r/, /w/, /y/	draw, dwell, (due)
/k/	/l/, /r/, /w/, /y/	close, crowd, queen, cure
/g/	/l/, /r/, /w/	glow, green, [Gwen]
/f/	/l/, /r/, /y/	fly, free, few
/θ/	/r/, /w/	three, [thwart]
/s/	/l/, /w/, /m/, /n/, /p/, /t/, /k/	sleep, swim, smile, snow, speak, stop, skate

Words in ( ) = Many people pronounce these words without /y/.
Words in [ ] = Very few words begin with this combination.

Table 4.10. Initial three-consonant clusters (sound 4.15).

First sound	Second sound	Third sound	Examples
/s/	/p/	/l/, /r/, /y/	splash, spring, spew
	/t/	/r/, /y/	string, (stew)
	/k/	/l/, /r/, /w/, /y/	[sclerosis], scrap, squirrel, skewer

Words in ( ) = Many people pronounce these words without /y/.
Words in [ ] = Very few words begin with this combination.

Consonant Clusters in the Middle of Words

In the middle of words, we often find combinations of up to four consonant sounds, as in *chapter, system, entry* or *obstruct* (**sound 4.16**). Many of these occur across syllable boundaries. That is, one syllable ends in one or more consonant sounds, and the next starts with one or more consonants (*chap•ter, sys•tem, en•try, ob•struct*).

Consonant Clusters at the Ends of Words

At the ends of words, we can have one, two, three, or four consonants together. Some of the longer clusters are in words with the grammatical endings *–s* or *–ed*, which add an extra sound. (See Chapter 6, "Pronunciation of Some Word Endings" for more details on the pronunciation of these endings.)

Here are some words ending in two-consonant clusters (**sound 4.17**):

> *help, felt, old, milk, shelf, curb, art, cord, mark, bump, ant, hand, tense, ranch, sink, else, bulge, course, march, arm, barn, girl, wasp, trust, ask, soft, act, tax, fourth*

Here are examples of words ending in three-consonant clusters :

> *text, sixth, exempt, waltz, world, glimpse, quartz, against*

Some words end in four-consonant clusters because a grammatical ending has been added:

> *texts, sixths, exempts, waltzed, worlds, glimpsed*

Simplification of Consonant Clusters

Teachers often encourage students to pronounce every sound in a consonant cluster, and this is generally good advice. However, there is one situation when it's acceptable to simplify a consonant cluster, that is, to omit one of the consonants. When there are three or more consonants in a row, the middle one is sometimes dropped. The first or last consonant is never dropped. This happens most often when the middle consonant is a stop, /θ/, or /ð/ (**sound 4.18**):

> *tests* might sound like /tɛsts/ or /tɛs/
> *asked* might sound like /æskt/ or /æst/
> *months* might sound like /mʌnθs/ or /mʌns/
> *sixths* might sound like /sɪksθs/ or /sɪks/

Native speakers are often not aware that they're omitting these sounds. However, these pronunciations are very common and are found in all but the most careful types of speech.

Another way native speakers make consonant clusters easier to pronounce is by **resyllabification**. That is, they split up a consonant cluster so that the last consonant in the cluster joins the syllable after it. For example, when we say: *The cats are sleeping,* the final /s/ in *cats* sounds like it joins the following word: *The cat sare sleeping.* We'll read more about this type of linking between words in Chapter 12, "Connected Speech."

Some Learner Problems with Consonants

Learners' problems in pronouncing new sounds vary, depending on the sound system of their native language. To predict the kinds of problems their students might have, teachers need at least a basic knowledge of the sound system of the learners' language. But whatever the student's language, the general types of problems are similar.

New Sounds

When learners try to pronounce a sound that doesn't exist in their own language, it's naturally difficult, and they may substitute a similar (but not identical) sound from their own language. For example, many languages don't contain the phonemes /θ/ or /ð/, so speakers of those languages often have a hard time hearing and distinguishing these new sounds. When they try to say the new sounds, they often substitute more familiar sounds, like /s/, /f/, or /t/ for /θ/ and /z/, /v/, or /d/ for /ð/. It's important to help students hear and understand that there actually is a difference between the new sounds and the familiar first-language sounds so they can begin to pronounce the new sounds more accurately. If we allow learners to assume that the new sounds are identical to sounds in their own language, they will have little chance of pronouncing new sounds well.

Familiar Sounds in Unfamiliar Environments

There can also be sounds that are easy for learners to pronounce in some phonetic environments, but difficult in others. For example, the glide /w/ is not a serious problem for Japanese or Korean speakers when followed by most vowels. Saying *wet, way,* or *wine* is not hard. However, when /w/ is followed by /uw/ or /ʊ/, it's more of a problem. Words like *woman, wood,* and *woo* are a pronunciation challenge. This is because Japanese and Korean have some sound combinations beginning with /w/, but not combinations like /wuw/ or /wʊ/. The fact that the sounds /w/ and /ʊ/ are very similar can also make it hard for learners to pronounce them in sequence, and *wood* can end up sounding like /ʊd/.

The same situation happens with /y/ before the similar vowel sounds /iy/ and /ɪ/. It's hard for many learners to distinguish *year* and *ear* or *yeast* and *east,* even though *yet* and *you* might not be a problem.

Final Consonants

Consonants at the ends of words are often more troublesome than the same consonants at the beginnings of words. This is especially true for students whose native language does not allow any consonants at the ends of words, or perhaps only a limited set of consonants.

When learners have trouble pronouncing final consonants, they cope in different ways, depending partly on their language background. Speakers of some languages tend to omit final consonants. For example, they might pronounce *meet* as /miy/ or *back* as /bæ/. Speakers of other languages might add an extra vowel after the final consonant, pronouncing *meet* as /miytə/ or *back* as /bæku/.

Another problem with final consonants affects speakers of languages such as German, Dutch, Russian, and Polish, where final stops, fricatives, and affricates (together called **obstruents**) are always voiceless, even if they're spelled with letters that normally represent voiced sounds. For example, the German word *Hand* (meaning "hand") is pronounced /hant/, not /hand/. When speakers of these languages pronounce English words that end in voiced obstruents, they may substitute voiceless sounds instead.

Because these substitutions fit the familiar patterns that the learners are used to using in their own language, they usually don't realize that they're changing anything. They unconsciously reshape new words to fit the comfortable pattern of their own language.

Consonant Clusters

Languages also have different restrictions on what kinds of consonant combinations are possible. Some languages don't have consonant clusters at all. Others have fewer clusters than English, or they allow different combinations of consonants. Learners whose languages have different syllable-structure rules than English may have trouble pronouncing some words with consonant clusters.

Learners cope with unfamiliar consonant clusters in different ways. They might omit one or more of the consonants. For example, they might pronounce *section* as /sɛʃən/ or *spring* as /spɪŋ/ or /pɪŋ/. Other learners add an extra vowel before or between the consonants. For example, *school* might become /ɛskuwl/ (if the speaker's L1 is Spanish) or *spray* might become /supʊrey/ (if the speaker's L1 is Japanese).

All of these are changes that learners unconsciously produce to make words easier and more comfortable to pronounce. However, they also make it harder for listeners to understand what the speaker is trying to say. Teachers need to help students understand and practice the patterns of English syllable structure to make their speech more understandable.

Some Troublesome Consonant Sounds

Let's look at a few of the consonant sounds that are difficult for many learners.

/r/

When pronouncing /r/, the lips are a little bit rounded, and the tip of the tongue does not touch the roof of the mouth. (This is different from sounds spelled with the letter *r* in some other languages. The /r/ sound in both American and British English is *not* a **flap** or a **trill**, as it is in Spanish, Russian, Arabic, and many other languages.)

There are actually two possible tongue positions for pronouncing the /r/ sound in English, and both can

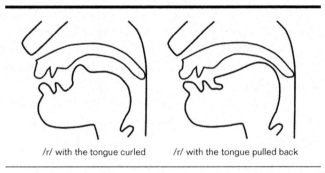

/r/ with the tongue curled   /r/ with the tongue pulled back

Figure 4.1. Two tongue positions for pronouncing /r/.

come out sounding the same. Some speakers of English pronounce /r/ with the tip of the tongue curled up a bit (a **retroflex** tongue position). Others say it with the back of the tongue pulled back and bunched up, without curling the tip (a **velarized** tongue position). Both ways can produce the same sound, and students should use the way that produces the best results for them.

/l/

As we read earlier, when we say /l/, the tip of the tongue touches the alveolar ridge, but the sides of the tongue are open, so air can flow around the tongue. This is a **lateral** tongue position. Unlike /r/, the lips are not rounded when we say /l/.

Here's one way to feel the difference between /r/ and /l/: Say /r/ and stop in the middle of the sound. Don't move your tongue or lips. Then breathe in quickly. The air rushing into your mouth should make *the underside of the tip of your tongue* feel cold. Now say /l/, again stopping in the middle of the sound and breathing in. Now the *sides* of your tongue should feel cold air. If a different part of your tongue feels cold, something may be wrong.

Learners can also check their pronunciation using a mirror. When they say /r/, their lips should be a bit rounded, and they should be able to see a little of the underside of their tongue. When they say /l/, their lips should not be rounded, and they should see just a little bit of the tip of their tongue.

/f/ and /v/

In pronouncing both /f/ and /v/, the top teeth gently touch just inside the lower lip, and air passes out under the teeth (Figure 4.2). Many students have been told to "bite their lip" when they say /f/ and /v/. This gives them a rough idea of where to put their teeth and lower lip, but it's a bit extreme for real speech. If students put their teeth too far forward on their lower lip or bite too hard, it will be hard to get enough air coming through to make the sound properly.

Speakers of languages that do not have labiodental sounds may substitute the bilabial /b/ for /v/, and some also substitute /p/ for /f/. If this happens and the speaker's lips really want to close when they say /f/ or /v/, have them put a finger on their top lip to hold it up out of the way. This makes it easier for just the top teeth to touch the lower lip.

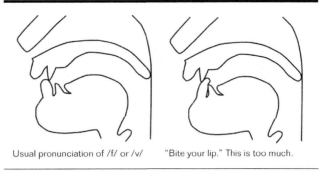

Usual pronunciation of /f/ or /v/   "Bite your lip." This is too much.

Figure 4.2. Pronouncing /f/ and /v/.

If students look in a mirror while saying /f/ or /v/, they should be able to see their teeth just a bit. If their lips are closed, or if they're too close together to see their teeth, they're not saying the sounds correctly.

/θ/ and /ð/

In pronouncing /θ/ and /ð/, the tip of the tongue gently touches the back or bottom of the top teeth (Figure 4.3). For these sounds, students may have been told to "bite your tongue" or "stick out your tongue." Again, this is a good hint for giving students a feeling of where to put their tongues, but in normal speech, the tongue doesn't stick all the way out of the mouth.

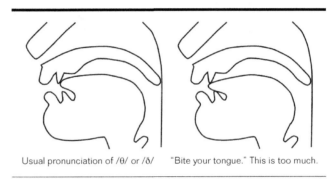

Usual pronunciation of /θ/ or /ð/   "Bite your tongue." This is too much.

Figure 4.3. Pronouncing /θ/ and /ð/.

When looking in a mirror while saying /θ/ or /ð/, you should see just a bit of your tongue, not your whole tongue sticking out.

Learning Takes Time

Learning to pronounce new consonant sounds can be challenging, and it won't happen all at once. It takes time for students to learn to recognize new sounds and get used to moving their mouths in strange new ways to produce them. (Figure 4.4 on the following page shows sagittal section diagrams of all the consonants in English.)

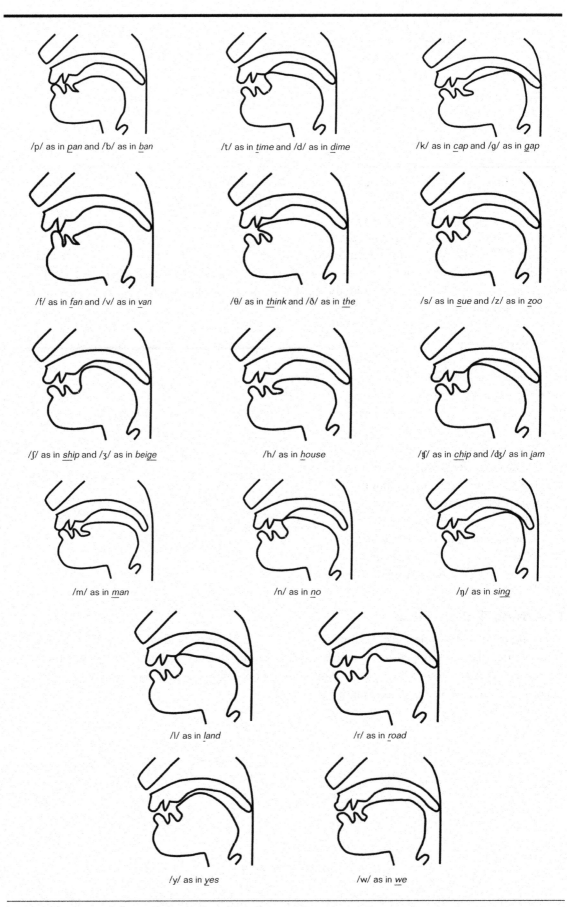

/p/ as in *pan* and /b/ as in *ban*

/t/ as in *time* and /d/ as in *dime*

/k/ as in *cap* and /g/ as in *gap*

/f/ as in *fan* and /v/ as in *van*

/θ/ as in *think* and /ð/ as in *the*

/s/ as in *sue* and /z/ as in *zoo*

/ʃ/ as in *ship* and /ʒ/ as in *beige*

/h/ as in *house*

/tʃ/ as in *chip* and /dʒ/ as in *jam*

/m/ as in *man*

/n/ as in *no*

/ŋ/ as in *sing*

/l/ as in *land*

/r/ as in *road*

/y/ as in *yes*

/w/ as in *we*

Figure 4.4. Sagittal section diagrams of all the consonants.

CHAPTER 5

The Vowels of American English

Vowels are sounds in which the airstream moves up from the lungs and through the **vocal tract** very smoothly; there's nothing blocking or constricting it. The first sounds in the words *extra, only,* and *apple* are vowels.

In general, every syllable has a vowel sound (although, as seen in the previous chapter, the consonants /n/, /l/, and /r/ can sometimes be lengthened to become a syllable in themselves). Vowels are the "heart" of syllables.

When comparing American, British, Australian, Irish, or other varieties of English, the vowels differ much more than consonants. Within each of these varieties there are many dialects, and their vowels may also differ greatly. The vowels I'll be describing here are for standard American English. If you look at books describing British, Australian, or other varieties of English, the description of vowels will be very different.

Sometimes people assume that there are five vowel sounds in English: *A, E, I, O* and *U*. However, this is a misconception. These are vowel *letters*, not vowel *sounds*. Each of these vowel letters can represent more than one sound. For example, the letter *a* can represent /æ/ as in *hat*, /ey/ as in *hate*, /ɑ/ as in *car*, or /ɛ/ as in *care*. Also, each vowel sound can be represented in more than one way in spelling: The sound /iy/ can be written as *ee* in *seem*, as *ea* in *seal*, as *ie* in *piece*, as *ei* in *seize*, as *ey* in *key*, as *i . . . e* in *machine*, and probably more. There's certainly not a one-to-one correspondence between letters and sounds, and English has many more vowel sounds than vowel letters.

For most speakers of American English, there are 14 vowel sounds, or 15 if the vowel-like sound in words like *bird, her* and *turn* is included. The phonemic symbols for the vowels are shown in Table 5.1, and the **sagittal section diagrams** showing the positions of the tongue, teeth, and lips in pronouncing all the vowels are in Figure 5.1. For each sound in Table 5.1, you'll see at least two symbols. This is because different textbooks and authors use different versions of the phonemic alphabet with different sets of symbols for vowels. Many American textbooks use symbols similar to those in the columns labeled "Symbols," while others use symbols like those in the columns labeled "Other symbols." The symbols in British textbooks are similar, but not identical, to the "Other symbols" column. In other places, you might see still more variations of the symbols in addition to the ones that are shown here. In this book, we'll use the symbols in the first column.

Describing vowels is trickier than describing consonants. The tongue is floating freely around

Table 5.1. The vowels of American English (sound 5.1).

Example word	Symbols used in this book	Other symbols	Example word	Symbols used in this book	Other symbols
b<u>ea</u>t	/iy/	/i:/	b<u>oo</u>t	/uw/	/u:/
b<u>i</u>t	/ɪ/	/i/	b<u>oo</u>k	/ʊ/	/u/
b<u>ai</u>t	/ey/	/eɪ/	b<u>oa</u>t	/ow/	/ou/
b<u>e</u>t	/ɛ/	/e/	b<u>ou</u>ght	/ɔ/	/ɔ:/
b<u>a</u>t	/æ/	/æ/	b<u>o</u>x	/ɑ/	/a/
b<u>u</u>t	/ʌ/	/ə/	b<u>y</u>	/ay/	/ai/ /aɪ/
sof<u>a</u>	/ə/	/ə/	c<u>ow</u>	/aw/	/au/ /aʊ/
h<u>er</u>	/ɚ/	/ər/ /ɜr/ /ɝ/	b<u>oy</u>	/oy/	/ɔy/ /ɔi/ /ɔɪ/

the mouth, not touching other parts of the vocal tract. This makes it harder to describe exactly what's happening inside the mouth. When we describe the vowels of English, we talk about

- **tongue position**;
- **lip rounding**;
- **tense** and **lax vowels**; and
- **simple vowels**, **glided vowels**, and **diphthongs**.

These categories are not as precise or reliable as those we use to describe consonants. Some of them are not even as firmly based on physical reality as we like to think, and they can vary a great deal among individual speakers. Still, the descriptions are useful in teaching, and it's important for teachers to know how vowels are traditionally described.

Tongue Position

The way you move and shape your tongue plays a big part in giving each vowel its own sound. When you pronounce a vowel, even a small change in the position of your tongue can make a big difference in how the vowel sounds.

When phonologists talk about tongue position, they mean where is the highest, tensest, or most active part of the tongue? The way they describe this position is something like graphing a point in math or finding a location on a map. They give two "coordinates" to describe where the point is, like the x- and y-coordinates of a point on a graph or a location on a map.

In describing a vowel, the vertical position of the tongue is listed first: high, mid, or low. That

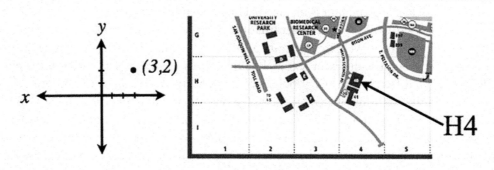

Illustration 5.1. Locating a point on a graph or map.

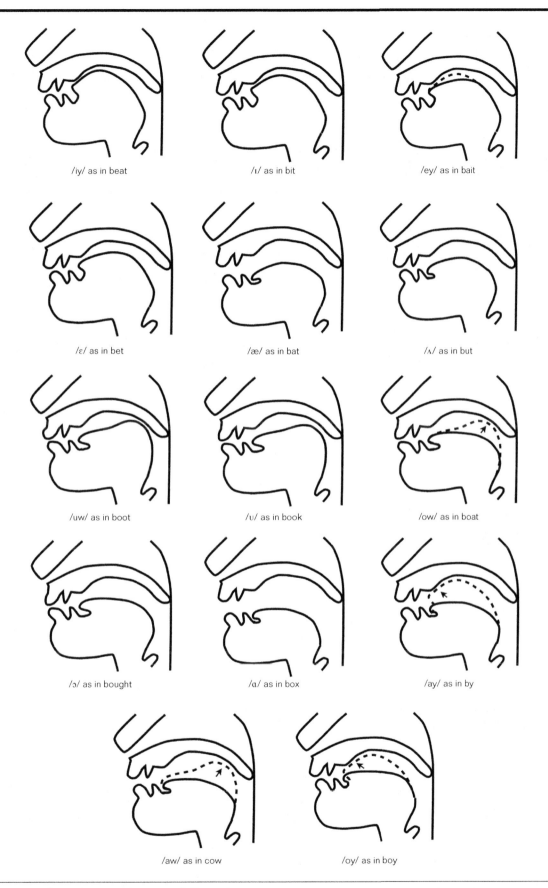

Figure 5.1. Sagittal section diagrams of all vowels.

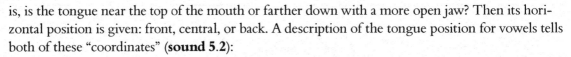

is, is the tongue near the top of the mouth or farther down with a more open jaw? Then its horizontal position is given: front, central, or back. A description of the tongue position for vowels tells both of these "coordinates" (**sound 5**.2):

/æ/ as in *cat* is a low front vowel. The most active part of the tongue is in the lower front part of the mouth.

/ʌ/ as in *cut* is a mid-central vowel. The tongue is resting in the middle of the mouth in a very neutral position.

/uw/ as in *boot* is a high back vowel. The back of the tongue is bunched up high at the back of the mouth.

We can show the tongue positions for different vowels by using a diagram called a **vowel quadrant**. This chart is divided into nine sections, each representing a different tongue placement, vertically and horizontally (Figures 5.2 and 5.3). The diagrams at the right show two versions of the vowel quadrant. The first shows the vowel quadrant alone, and the second shows how the sections of the vowel quadrant are related to the parts of the vocal tract.

	Front	Central	Back
High	iy ɪ		uw ʊ
Mid	ey ɛ	ʌ, ə	ow
Low	æ	ɑ	ɔ

Figure 5.2. Vowel quadrant: basic version.

Vowels that are near each other in the vowel quadrant are pronounced with tongue positions that are close to each other, and their sounds are similar, so learners are more likely to confuse them than pairs that are farther apart in the vowel quadrant. For example, learners often confuse *sheep* (/iy/) and *ship* (/ɪ/), whose symbols are in the same box, but they seldom confuse *sheep* (/iy/) and *shop* (/ɑ/), which are farther apart.

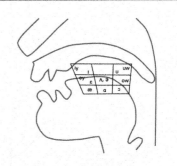

Figure 5.3. Vowel quadrant superimposed on sagittal section diagram.

Lip Rounding

Vowel sounds are also affected by the shape of the lips—whether they're very rounded, just a little rounded, relaxed, or stretched a bit wide.

In English, the back vowels—/uw/, /ʊ/, /ow/, and /ɔ/—are pronounced with varying degrees of lip rounding. In addition, /r/ also has a little bit of lip rounding, whether it's used as a consonant (/r/) or a vowel (/ɚ/). The front and central vowels—/iy/, /ɪ/, /ey/, /ɛ/, /æ/, /ʌ/, /ə/, and /ɑ/—are unrounded. For the vowels /iy/ and /ɪ/, the lips may be spread or stretched a bit wide, and some textbooks even tell students to "smile" when they say the vowels in *heat* or *hit* (**sound 5**.3). Table 5.2 shows typical lip positions for American English vowels.

In reality, however, the lip positions that native speakers use for vowel sounds vary quite a bit. Some people don't move their lips much, and others move them much more. Their lip positions may not look just like those in the chart, but they can still produce perfectly normal vowel sounds. Still, knowing and imitating these "standard" lip positions can help students pronounce vowel sounds more understandably.

Table 5.2. Lip positions for American English vowels.

Vowel	Lip position	Picture
/iy/	Unrounded, can be stretched a bit	
/ɪ/	Unrounded, can be stretched a bit	
/ey/	Unrounded, not so stretched	
/ɛ/	Unrounded, not so stretched	
/æ/	Unrounded, open wide	
/ɑ/	Unrounded, open wide	
/ʌ/, /ə/	Unrounded, neutral and relaxed	
/uw/	Very rounded	
/ʊ/	Moderately rounded	
/ow/	Rounded at the end of the vowel	
/ɔ/	Open and a bit rounded	
/ɚ/	A bit rounded	
/ay/	Unrounded → unrounded	
/aw/	Unrounded → rounded	
/oy/	Rounded → unrounded	

Tense and Lax Vowels

Vowels can also be divided into two categories called tense and lax vowels. This is a distinction that separates pairs of vowels like those in *sheep* (/iy/) and *ship* (/ɪ/); *late* (/ey/) and *let* (/ɛ/); *fool* (/uw/) and *full* (/ʊ/). Phonologists have traditionally thought of the difference between these two categories as being a change in the tension or tightness of the muscles of the tongue or lips while saying the sound, but again, this is an oversimplification. There is sometimes not a great difference in physical tension between tense and lax vowels (Ladefoged, 2006).

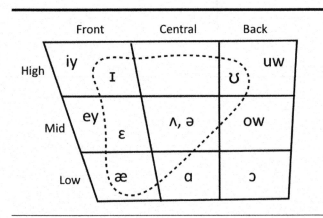

Figure 5.4. Tense and lax vowels.

Which vowels are in each group? The vowel quadrant in Figure 5.3 shows the tense and lax vowels, based on Celce-Murcia, Brinton, and Goodwin (2010). The vowels whose symbols are inside the dotted line are lax; the vowels outside the dotted line are tense. If you look at the dotted line that divides the two groups, you can see that the tense vowels are mostly toward the outside edges of the quadrant, indicating that they have more extreme tongue positions, and the tongue has to stretch or push a bit farther to get there. The lax vowels are closer to the middle of the quadrant; the tongue is not pushing out toward the extreme edges of the mouth, so in a sense, it is more relaxed.

Another difference between tense and lax vowels is the positions in which they can be used in words. Tense vowels can occur both in **closed syllables** (those that end in a consonant sound, like *meet* or *goal*) and **open syllables** (those that do not have a consonant sound after the vowel, like *me* or *go*). Lax vowels can occur in closed syllables, but not in stressed, open syllables. This means that we often find words that end in tense vowels: *Me, day, shoe, show, saw, happy, today, subdue,* and so forth. However, we never find words that end in stressed lax vowels. That is, American English doesn't have words like /mɪ/, /dɛ/, /ʃæ/, or /bʊ/. (Of course, many words end in the unstressed lax vowel /ə/, like *sofa,* banan*a,* and pizz*a.*)

For the purposes of teaching pronunciation, tenseness or laxness is only important when working with three pairs of vowels that are very similar, but differ in tenseness (**sound 5**.4):

/iy/ as in *seat* (tense) vs. /ɪ/ as in *sit* (lax)
/ey/ as in *wait* (tense) vs. /ɛ/ as in *wet* (lax)
/uw/ as in *pool* (tense) vs. /ʊ/ as in *pull* (lax)

For other vowels, such as /æ/, /ɔ/, or /ɑ/, it's not necessary to analyze tenseness or laxness; it's enough to concentrate on other characteristics: tongue position, lip rounding, and tongue movement (coming in the next section).

Simple Vowels, Glided Vowels, and Diphthongs

The last classification of vowels is based on how far the speaker's tongue moves while pronouncing the vowel (Table 5.3). For example, when we say /æ/ as in *bad,* the tongue position and quality of the vowel stay constant throughout the sound, even if we continue to say the vowel for a long time. This type of vowel is called a simple vowel or a pure vowel.

Some other vowels have a small change in tongue position from the beginning to the end. For example, when we say /ey/ as in *day,* our tongue moves just a bit, from the position of /ɛ/ to

Table 5.3. Vowels categorized by degree of tongue movement.

None	Very little	Some	A lot
Simple vowels	**Glided vowels**		**Diphthongs**
ɪ	iy	ey	ay
ɛ	uw	ow	aw
æ			oy
ʌ			
ʊ			
ɑ			
ɔ			

the position of /iy/. These types of vowels are called glided vowels or vowels with glides. (In some textbooks, glided vowels aren't considered a separate group. Some authors include them with the simple vowels, while others group them with the diphthongs.)

It may be difficult to hear the difference between the simple vowels and glided vowels when someone is speaking at a normal speed, but when you say the vowels slowly, you should be able to hear and feel the change in tongue position. In particular, it's the slight glide at the end of /ey/ as in *day* and /ow/ as in *go* that makes them sound different from /e/ or /o/-type vowels in many other languages.

Finally, some vowels have a big change in tongue position and sometimes also in lip rounding from the beginning to the end of the sound. For example, /ay/ as in *buy* sounds like a blended combination of the vowels /ɑ/ and /iy/, with the first part longer and more prominent and the second part lasting a shorter time than the first. These vowels are called diphthongs. The vowel quadrant in Figure 5.5 illustrates the three diphthongs of American English, /ay/ as in *hi,* /aw/ as in *cow,* and /oy/ as in *boy* by drawing arrows from the beginning to the ending tongue positions for each one.

In addition to the change in tongue position, the diphthongs /aw/ and /oy/ also have a change in lip rounding; /aw/ begins with unrounded lips and changes to rounded lips, and /oy/ moves from rounded to unrounded.

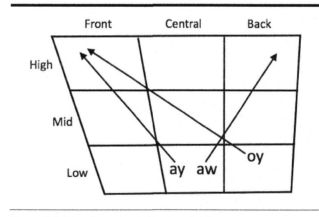

Figure 5.5. Vowel quadrant showing diphthongs.

The glided vowels and diphthongs in American English all end in the **glides** /y/ or /w/. We've already seen glides listed as a category of consonants, which are also called **semivowels**. We can see now why they have this name, which means "half-vowel." They sound like quick vowels, but function as either vowels or consonants, depending on the context.

The Vowel /ɚ/

There is one more vowel-like sound in English, found in words like *bird, first,* and *her* (**sound 5.5**). This sound can be represented by the symbol /ɚ/ (like a **schwa** with a tail). In many textbooks this sound is analyzed as a combination of a vowel plus a consonant and represented by symbols

like /ər/, /ɜr/, /əʳ/, or /ɝ/. In others, it's
represented by a single symbol, /ɚ/.
Whichever symbol we use, this sound
is best thought of as a single vowel
sound rather than a vowel sound
followed by a consonant. The only
difference between the vowel /ɚ/ and
the consonant /r/ is in timing: /ɚ/ lasts
longer so that it becomes the "heart"
of the syllable.

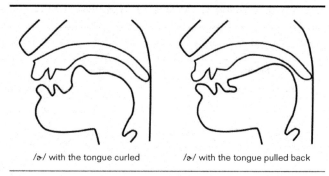

/ɚ/ with the tongue curled   /ɚ/ with the tongue pulled back

Figure 5.6. Two ways to pronounce /ɚ/.

There are two ways to pronounce
the /ɚ/ sound (Figure 5.6), just as
there are with the consonant /r/. Some people pronounce /ɚ/ with the tip of the tongue curled back
a bit. In fact, the /r/ and /ɚ/ sounds are often called **retroflex** sounds, a name that comes from a
Latin word meaning "bent backward." However, other people pronounce /r/ and /ɚ/ with the back
of the tongue bunched up, without curling the tip. Both ways can produce the same sound. With
both tongue positions, the lips are slightly rounded.

An Endangered Vowel Sound: /ɔ/

As you know, languages and their sounds are changing all the time. One change happening now
in American English involves the vowel sound /ɔ/. For many speakers, the vowel /ɔ/ is **merging**
with /ɑ/. This means that these speakers pronounce words whose pronunciation is listed in most
dictionaries with the vowel /ɔ/, like *caught, saw,* and *walk,* with an /ɑ/ sound instead. So *caught* and
cot sound alike: /kɑt/, and *dawn* and *don* sound alike: /dɑn/ (**sound 5.6**).

The merging of /ɔ/ and /ɑ/ is occurring mainly in the Western and Midwestern areas of the
United States and is more common among younger speakers than older speakers (Ladefoged,
2005, p. 28). In many areas of the United States, it could be said that /ɔ/ is an "endangered sound."
As time goes by, it's being used less and less in certain words and eventually could even die out as a
separate phoneme.

Because of this merging of sounds, for teaching purposes it's much less important to concentrate on the difference between /ɔ/ and /ɑ/ than it is to teach the difference between, for example,
/ɑ/ and /æ/. If students pronounce *cot* and *caught* the same way, they'll be understood, but if they
pronounce *cot* and *cat* in the same way, people could be confused.

"Invisible /y/"

Learners sometimes have trouble knowing how to pronounce words spelled with the vowel letters
u, ue, eu, ew, or *ui.* In American English, these letters sometimes represent the sound /uw/, as in
the words *suit* (/suwt/) or *true* (/truw/), and sometimes /yuw/, as in the words *music* (/ˈmyuwzɪk/),
computer (/kəmˈpyuwtɚ/), and *pew* (/pyuw/). In some words spelled with these letters, the vowel

sound can even be pronounced either way, such as *new* (/nuw/ or /nyuw/) (**sound 5.7**). What's
happening here?

We sometimes say that the /yuw/ pronunciation in words like this has an **"invisible /y/"**
because we hear a /y/ sound, but it's not represented in spelling. We might think of /yuw/ as
another diphthong, but with the glide at the beginning instead of the end.

In standard American English, invisible /y/ is almost never found after certain alveolar and palatal sounds: /r/, /ʃ/, /ʒ/, /s/, /z/, /dʒ/, and /tʃ/, and it's seldom found after the sounds /t/, /d/, /n/, and /l/,
although some people do pronounce it in words like *new* (/nuw/ or /nyuw/) or *Tuesday* (/tuwzdey/
or /tyuwzdey/). In British English, the invisible /y/ is more common after alveolar sounds, with
pronunciations like /syuwt/ for *suit* or /tyuwb/ for *tube.*

The invisible /y/ is never found in words spelled with *oo* or *o*, like *food* (fuwd), *moon* (muwn), or *move* (muwv). This is true in both American and British English.

Invisible /y/ can cause confusion if the learner's language has words that are similar to those in English, but which are pronounced without the "invisible /y/." This is especially true for some words in languages that are also written with the Latin alphabet, like German *Musik*, pronounced (/muzik/, not /myuzik/) or Spanish *regular* (/řegular/, not /řegyular/).

Vowel Length

Sometimes teachers talk about "long vowels" and "short vowels." These terms are used in different ways by different groups of people, and this can be confusing. When **linguists** say that a vowel is long or short, they mean its duration in time is actually longer or shorter. The sound quality is the same—the sound just lasts longer. In teaching **phonics**, teachers say that each vowel letter has a "long sound" and a "short sound." These terms don't mean that the "long" sounds really last longer than the "short" sounds; they're just names for different categories of sounds (see Chapter 15, "Spelling, Sounds, and Phonics.")

Many **pronunciation** textbooks, especially those by British authors, call tense vowels like /iy/ and /ey/ "long vowels," and lax vowels like /ɪ/ and /ɛ/ "short vowels." While there may be a slight difference in how long these sounds last in some circumstances, the most important difference between pairs of sounds like these is *not* length.

Teachers don't want students to think that the only difference between the pairs of vowels /iy/ and /ɪ/, /ey/ and /ɛ/, or /uw/ and /ʊ/ is that one is longer in **duration** and the other is shorter. This is simply not the case. Many students have learned this, but it doesn't work as a way of producing understandable vowel sounds (Ladefoged, 2006; Celce-Murcia et al., 2010; and others).

In reality, the difference between the vowels in each of these pairs depends primarily on two points: (1) tongue position and (2) tenseness or laxness of the vowel. As we saw earlier in this chapter, these factors change the quality of the vowels and make them sound different. Students *must* pronounce these pairs of vowels with different vowel quality, not simply with a difference in length.

What Affects Vowel Duration?

In reality, the time duration of any vowel sound varies quite a bit, depending on where it is in a word and in a sentence. All vowel sounds tend to be longer in some environments and shorter in others. Two important principles affect the time duration of vowels.

Vowel length and stress. All vowel sounds tend to last longer in stressed syllables than in unstressed syllables. This is an important factor in making stressed syllables stand out and be noticed. For example, the first syllable in *city* /ˈsɪtiy/ will last longer than the second syllable because it's stressed. The fact that /ɪ/ is sometimes called a "short vowel" and /iy/ is called a "long vowel" doesn't matter. It's important for students to know that within a **polysyllabic** word (a word with more than one syllable), the stressed syllable will last longer than the unstressed syllable or syllables. (More about word stress is coming in Chapter 8, "Syllables and Word Stress.")

In the same way, within a sentence, words that have more emphasis will last longer than words that have less emphasis. For example, in this sentence:

My **friend** should have **called** me.

The words *friend* and *called* are stressed more than the others, and so they last longer **(sound 5.8)**. And *called* lasts the longest because it is has **prominence**. That is, it's the one word in the sentence that has the most stress of all. The words *my, should, have,* and *me* are unstressed, and so they are very short. The words last different lengths of time, even though they each have one syllable. (We'll learn more about prominence in Chapter 10, "Thought Groups and Prominence.")

Table 5.4. Changes in the duration of vowels (sound 5.9).

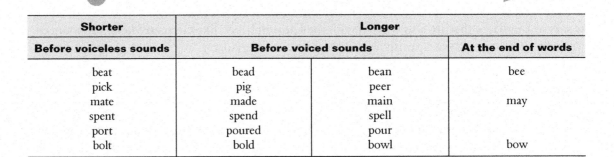

Shorter	Longer		
Before voiceless sounds	Before voiced sounds		At the end of words
beat	bead	bean	bee
pick	pig	peer	
mate	made	main	may
spent	spend	spell	
port	poured	pour	
bolt	bold	bowl	bow

The following sound. The duration of a vowel depends greatly on the sound that comes after it. Vowel sounds are usually shorter in duration before voiceless sounds and longer before voiced sounds. They're longest of all when they come at the end of a word (Table 5.4).

There are also slight variations in vowel length before different kinds of voiced sounds. Vowels are longer before "smooth" sounds like nasals and liquids (which are all voiced in English) than before "rough" sounds: voiced stops, affricates, and fricatives. However, this length difference is so small that it's hard to detect without special measuring instruments.

The same changes in vowel length also happen in words like *spent* and *spend*, *port* and *poured*, *bolt* and *bold*, even though another consonant—/n/, /r/, or /l/—comes between the vowel and the final sound. The vowel in the first word in each of these pairs is shorter than the vowel in the second word because the first word in each pair ends in a voiceless sound, and the second ends in a voiced sound.

Why is this change in vowel length important? For one thing, it's often hard to hear the difference between final voiced and voiceless sounds in English. As I pointed out in Chapter 4, "The Consonants of American English," stop consonants at the ends of words are often unreleased; that is, they're not pronounced completely. This makes pairs of sounds like /p/ and /b/, /t/ and /d/, /k/ and /g/ hard to distinguish on their own when they're at the end of a word. Because of this, the listener's brain uses the length of the preceding vowel sound to help figure out which consonant was heard. For example, listeners unconsciously tell the difference between words like *seat* and *seed* mainly from the length of the vowel, not so much from the difference in the final consonants. This is why it's important for speakers to make vowel sounds a bit longer before voiced consonants.

What Do Students Need to Know About Vowel Length?

From a teaching perspective, there are three points that are the most important for students to know:

- The difference between pairs of tense and lax vowels like /iy/ and /ɪ/, /ey/ and /ɛ/, /uw/ and /ʊ/ is more than just length. We have to pronounce the sounds differently, too.
- Vowels are longer in stressed syllables and shorter in unstressed syllables.
- Vowels are longer before voiced sounds or at the end of a word and shorter before voiceless sounds.

Vowels in Unstressed Syllables

We know that words can be divided into **syllables**—rhythmic units of sound that each get one "beat." In a word with more than one syllable, one of the syllables is **stressed**, or emphasized. Other syllables are unstressed. In English, vowels in unstressed syllables are often different from

Table 5.5. Vowels in unstressed syllables (sound 5.10).

Vowel	Examples	Vowel	Examples
/ə/	'sof<u>a</u>, 'glass<u>es</u>, <u>a</u>'bout	/ey/	m<u>ai</u>n'tain, 'rot<u>a</u>te
/ɚ/	'wat<u>er</u>, c<u>ur</u>'tail, 'ord<u>er</u>ly	/ɛ/	S<u>ep</u>'tember, m<u>e</u>di'cation
/ɪ/	'mus<u>i</u>c, 'van<u>i</u>sh, <u>in</u>'tense	/u/	'child<u>hoo</u>d, 'hand<u>boo</u>k
/iy/	'cit<u>y</u>, 'happ<u>y</u>, 'twent<u>ie</u>th	/ay/	l<u>i</u>'brarian, c<u>i</u>'tation
/ow/	'shad<u>ow</u>, h<u>o</u>'tel, pi'an<u>o</u>	/aw/	'eyebr<u>ow</u>, <u>out</u>'side
/uw/	'men<u>u</u>, <u>u</u>'surp, 'ven<u>ue</u>	/oy/	'hard-b<u>oi</u>led, expl<u>oi</u>'tation

those in stressed syllables. They become weaker, quicker, and less clear than vowels in stressed syllables. We say these syllables and their vowels are **reduced**.

Vowels in unstressed syllables often (but not always) become a sound represented by the symbol /ə/ (called *schwa*). This is a sound that, for speakers of American English, is very similar to /ʌ/: a mid-central, lax, unrounded vowel. When saying /ə/, the tongue is in a relaxed position in the middle of the mouth. The difference between the phonemic symbols /ʌ/ and /ə/ is that /ʌ/ is customarily used to represent a vowel in a stressed syllable, and /ə/ is used to represent only an unstressed vowel. Because /ə/ is found in so many unstressed syllables, and because there are more unstressed syllables than stressed syllables, /ə/ is the most common vowel sound in English. Table 5.5 shows some examples of vowel sounds in unstressed syllables.

Reduced Function Words

We've just seen that unstressed syllables in words can have weak, reduced forms. In a similar way, whole words can sometimes have reduced pronunciations when they're unstressed. This happens most often with **function words**—words that have **grammatical meaning** rather than **lexical meaning**, such as articles, pronouns, prepositions, and conjunctions. These "small" words can be pronounced in two ways—as a **citation form** or as a **reduced form**. The citation form is the way we pronounce the word when we're saying it very carefully—the pronunciation that's described in a dictionary. For example, the citation form of *to* is /tuw/. When we say *to* in normal speech, however, we don't usually say /tuw/. We're much more likely to pronounce it /tə/. This is its reduced form, the way it's pronounced in normal, connected speech when it isn't being emphasized.

Because unstressed function words and syllables are closely connected to the rhythm of English, we'll look at reduced forms of function words in more detail in Chapter 9, "Rhythm." There are lists of common reduced forms of function words in that chapter.

Vowels and Consonants: A Blurry Line

In this chapter and the previous one, we've seen something surprising: The differences between vowels and consonants are not as clear-cut as we might imagine, and some sounds can have qualities of both. For example, we've seen that a few consonants (/n/, /r/, and /l/) can also be used as the "heart" of syllables when they become vowel-like syllabic consonants. They're consonants, but they can sometimes function as vowels. Also, the consonant /r/ and the vowel /ɚ/ are actually the same sound—the difference is in duration and function within a syllable. Finally, the glides /w/ and /y/ are used as consonants in words like *win* and *yes,* but they can also be the last part of the diphthongs /ay/, /aw/, and /oy/. Like many rules and categories in language, the boundary between vowels and consonants is a little blurry.

Sources of Learner Problems With Vowels

While there are a number of problems learners can have pronouncing vowel sounds, they tend to fall into a few categories.

New Sounds

English has more vowel sounds than many other languages. According to the *World Atlas of Language Structures Online* (Dryer & Haspelmath, 2013), the average number of vowels in the languages of the world is five or six. English has more than twice that number! Vowels that are found in English but not in the learner's language are often challenging, since the learner's tongue and lips need to get used to unfamiliar positions and new combinations of movements.

Differences Between the Phonemes of Different Languages

Some pairs of vowels that are separate phonemes in English may be allophones of the same phoneme in other languages. For example, /iy/ and /ɪ/ are separate phonemes in English, and we find many minimal pairs such as *sleep* and *slip* or *least* and *list*. But these sounds are variations of a single phoneme /i/ in Japanese, Spanish, Korean, and many other languages. Other pairs of tense and lax vowels are also often confused in this way: /iy/ and /ɪ/, /ey/ and /ɛ/, /uw/ and /ʊ/. Other similar vowels, such as /ɛ/ and /æ/ or /ʌ/ and /ɑ/, may also be heard as variations of the same sound in some languages.

Glided Vowels

English vowels that end with a /y/ or /w/ glide can also cause problems, particularly /ey/ and /ow/. Many languages have vowels that are similar to these, but without the final glide. Speakers of these languages may keep the vowel sound consistent throughout the vowel instead of adding the final glide, leading to vowel sounds that may be hard to recognize.

Vowels Followed by /r/

Learners from some language backgrounds have particular problems with vowels followed by /r/. They may have trouble differentiating pairs of words like these (**sound 5.11**):

stir and *star*	*stir* and *store*
curd and *card*	*curd* and *cord*
were and *wore*	*word* and *ward*

Reduced Vowels

As I've said, many unstressed vowels are reduced to /ə/ in English. In many languages, this does not happen; vowels retain their "full" quality, whether they're stressed or unstressed, spoken slowly or quickly. Speakers of these languages may pronounce unstressed syllables in English with "full" vowels too, and this can make it hard for listeners to understand which words are meant.

CHAPTER 6

Pronunciation of Some Word Endings

In English, some grammatical word endings (called **inflections** or **inflectional suffixes**) are pronounced in more than one way, depending on the sound that comes before them. You can't always predict the pronunciation of an ending by looking at the spelling of the word. You have to think about the *sounds* that are around it. (In this chapter I'm only going to talk about the *sounds* of these endings, not their spelling. There is a separate and independent set of rules about changes in the spelling of words when these endings are added.) First, let's look at the pronunciation of the endings *-ed* and *-s*.

Pronunciation of *–ed* Endings

The *-ed* ending is added to regular verbs to show their past tense and past participle forms. The *-ed* ending is pronounced in one of three ways (Table 6.1):

1. If the base verb ends in /t/ or /d/, we add an extra syllable: /əd/ or /ɪd/.
2. If the verb ends in any *voiced* sound except /d/, we add a voiced ending: /d/. We add just one sound, not an extra syllable.
3. If the verb ends in any *voiceless* sound except /t/, we add a voiceless ending: /t/. Again, we add just one sound, not an extra syllable.

Table 6.1. Pronunciation of *–ed* endings (sound 6.1).

Final sound of word	The *–ed* ending pronunciation	Examples
/t/, /d/	/əd/ or /ɪd/	*chatted, waited, added, needed*
Any *voiced* sound besides those listed above	/d/	*cried, viewed, moved, robbed, buzzed, judged*
Any *voiceless* sound besides those listed above	/t/	*stopped, walked, passed, laughed, washed, matched*

The first form of the ending is listed above as "/əd/ or /ɪd/." This is because the exact vowel of the ending might vary a little. It can sound like /ə/, like /ɪ/, or like a vowel between the two. The important thing is that an extra, unstressed syllable is added when we put an *-ed* ending on regular verbs that end in /t/ or /d/.

Pronunciation of –s Endings

The *-s* ending can be used in four different ways (Table 6.2) (**sound 6.2**).

1. It can be added to regular nouns to make the plural form:

   box → boxes   *pen → pens*   *book → books*

2. It can be added to all nouns, both regular and irregular, to make a possessive form, either singular or plural. Although the spellings of the singular and plural possessive forms are different, they both sound the same.

   boy → boy's book   elephant → elephant's trunk
   boys → boys' books   elephants → elephants' trunks
   child → child's toy   children → children's toys

3. It can be added to verbs to make the third-person singular present tense form.

   kiss → kisses   run → runs   walk → walks

4. In contractions, it can be a reduced form of *is* or *has*. (Contractions of *is* and *has* sound the same.)

   he is → he's   it is → it's   he has → he's   it has → it's
   what is → what's   where is → where's   what has → what's

All of these *-s* endings follow the same pronunciation rules, no matter what their meaning. The *-s* ending is pronounced in one of three ways:

1. If the word ends in /s/, /z/, /ʃ/, /ʒ/, /ʧ/, or /ʤ/ (the sounds that are similar to /s/, called **sibilant** sounds), we add an extra syllable: /əz/ or /ɪz/.
2. If the word ends in any *voiced* sound except the ones listed above, we add a voiced ending: /z/. We add just one sound, not an extra syllable.
3. If the word ends in any *voiceless* sound except the ones listed above, we add a voiceless ending: /s/. Again, we add just one sound, not an extra syllable.

Just as with the *-ed* endings, the vowel in the first form of the *-s* ending can sound like /ə/, like /ɪ/, or like a vowel between the two. Here too, the important thing is that an extra, unstressed syllable is added when we put an *-s* ending on words that end in /s/, /z/, /ʃ/, /ʒ/, /ʧ/, or /ʤ/.

Table 6.2. Pronunciation of –s endings (sound 6.3).

Final sound of word	The –s ending pronunciation	Examples
/s/, /z/, /ʃ/, /ʒ/, /ʧ/, /ʤ/	/əz/ or /ɪz/	boxes, roses, bushes, judge's, bosses', Max's, kisses, catches, wishes
Any *voiced* sound besides those listed above	/z/	pens, bags, birds, eyes, boy's, Betty's, children's, runs, sees, returns, goes, he's, she's, where's, Bob's
Any *voiceless* sound besides those listed above	/s/	books, boats, laughs, Mike's, cat's, cats', walks, laughs, stops, it's, what's, Elizabeth's

Problems with *–ed* and *–s* Endings

Learners from many language groups tend to have some of the same problems with *-ed* and *-s* endings. Here are some reminders for learners.

Don't Add an Extra Syllable When It's Not Needed

Learners sometimes add unnecessary extra syllables with *-ed* and *-s* endings, especially when adding the ending results in a troublesome consonant cluster. For example, *watched, judged, stopped,* and *walked* need to have just one syllable each, even though some of the final consonant clusters may be hard to pronounce. Learners should be careful not to say *watch•ed, stopp•ed,* or *walk•ed.*

Don't Confuse the Sounds That Trigger Each Ending

The final sounds that cause the ending to have an extra syllable are different depending on whether the ending is *-ed* or *-s*. When students learn the rules for both endings, they sometimes forget which sounds go with which rule. It's important to help them see *why* particular sounds trigger an extra syllable: Sounds that are very similar to the sound of the ending need an extra vowel to separate them from that similar sound. This helps the ending to be heard more clearly.

Don't Omit the Endings

Learners sometimes omit *-ed* or *-s* endings entirely, especially if their native language has few or no consonants at the ends of words or if adding the endings results in unfamiliar consonant clusters. The endings are important; the listener needs to hear them to get grammatical information to help understand the whole meaning of what's being said.

Think About Sounds, Not Letters

Sounds and letters are not the same. For example, the verb *hope* ends in a vowel *letter,* but a voiceless consonant *sound.* When we add an *-ed* or *-s* ending, the ending is voiceless: *hoped* /howpt/ or *hopes* /howps/.

Hearing Voiced and Voiceless Sounds

It's sometimes hard to hear the difference between the voiced and voiceless endings /z/ and /s/ or /d/ and /t/. This is because in English, voiced **obstruents (stops, fricatives,** and **affricates)** are usually not very strongly voiced at the ends of words. This can make final voiced and voiceless obstruents sound very similar. Also, as seen in Chapter 4, "The Consonants of American English," voiced and voiceless stops are both often unreleased at the ends of words, so they sound very similar.

In addition, hearing and producing the difference between the voiced and voiceless endings can be difficult for speakers of some languages. Learners whose native language is German, Russian, or other languages that don't have final voiced obstruents may have trouble with the voiced endings. Speakers of Spanish or Portuguese may also produce all of the *-s* endings in their voiceless forms, since those languages have plural *-s* endings that are always pronounced as a voiceless /s/.

Fortunately, mixing up the voiced and voiceless endings causes less misunderstanding than omitting a syllable or adding an extra one. Therefore, for the purpose of teaching the pronunciation of these word endings, it's less important for students to differentiate between the voiced and voiceless endings than between the "extra syllable" and "no extra syllable" endings.

Some Adjectives That End in *–ed*

We've just looked at the pronunciation of the past tense and past participle verb ending *-ed.* Past participles are also often used as adjectives: *tired, surprised, excited, broken.* For a few of these past-participles-turned-adjectives that end in *-ed,* the verb form is still pronounced according to the regular rules, but the related adjective is pronounced with an extra syllable: /əd/ or /ɪd/. For example:

Verb + -ed used as a verb (**sound 6.4**):
We *learned* some new words.	/lɚnd/
The priest *blessed* the people.	/blɛst/
You haven't *aged* a bit.	/eydʒd/

Verb + -ed used as an adjective:
a *learned* professor	/ˈlɚnəd/
blessed freedom	/ˈblɛsəd/
my *aged* grandparents	/ˈeydʒəd/

This extra-syllable pronunciation only happens with a very limited group of words, often old-fashioned, formal, or poetic sounding words. Not all verb/adjective pairs ending in -ed are pronounced differently. For example, *tired, surprised, bored,* and many others, are pronounced the same whether they're verbs or adjectives. Some examples of both types are shown in Table 6.3.

Table 6.3. Pronunciation of some verbs and adjectives ending in –ed (sound 6.5).

Pronounced differently (These and very few others)				Pronounced the same (These and many others)			
Verbs		**Adjectives**		**Verbs**		**Adjectives**	
blessed	/blɛst/	blessed	/ˈblɛsəd/	tired	/tayrd/	tired	/tayrd/
learned	/lɚnd/	learned	/ˈlɚnəd/	surprised	/səˈprayzd/	surprised	/səˈprayzd/
aged	/eydʒd/	aged	/ˈeydʒəd/	bored	/bɔrd/	bored	/bɔrd/
beloved	/bəˈlʌvd/	beloved	/bəˈlʌvəd/	confused	/kənˈfyuwzd/	confused	/kənˈfyuwzd/
dogged	/dɑgd/	dogged	/ˈdɑgəd/	worried	/ˈwəriyd/	worried	/ˈwəriyd/

There are also some adjectives ending in -ed that do not come from past participles of verbs. They often (but not always) have the form of a noun followed by -ed. Most of these are also pronounced with an extra syllable /əd/ or /ɪd/ (**sound 6.6**).

a *crooked* line	/ˈkrʊkəd/
a *naked* man	/ˈneykəd/
ragged clothing	/ˈrægəd/
rugged mountains	/ˈrʌgəd/
a four-*legged* table	/ˈlɛgəd/
a *wretched* feeling	/ˈrɛtʃəd/
a *wicked* witch	/ˈwɪkəd/

Pronunciation of –*ing* Verb Endings

The -*ing* ending found on present participle verb forms can also be pronounced in different ways (Table 6.4). However, these don't follow definite phonological rules like the -*ed* and -*s* endings. Instead, they vary depending on the degree of formality or informality and the speed of speech, and they act more like the full and reduced forms of function words that are described in Chapters 5 and 9. When the -*ing* ending is pronounced carefully, it sounds like /ɪŋ/. However, in more casual speech, it often sounds like /ən/ or /ɪn/. This pronunciation is sometimes represented in writing as -*in'* when the writer wants to seem casual or folksy, as in the old song "Blowin' in the Wind" or the even older movie *Singin' in the Rain.*

Table 6.4. Pronunciation of –*ing* verb endings (sound 6.7).

In careful speech (citation form)	In casual speech (reduced form)
I'm doing my homework.	I'm doin' my homework.
We're learning about sounds.	We're learnin' about sounds.
Are you coming?	Are you comin'?
blowing in the wind	"Blowin' in the Wind"
singing in the rain	*Singin' in the Rain*

It's helpful to know that the /ən/ or /ɪn/ pronunciation of the -*ing* ending is not always appreciated by strict teachers or parents who want to encourage "correct" pronunciation. They may warn children not to "drop their g's," although of course there was never a /g/ sound in this ending to start with—just a single consonant sound /ŋ/. It's probably best to help students understand the reduced pronunciation of the -*ing* ending when they hear it, but not encourage them to use it themselves.

Verbs with –*ing* Used as Adjectives or Nouns

Verbs with -*ing* are often used as adjectives (*boring, interesting, tiring, exciting*) or as nouns *(Swimming is fun. I like reading.)* Interestingly, these adjectives or nouns ending in -*ing* are less often pronounced with a reduced ending, even in casual or rapid speech (Shockey, 2003; **sound 6.8**).

Was the movie *interesting* or *boring?*	/ɪntrəstɪŋ/ /bɔrɪŋ/
We had a *tiring* day.	/tayrɪŋ/
What a *fascinating* story!	/fæsəneytɪŋ/

CHAPTER 7

Teaching Consonants and Vowels

In this chapter I'll show you ways to introduce and practice consonant and vowel sounds—alone, in words, in sentences, and in speaking. Examples of some of the activities are available online. Ways of practicing other pronunciation skills, emphasizing **suprasegmental features** such as **intonation**, **stress**, and **rhythm**, are in Chapter 13, "Teaching the Musical Aspects of Pronunciation."

Planning Pronunciation Practice

In many traditional classrooms, learning pronunciation has meant mainly repeating words and sentences after the teacher or a recording. But "repeat after me" is not enough to help students achieve clear pronunciation. Students need help in learning to notice how the sounds are pronounced and to understand them when they hear them. They also need to practice using new sounds in context and eventually use them in communicative activities too. As a teacher, you'll need to plan a sequence of activities to lead students through the whole process of mastering a new sound, beginning with hearing and trying it out for the first time and continuing through practicing it in several ways, from simple to more complex.

When you're planning a practice sequence, you need to think about more than just what you, as the teacher, are going to do. You should also think about the lesson from the students' point of view: How will they notice and begin to understand the new sounds? What will they be doing to help them master the sounds? How will they experience and practice using them? Will they understand your presentation easily? Will they feel interested and engaged?

Steps in Practicing a New Sound

In language teaching in general, it is widely accepted that learners need plenty of practice with language in realistic contexts to master its use, and the same is true about teaching pronunciation. Celce-Murcia, Brinton, and Goodwin (2010) recommend using a communicative framework for teaching pronunciation, with a series of steps building from simple practice to using the new sounds in realistic communication. They suggest the following steps in introducing and practicing a new sound or sound contrast.

Description and analysis. Introducing the sound and explaining or showing how it's produced through spoken descriptions and visual demonstrations.

Listening discrimination. Listening practice aimed at helping students learn to recognize the new sound when they hear it and recognize the difference between the new sound and other similar sounds.

Controlled practice. Very structured practice using language supplied by the teacher or textbook. Learners are mainly reading or repeating words, sentences, or dialogues containing the sound, alone or as a class.

Guided practice. Somewhat freer practice using the sound being learned. The teacher supplies a framework or structured activity, such as an information gap, that guides the learners toward using specific sounds, but the learners must choose exactly what to say.

Communicative practice. Activities involving discussions, planning, role plays, or conversations using the sounds being practiced. When these activities are planned to include the use of words with particular sounds, they help students build fluency in both pronunciation and speaking.

These steps do not have to be done all in one lesson. They could easily extend over many practice sessions, especially if pronunciation is only one element among many in your curriculum. You'll also find that the steps overlap to some extent, and there's not always a clear distinction between them. If you're not sure which category an activity belongs to, don't worry too much. It's more important to do a variety of activities leading from simple to more complicated than to classify the category of each activity.

Finally, the sequence of activities doesn't have to be a one-way street. Even after you've gone through all the steps, you might want to circle back to an earlier stage and do more practice. Review is a good thing.

Let's look more closely at each step in the process of teaching and practicing sounds.

Description and Analysis

A better name for this first step might be "introducing the sounds," since it doesn't necessarily have to include verbal explanations or explicit analysis. There are several ways to introduce sounds, depending on the age and abilities of the students and the preferences of the teacher.

Demonstrations. *Show* how to produce the sound. Use your own voice and mouth as a model. You can supplement this by using a dental model to show how to produce many of the sounds. Use your hand to represent the tongue and show its position and movement.

Explanations. *Tell* students how to produce the sound, using clear, simple, concrete descriptions. Where does the tongue touch? What are the lips doing? For most groups of learners, avoid technical language as much as you can. Explain in a way that is suited to your students' age and level of understanding. Remember that explanations alone are not enough, and simply telling is not teaching. Descriptions are a good beginning, but they need to be combined with demonstrations and other visuals to be effective.

Videos demonstrating sounds. Several websites have short videos giving explanations and demonstrations of how to produce sounds. However, check the quality of the video contents carefully before you use it in class. Some look good at first glance, but are actually inaccurate or misleading. Links to some reliable sources can be found in the Resources section at the end of the book.

Visual symbols. Some teachers and students like to use phonemic symbols to represent sounds; others hate them. For young children, phonemic symbols are too abstract and just won't work well.

For adults, especially visual learners, phonemic symbols can provide an "anchor" for new sounds and help keep all those strange new sounds from seeming like a shapeless, confusing mass. However, some students are just confused by the symbols, especially if they're also just starting to learn the English alphabet. Used judiciously, phonemic symbols can be helpful, especially for sounds that don't have a consistent spelling in English. (See also the section "Should You Use Phonemic Symbols in Teaching?" in Chapter 14, "Different Places, Different Learners.") Sounds can be represented visually in other ways if phonemic symbols don't seem helpful:

- Represent each sound with a color, either one whose name contains the sound it represents (red for /r/, yellow for /y/) or one that just seems to fit the sound.
- For vowel sounds, consider using the Color Vowel Chart. Developed by ESL teachers Karen Taylor and Shirley Thompson, the chart shows the vowels of American English, each represented by a color and phrase containing that sound. For example, *green tea* stands for /iy/ and *blue moon* stands for /uw/. Their website shows the complete chart and explains how to use it.
- Represent each sound with a picture of an object or animal that contains the sound: a dog for /d/, a monkey for /m/, an elephant for /ɛ/, and so forth.

For young learners, any of these representations can seem friendlier, less threatening, and easier to remember than traditional phonemic symbols.

Gestures and movements. Gestures or body movements can be used to represent sounds and remind students of how they're pronounced. For example, holding one hand with the fingers curled up could represent /r/, to mimic the movement of the tongue. Some teachers create whole sets of gestures to use in representing sounds.

Deductive or Inductive Teaching?

Some teachers prefer to introduce new information **deductively**. That is, they give an explanation, rule, or generalization and then have students practice using what they've learned. Others prefer to introduce new material **inductively**. They give several examples of a rule or pattern and guide students as they try to figure out the general principle for themselves. Both of these can be effective ways of introducing new pronunciation information, and you might want to use both methods at different times. However, here are some tips for using each way of introducing new material.

If you introduce new sounds or rules deductively, keep your explanations short, simple, and easy to understand, and move quickly toward the practice stage. Don't let your explanations and analysis be so lengthy and detailed that students are overwhelmed, bored, or confused. Simply listening to an explanation is not learning. Students have to *use* what they're learning.

If you introduce new sounds or rules inductively, be sure that the examples you present will be more than enough to lead students to the rule or generalization. Inductive teaching is not supposed to be a guessing game; the conclusion should be obvious after students think about it for a while. Remember that students can't read your mind. Sometimes the rule you're trying to get across is perfectly clear to you, but still a complete mystery to your students. If they just don't seem to be "getting it," there's nothing wrong with going ahead and giving them more hints or even telling them the rule you're trying to teach.

More Advice for Introducing New Sounds

- Don't try to introduce too many sounds at once. Students will just be confused by too much information.
- Practice slowly at first. Pronunciation is a muscular activity, and the muscles in learners' tongues, lips, and jaws have to get used to moving in new ways when they pronounce new sounds. It's like learning a new dance—you have to practice the steps slowly at first, and

then you can gradually speed up. In pronunciation, too, you can't expect students to speak at a normal speed from the beginning.

- When explaining or demonstrating a sound, give students many chances to practice during your explanation. They need to try out each element that you explain right away. Explain or introduce a small point briefly and then spend lots of time practicing. If students hear too much explanation before they have a chance to practice, they'll forget everything and won't be able to use what you've told them. In other words, your lesson should look like this:

Explain → **PRACTICE** → Explain → **PRACTICE** → Explain → **PRACTICE**

Not like this:

EXPLAIN → **EXPLAIN** → **EXPLAIN** → **EXPLAIN** → Practice

Listening Discrimination

If students can't hear the difference between two sounds, then it will be very difficult for them to pronounce those sounds correctly. Students need to build up their ability to recognize new sounds and differentiate them from each other and from sounds in their own language. Here are some types of practice that emphasize listening, moving roughly from easier to more demanding:

Same or different. Students hear two words and decide whether they're the same or different. For example, if they hear *right, right,* they say "same," but if they hear *right, light,* they say "different."

"Odd one out" listening. Students hear a series of three or four words, all the same except one. They have to identify which one is different (the "odd one out"). For example, if they hear *right, light, right, right,* they'll say that the second word is different.

Matching spoken words to written words or pictures. Students see a series of pairs of pictures representing minimal pair words (for example, pictures of a sheep and a ship or a piece of paper and a pepper shaker). As they hear words, they choose the matching picture. This can also be done with written words instead of pictures, or with spoken sentences matched to written sentences or pictures. If you do the activity with pictures, be sure students know what word each picture represents. For example, does a picture of a smiling man holding a book represent *man, boy, teacher, student, person, happy,* or *smile*? Sometimes it's hard to tell.

Sound sorting. Prepare a handout with boxes for the sounds you've been practicing, each labeled with a phonemic symbol, example word, or picture, depending on your students. Give students a set of words containing the sounds, either in writing or verbally. Students read or listen to each word, decide which sound it represents, and write the word in the correct box.

Listening practice using minimal pairs. There are many ways to use **minimal pairs** for listening practice:

- Choose a minimal pair that contains the sounds you're practicing. For example, for /r/ and /l/, you might choose *rock* and *lock* or *right* and *light*. Choose words that your students know; uncommon words like *roam* and *loam* are not the best choices. Write the two words on the board or draw pictures to represent them if your students are not yet able to read.
- Say the words, and have students repeat them. Show and explain differences in how the sounds are pronounced by using demonstrations, mirrors, or a dental model. (See "Your Pronunciation Toolbox" later in this chapter for more about using a dental model.)
- Label the words on the board "1" and "2." Say one of the words, and have students tell you which word you've said, holding up one or two fingers. Keep this up until they can identify the sounds easily. To make it more challenging, hold a piece of paper in front of your mouth as you say the words.

- Have students do the "1 or 2" practice with a partner for a few minutes while you go around and check their pronunciation. Students take turns saying one of the words for their partner to identify.
- Practice in the same way again, whispering or saying the words without making any sound, and have students decide which word you're saying. This pushes them to pay attention to lip rounding, tongue movement, and so forth. (Don't use this method to practice differentiating voiced/voiceless pairs like /b/ and /p/! All sounds are voiceless when you whisper.)

Just as minimal pairs are words that are the same except for one sound, minimal pair sentences are sentences that are exactly the same except for one sound (**sound 7.1**):

We enjoy **voting**. We enjoy **boating**.
He's a **pirate**. He's a **pilot**.
Give me the **paper**. Give me the **pepper**.

Pairs of sentences like these are useful for practicing in the same way as minimal pair words, and they offer at least a little bit of context. You'll probably find, though, that creating minimal pair sentences is much harder than thinking of minimal pair words because the sounds, meaning, and grammar all have to fit together perfectly.

Cloze listening with sentences or paragraphs. Prepare a handout with several sentences or a paragraph with some words replaced by blanks. (The words should contain the sounds you're practicing.) As you read or play a recording of the text in the handout, have students try to hear and write down the missing words. When planning this activity, keep in mind the time it takes for students to hear, understand, and write the missing words. Don't put the blanks too close together; give students enough time to finish writing each one without feeling too rushed. You might pause after each sentence to give students a little more time to write. To make the activity simpler, you could supply two or three word choices for each blank instead of asking students to think of words entirely on their own.

Teacher dictation. Prepare several sentences that include the sounds you're working on. Make sure the vocabulary and sentence structure are well within the students' ability; if they have to struggle to understand the meaning of the sentences, the activity is much less effective. Read or play a recording of the sentences and ask students to write them down as well as they can. Repeat a couple of times, pausing during the sentence if it's too long to remember all at once. Next, have students compare their writing with a partner, and then check what they've written against the correct sentences. Finally, ask students what words were difficult for them to understand. This can lead to a discussion of *why* they misheard some words and how they can improve their listening. ("I thought you said *sick*, but you really said *thick*. Why couldn't I tell the difference?") Of course, dictations can only be used if your students already have some ability to write in English.

Partner dictation. Prepare a pair of handouts, each with two or three simple sentences and space below to write other sentences. (Use different sentences for each of the pair of handouts.) Put students in pairs and give each partner a different handout. Students take turns dictating their sentences to their partner, who writes them down. Then both students check what they've written, trying to see which sounds they've misheard. This activity gives students practice in both hearing and producing sounds.

Controlled Practice

In controlled practice, students work with new sounds in a very structured way. The words to be practiced are supplied by the teacher or textbook; the students just have to repeat them. Learners need this controlled practice when they begin to learn a new sound. It gives them time to concentrate on reproducing the necessary tongue and lip movements without also having to decide what words they're going to say or what grammatical forms they need to use. Repetition helps students build **muscle memory**—an increased ability to do a physical activity easily after practicing many times.

At this stage it's especially important for students to have **feedback** about the accuracy of their pronunciation. That is, they need comments and corrections from the teacher. They need to know if they're doing something wrong so they can change it and not keep practicing mistakes. Famous American football coach Vince Lombardi once said, "Practice does not make perfect. Only perfect practice makes perfect." While this is an exaggeration, it helps us see that students will not improve if they unknowingly practice the same mistakes over and over.

Choral and individual repetition. In the simplest types of controlled practice, students repeat words, minimal pairs, or sentences after a model provided by the teacher or a recording, with feedback on how well they're doing. While learners need lots of practice of this type to be able to produce sounds automatically, it's best not to continue simple repetition for too long at one time. Follow up with more contextualized and meaningful practice to avoid boredom—for the students *and* the teacher.

Find or write sentences using words with the sounds you're practicing, or have students write sentences on their own. They may enjoy practicing sentences they've created themselves more than those from a book. It can also be fun to include students' names or something about the class in the practice sentences. Don't choose sentences that are too difficult, especially in the beginning, or students will get frustrated and discouraged. Have students practice repeating the sentences as a group and then individually or with a partner.

Tongue twisters can also be used for repetition practice, but they should be used with caution. See "Some Thoughts on Tongue Twisters" later in this chapter.

Proverbs and famous quotations. These are also good for repetition practice, especially with more advanced learners (**sound 7.2**):

Time flies. (practice with /ay/ or /l/)
Birds of a feather flock together. (/f/ and /v/ or /ð/)
All's fair in love and war. (/l/ and /r/)

Be sure the students understand the meaning—both literal and figurative—of what they're saying. If you have students discuss the proverbs or quotations with a partner or group and try to work out their meaning, they'll be able to do valuable communicative practice along with their pronunciation practice.

Dialogues and skits. Dialogues and skits provide controlled practice with the possibility of more context and more meaningful use of language. Choose dialogues that fit situations the students might encounter or words and expressions that they need to know. Make sure the dialogues make sense and sound as realistic and natural as possible. In other words, don't try to cram in as many words with a particular sound as you can if it will make the dialogue sound forced and phony. Have students repeat after the model and then practice the dialogue with a partner. Even when doing controlled practice, encourage learners to speak with feeling, as if they were really in the situation of the dialogue.

Stories and anecdotes. Reading prepared stories out loud can provide good controlled practice if the material contains the pronunciation elements that you're practicing. However, a disadvantage of reading aloud is that it divides students' attention and effort between pronunciation and decoding the written symbols. Be sure that the story contains language that students are familiar with and can read easily so that they can give more attention to pronunciation. (Chapter 14 has more suggestions about reading aloud as a form of pronunciation practice.)

Strip stories. Find a simple story containing the sounds you want to practice. Cut the story into individual sentences, and mix them up. Give the sets of strips to pairs or small groups of students and ask them to reassemble the story. The pronunciation practice comes as students read the strips while arranging them and then read the whole story after it's assembled.

Guided Practice

Guided practice is a bit freer than controlled practice. Words, phrases, and examples are given or suggested, but complete sentences or dialogues are not predetermined. The teacher gives a framework, but students have to create their own "script" or figure out what to say to accomplish a task. Some of the activity types listed below are most often thought of as speaking activities, but if they are planned so that students must use the sounds being practiced to complete the task, they are also good pronunciation practice. Here are some examples of types of guided practice activities.

Information gaps. An information gap activity, or info gap, is a pair-work activity in which each partner has some of the information needed to complete a task, but neither one has all of it. The partners need to talk to each other and combine their information to solve a problem, fill out a chart, or complete a task. In the simplest kind of info gap, the partners might each have a grid in which some boxes are empty and others have a picture or word containing the target sound. They ask each other questions like "What word is in Box 2?" and fill in the blanks with the information they learn. There are many variations of info gap activities that make good guided pronunciation practice if the words or names are chosen to include the sound being practiced. The next paragraphs describe some of these.

Calendars and schedules. Each partner has a schedule of his or her imaginary daily activities. They try to find a meeting time that works for both of them by asking and answering questions about their schedules.

People charts. Create a family tree, sports team roster, or organizational chart of workers in an office that includes names, titles, or other words with a particular sound. Have students ask and answer questions about the people. Create two versions of the chart, each with some names missing, and have students talk together to discover the missing names.

Maps, floor plans, and diagrams. Find or create a map, floor plan, or diagram with labels using the sounds you want to practice. Pairs of students ask and answer questions about the map or plan. They might give each other directions to particular places or plan where to add features to the diagram. For example, they could discuss where to add furniture on a floor plan of a house or where to build a new shopping center, amusement park, or university on a city map.

Journals and diaries. To practice the pronunciation of past tense -*ed* endings, students look at a journal or list of someone's actions in the past and tell each other about them. These can be real events in the students' lives, news stories, or actions by famous people, real or imaginary. (If it turns out that some of the verbs students use are irregular and don't illustrate the -*ed* endings, that's all right. Students need practice with irregular verbs too.)

Sound scavenger hunt. Ask students to find things in detailed drawings or photographs, in pictures cut from a magazine, or in the real-life classroom that contain a particular sound or sounds. Pairs can work together to make lists and see who can find the most words.

Brainstorming lists of words. Ask students to think of words in particular categories that contain the sound you're practicing. For example, ask them to think of names of countries, types of food, animals, words related to sports, or some other category that all begin with /v/. Pairs or groups can try to see who can think of the most words. They'll practice pronunciation as they brainstorm the word lists and then tell their words to the rest of the class. (This is very much like the commercially available game Scattergories.)

Communicative Practice

Communicative activities in which students have freedom to choose their own words to express their own ideas can be useful for pronunciation practice. Because these same types of activities are also used for speaking practice, adult students sometimes don't understand why they're doing them in a pronunciation class. It's important to explain the reason for using communicative practice in teaching pronunciation: Sounds don't exist in isolation—they live in words, stories, conversations, and other kinds of real language. If learners can only say words in isolation but not in real speaking, their skill is not very useful. Many learners can say a sound perfectly when it's alone or in a single word, but they forget it entirely in conversation. This is why we use communicative activities for pronunciation practice—to help learners get ready to use sounds in real conversation.

Here are some examples of communicative activities that can be used to practice sounds if we fill them with words containing those sounds.

Role plays and simulations. Give students a situation and a list of suggested vocabulary words containing the sounds you want to practice. Ask them to create and practice a conversation to fit the situation. The activity can be based on a handout with authentic or teacher-created materials, such as a menu (for a conversation between a waiter and customer); a Web page showing items for sale (for a conversation discussing which things to buy); advertisements for movies, plays, or concerts (to discuss which one to attend); or many other possibilities. If many of the names and words on the handout contain the sounds you're practicing, students will have to produce those sounds during their role play.

Lists, ranking, and problem solving. Give students a task involving listing ("If you were stranded alone on an island, what 10 items would you want to take?"); evaluating and making choices (Read descriptions of three job applicants, and decide who should be hired); or ranking (Look at a list of 10 hobbies, and arrange them in order of students' preference).

Writing stories. Give students a list of words containing particular sounds and ask them to write sentences or a story using some of them. It's best if you give a context or purpose for the story; writing random sentences without context is less meaningful. Students can then practice reading their story and share it with others in the class.

Dialogues and drama. Have students create dialogues using words with the chosen sound. Encourage them to say the lines with feeling as they practice with a partner. Then it's only a short step to using drama—short skits or plays—that encourages students to use what they've been practicing.

Teaching with Authentic Materials

We can find plenty of materials for practicing pronunciation in textbooks. However, we can also use **authentic materials** as a basis for interesting and effective pronunciation practice. Authentic materials are things that were created for real-life purposes—such as newspapers, magazines, TV or radio programs, movies, YouTube videos, advertisements, recipes, menus, poems, and songs—not just for teaching. Materials like these will often keep students' interest more than the usual textbooks. For learners living in English-speaking countries, they show students how they can use the sounds and words they've been practicing in their lives. For those living in areas where English is seldom spoken, they give learners a taste of everyday life in new and interesting places and may give them a stronger motivation to learn.

To use authentic materials, look for sources that contain words with the sounds you're practicing or things that can be described or discussed using those sounds. Then plan what you'll have students do with the material. The activity types listed earlier in the "Guided Practice" and "Communicative Practice" sections will often work. Depending on the type of material, you might ask students to

- practice reading the material aloud;
- summarize or tell a story about it;
- ask and answer questions about it;
- write and practice a dialogue that fits the material;
- do impromptu role plays based on it;
- compare two items and describe the differences between them;
- make a list of things that they see or words that can describe them;
- make predictions about what something is or what will happen; or
- brainstorm solutions to a real or imagined problem related to the material.

Some Thoughts on Tongue Twisters

Tongue twisters are phrases or sentences that are designed to be challenging to say. They usually contain several words with the same sound or with two sounds that are easily confused. You may remember practicing tongue twisters like this very famous one: She sells seashells by the seashore.

Many teachers like to use tongue twisters in pronunciation practice, and they can be valuable tools if used wisely. However, if they're misused, they can lead to frustration and discouragement. Here are some recommendations:

- Use tongue twisters sparingly. They may be fun once in a while, but students will get tired of them quickly if they have to practice them too often.
- Make sure students understand what they're saying. If they don't understand the words, a tongue twister becomes just a difficult tongue exercise, and that's not much fun.
- Don't make the tongue twisters too hard or too long, or they become pointless. If *you* can't say a tongue twister easily, your students probably won't be able to say it at all. For example, here's one that is hard enough to discourage even the most eager student: The sixth sick sheik's sixth sheep's sick.
- Don't emphasize speed too soon. We've probably all practiced tongue twisters in our own language, trying to say them several times very quickly, but it's much harder to do that in a new language. Don't rush until students are ready.
- Don't jump too quickly from explanation and very controlled practice directly to a difficult tongue twister. Do some practice with simple, ordinary sentences first. (After all, you wouldn't give somebody one tennis lesson and then send them to play at Wimbledon, would you? They need lots of easier practice first!)

Here are some examples of tongue twisters that are simple and reasonably easy to understand (**sound 7.3**):

- We took a cheap ship trip.
- Funny Frank fell fifty feet.
- Orange Jell-O, lemon Jell-O.
- The three trees.
- Betty loves the velvet vest best.

Meeting Students' Real-Life Needs

With adult or young adult students who need to use English in their everyday lives, especially in an English as a second language (ESL; rather than **English as a foreign language**, or EFL) context, taking a few minutes to answer questions that students bring in can be a good way to begin a pronunciation lesson. Ask students to write down and bring to class the words or phrases that they've had trouble pronouncing or understanding in their daily activities, such as street names (*Harbor Boulevard* vs. *Harvard Boulevard*); cities (*Irvine, Las Vegas, La Jolla*); words they need in their jobs or studies (*cash register, availability, anesthesiologist*); or even beverages at Starbucks (*vanilla spice latte*). These can be used as the basis for practice with common words and sound combinations. Students might also appreciate help in practicing the pronunciation of their own address, phone number, or other basic information. This practice gives students a sense that they have a say in what they do in class, and it often fits their needs better than using only what's in a textbook. Getting the specific help they need can empower them and make a real difference in their lives.

Auditory, Visual, and Kinesthetic Learning

People learn in many ways: by hearing, by seeing, and by touching and manipulating objects. Everyone can use all these skills, although most people are stronger in some types of learning than in others. In planning pronunciation teaching, we should try to include all three **learning modalities:**

- **Auditory learning (learning through listening).** Listening to a model provided by the teacher or a recording.
- **Visual learning (learning through seeing).** Watching how the teacher or someone on a video produces sounds, using mirrors so students can see how their own mouths move, looking at sagittal section diagrams or a dental model to see how sounds are produced, or using phonemic symbols as a visual representation of sounds.
- **Kinesthetic learning (learning through doing).** Using gestures and movements to represent sounds, using feathers, straws, rubber bands, or other gadgets to help students understand how sounds are produced or to guide their own pronunciation.

Your Pronunciation Toolbox

To help you teach using all three learning modalities, you'll need to have the right tools. Explanations alone aren't enough to help students achieve good pronunciation; merely pointing out what they should do is sometimes meaningless. Tools and gadgets that students can see and touch can help them understand pronunciation better.

But before you start using any of these tools and gadgets, think carefully about whether they're appropriate for your group of students. Ask yourself: Is this tool safe for my students, given their age and maturity level? Will it hurt them, or will they hurt it? Is there any possible way my students can use this tool to get into mischief or cause serious distractions? Will it make a mess in the classroom or disturb nearby classes? Will my students understand the purpose of using this tool? Most important, will it help the students achieve a learning goal? Some of the most useful tools for teaching pronunciation are described here.

Mirrors are absolutely necessary in teaching pronunciation. It's not always easy for students to feel whether their lips are rounded or whether their tongue is touching their teeth, but with a mirror they can see what's happening. If you can't find enough small mirrors, try using blank CDs. They don't reflect as well as real mirrors, but they're cheap, easy to get, and not easily breakable. If your students have cell phones with front-facing cameras, these can also be used to let students see themselves as they speak.

A **dental model** (the kind dentists use to teach children how to brush their teeth) is a good way to show students what's happening inside their mouths (Figure 7.1). Use your hand as a "tongue" to show the position of the tongue in the **articulation** of sounds. You can make a "tongue puppet" out of red or pink felt or other fabric to cover your hand to make a more realistic "tongue," or put a sock over your hand. It's much easier to see what's inside the mouth with the dental model than by trying to look inside the teacher's mouth, and probably more pleasant, too! A list of sources for dental models is in the Resources section at the end of the book.

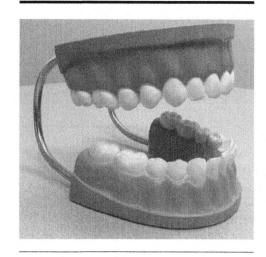

Figure 7.1. Dental model.

If you don't have a dental model, you can use Marsha Chan's technique of using your own hands to show the pronunciation of sounds. Hold one hand with the palm down to represent the roof of the mouth. Bend your fingertips down a bit to represent the teeth. Use your other hand as the tongue, showing how it moves and touches parts of the roof of the mouth. (Source: "Using Your Hands to Teach Pronunciation," a teacher training video from Sunburst Media. See a short demo video at http://www.sunburstmedia.com /UsgHands-demo.html.)

The disadvantage of using either a dental model or your hands is that they have no lips. Both tools are great for demonstrating sounds and contrasts like /θ/ and /s/, /z/ and /dʒ/, or /n/ and /ŋ/, but not so helpful for /f/, /v/, /m/, /w/, or other sounds that involve the lips.

Listening tubes like those sold under the names Whispy Reader, Toobaloo, Hear Myself Sound Phone, WhisperPhone, and others are basically a curved tube (Figure 7.2). When learners hold the tube like a telephone receiver, speaking into one end and listening to the other, they can hear their own voices more clearly while background noise in the classroom is lessened. Listening tubes are useful for both children and adults, although some companies' models are too small to be comfortable for adults.

A cheap-and-quick version can even be made out of folded paper. (See Figure 7.3 below and online.) You can also make listening tubes yourself from PVC pipe (see bottom picture

Figure 7.2. Listening tubes.

in Figure 7.2). Get the fittings you need at a hardware or building supply store and assemble them easily. For each listening tube you'll need a straight piece of pipe about 5 inches/ 12 cm. long and two elbow joints. You can glue the pieces together, but they usually stay together well enough without glue. Be careful not to make the middle (straight) section too long, or the phone will be too long to fit between the user's ear and mouth.

Paper Listening Tube

1. Cut out the pattern below along the solid lines.
2. Fold up on the dotted lines.
3. Lap tab A over tab B as far as the light dotted line and tape in place to make a small tubelike area. Do the same with tabs C and D.
4. Lap E over F as far as the light dotted line and tape together. Do the same with G and H.
5. Fold the tubelike ends up and tape I and J to their sides. Do the same thing with K and L.
6. Bring the long edges of the middle section together and tape together.
7. Hold the finished tube to your ear and mouth like a telephone receiver and speak into it to make your voice sound louder.

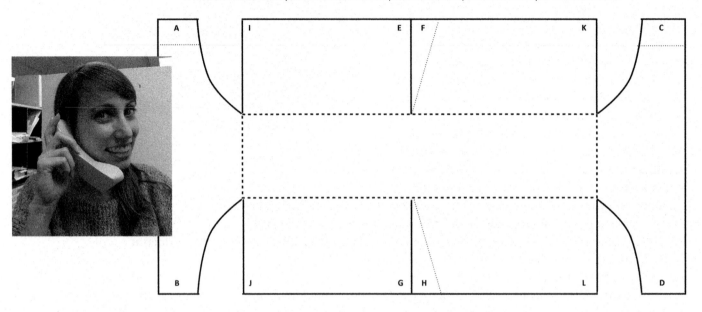

Figure 7.3. Paper listening tube: Picture of woman using listening tube. Pattern for making listening tube.

The Make, Take, & Teach website has a video that shows how to make listening tubes from PVC pipe. See http://blog.maketaketeach.com/how-to-make-a-phonics-phone/#.

Rubber bands can be used to illustrate the difference between tense and lax vowels. Have students hold a thick rubber band and stretch it as they say words like *seat, late,* or *shoe* to help them feel the tension in their tongues and lips during those tense vowels. Have them hold the rubber band loosely when they say *sit, let,* or *should* to illustrate that those lax sounds are pronounced in a more relaxed way. Be sure to use the thickest rubber bands you can find. (The ones I use are #84.) Thin ones stretch or break too easily, and they're easier for students to get in trouble with by snapping each other or flinging them across the room.

Drinking straws are useful for practicing several sounds. To help students get a feeling for the tongue position for /r/, have them grip a straw horizontally between their teeth (like a dog holding a bone in its mouth) so that their tongue is guided backward and can't reach the alveolar ridge. For /l/, have them bite gently on the end of a straw, with the last 1/4 inch (0.5 centimeter) in their mouths. Have them put the tips of their tongues above the short bit of straw that extends into their mouths. The straw will push the tip of the tongue up to the alveolar ridge.

When practicing /w/, /kw/, and /uw/, which all require rounded lips, have students put the end of a straw in their mouths and tighten their lips around it to encourage lip rounding. For /ʊ/, use a bigger straw (a milkshake or "boba" straw) or a finger-sized rolled-up paper so that the lips are a little less rounded.

Feathers or thin tissue paper can be used to illustrate the aspiration of initial stops /p/, /t/, and /k/. Have students hold the feather or paper in front of their mouths. When they say words beginning with these sounds, there should be a small puff of air that makes the feather or paper move slightly. If students are not aspirating the stops enough, the feather or paper won't move.

(Some books recommend using a lighted candle for this purpose. However, this can be quite dangerous, and is not a good idea, even for adult students.)

Using Gadgets with Adults

Some teachers wonder if it's all right to use kinesthetic teaching aids with adult students. I've found that most tools work well with adults, as long as you explain the purpose of what you're doing and tell them how it will help them improve their pronunciation. Most adults appreciate these learning aids if they see that they have a solid learning purpose. While you won't want to do extremely childish or cute things with adults, you don't have to be businesslike 100% of the time either, even with business-oriented adults.

Games for Teaching Sounds

We've been looking at activities for teaching pronunciation. Games can also be effective teaching tools. First let's consider the difference between an activity and a game.

Games have an element of competition—between individuals, between teams, or even with individuals competing against their own past performance. Games have rules that need to be followed, and there are usually winners and losers (or to be kind, I suppose we could say "non-winners.") In activities that are not games, the main purpose is not to win, but to accomplish a task or learning purpose. Everybody can succeed at the same time. Even though some students may be checking their own work against that of others to see who is doing the best, competition is not the main goal.

You can turn many activities into games by adding an element of competition. Divide the class into teams and have them take turns doing bits of practice: They could read words with correct pronunciation, identify which sound they hear, think of a word that rhymes with a given word, list words starting with a given sound, or many other possibilities. Whether you count points or award prizes is up to you. (A round of applause can be a great prize, and it's free!) You can also turn many common games into pronunciation teaching tools. For example:

Bingo. Make bingo grids with minimal pairs using vowels or consonants or pairs of words that are the same except for stress. For additional practice, students can take turns calling the bingo words.

Card games. Children's card games like Go Fish and Crazy Eights can be used to practice pronunciation if you make cards with symbols or pictures of objects that contain the sounds you want to practice instead of the usual hearts, diamonds, clubs, and spades. Look here for instructions for card games that can be adapted for pronunciation practice: http://www.activityvillage.co.uk /card-games.

Concentration. This is a game played with cards or pictures that match up in pairs: A sound symbol and a picture of a word starting with it, a picture and its word, and so forth. The cards are mixed up and arranged upside down. Players take turns choosing two cards to see if they match. If they do, they are left face up, and the player gets a point. If they don't match, they're turned upside down again, and the next player chooses two cards. The object of the game is to find as many matching pairs as possible.

Board games. Find or make a game board with spaces leading from the first to the last space. Write questions or instructions on cards or slips of paper. Change the questions to practice different subject matter. Players throw dice, move the indicated number of spaces, choose a card, and answer the question. The object of the game is to reach the "finish" square first.

Unless you're teaching young children, be careful about how many games you use. They're the icing on the cake, not the cake itself. Students will overdose if they have too much.

Classroom Management While Using Activities, Games, and Gadgets

Teachers sometimes worry that if they use pair work, games, toys, and gadgets in teaching, the class will be noisy and out of control. This can certainly happen, especially with elementary or junior high school age learners. However, if you have a plan for good classroom management, your class can be purposeful and under control even while students are having fun. Here are some suggestions that can be adapted to fit the age and attitudes of your students:

- **Choose your game or activity carefully** to fit the needs, abilities, and age of your students. If the activity is too complex for young learners or too childish for older learners, it won't be successful.
- **Be purposeful**. Don't treat an activity, game, or gadget as *just* silly play. Yes, it's fun, but it should also have a serious learning purpose. Help students feel that they're learning and accomplishing something as they play.
- **Build accountability** into your activity. Give students a specific task to do, something to produce, or a chart to fill out to ensure that they're on task.
- **Explain** what the students are going to do and why. For example, you might say, "This game will help you practice the /v/ sound" or "When you imitate this video, it will help your intonation sound more natural."
- **Give simple, clear instructions** step by step. Plan how you'll give instructions. Exactly what are the steps for students to follow? What words will you use to explain them? What misunderstandings could arise, and how can you avoid these by making the instructions very clear? Check to be sure students understand the instructions. Some teachers like to ensure understanding by having students repeat the instructions back to them. Demonstrate what to do by doing it yourself or by trying the activity with a student.
- **Remind students** of your expectations for behavior, especially with younger learners. They shouldn't be allowed to goof off or misbehave just because they're doing something "fun." Make your expectations stick.
- **Walk around** the room and monitor students' work during the activity. Nip problems in the bud. Keep students on task.
- **Don't overdo** the "fun stuff," or students will get bored. Use games or gadgets as the dessert, not the whole meal.

Correcting Pronunciation Errors

When and how should we correct students' pronunciation errors? Students need feedback so they'll know what they're doing wrong and they can try to do it differently and begin to improve, but we don't want them to feel discouraged by focusing too much on what they *can't* do. Adult students sometimes ask the teacher to correct all their pronunciation mistakes, but this really isn't practical or even very helpful. To a student who is having trouble, constant corrections might feel like nagging or scolding and have a negative impact on his or her motivation. So we have to be selective about which errors we choose to correct and how we do it. Goodwin (2001, p. 130) makes this suggestion:

> Which errors should we correct? Rather than overwhelming the student with feedback on every possible error, follow the guidelines below:
>
> - Errors which cause a breakdown in communication
> - Errors which occur as a pattern, not as isolated mistakes
> - Errors which relate to the pronunciation points we are teaching

When you do make a correction, there are many ways to do it. Choose the way that works best for you, your students, and your teaching style. Here are a few possibilities:

- Model the correct pronunciation, and have the student imitate it. Make sure the student realizes that what you're modeling is different from what was originally said.
- Explain the difference between the correct way and the student's mistake, giving instructions for the correct pronunciation. Then have the student repeat.
- Demonstrate the student's way and then the correct way so the student can hear the difference. Then have the student repeat.
- During pair or group work, take notes of errors that many students are making and practice those points with the whole group afterwards. This has the advantage of not calling attention directly to the student who has made the mistake. On the other hand, it has the disadvantage that the students who made the mistakes might still not realize that they were doing something wrong.
- Know when to quit. If a student tries and tries and still can't "get it," pushing further at that moment could just lead to frustration, anger, and resistance in the future. Sometimes it's better to say, "It's OK. We'll keep working on it," move on to something else, and come back to that problem later. Reassure students that learning pronunciation is a process that takes time. They don't have to be perfect immediately.

Review Is Important!

Don't be afraid to teach the same point more than once or to review often. If students wonder why they have to practice the same sounds again and again, make an analogy with learning to play a musical instrument. Someone who is learning to play the violin can't say, "Oh, I've already played that song. I don't need to play it again." They know that they have to play the same song many times, haltingly at first and then more smoothly, before they can play it really well.

Example Activities

You can see examples of some of the activity types mentioned in this chapter on the accompanying website, www.tesol.org/beyondrepeatafterme. Most of these activities come with handouts that you can distribute to your classes, and any of them can be adapted to practice other sounds or to fit the needs of your students.

CHAPTER 8

Syllables and Word Stress

Until now I've been talking about individual phonemes—consonants and vowels—which together are called the **segmental features of pronunciation.** The next five chapters go beyond just the individual sounds to **suprasegmental features**—aspects of pronunciation that affect more than just a single sound. The following are the most important suprasegmental features in English:

- **Word stress.** The extra emphasis given to one syllable in a polysyllabic word.
- **Thought groups.** Groups of spoken words that form a grammatical and semantic unit and seem to fit together.
- **Prominence.** The one word or syllable in each thought group or sentence that receives more stress than the others.
- **Intonation.** The pitch pattern of a sentence—the up-and-down melody of your voice as you speak.
- **Rhythm.** The characteristic pattern of longer and shorter, stressed and unstressed syllables in a language.
- **Connected speech.** Changes in pronunciation when words come together when you talk and are linked to the words around them.

How important is it for these features of pronunciation to be taught, learned, and used? These days, teachers and scholars recognize that stress, rhythm, intonation, and other suprasegmental features are very important in helping speakers sound natural and be understood, but this hasn't always been the case. Until the 1970s, suprasegmental features were mostly ignored in language classes, and pronunciation teaching usually concentrated on individual sounds. With the growing popularity of **communicative language teaching** beginning in the late 20th century and continuing into the 21st, however, many scholars began to emphasize the importance of suprasegmentals. In fact, some claimed that in order to make speech understandable, pronouncing individual sounds accurately was much less important than using word stress, rhythm, and intonation well. More recently, scholars and teachers have begun to look for a more balanced approach that helps learners use both aspects of pronunciation more effectively (Celce-Murcia, Brinton, & Goodwin, 2010). As classroom teachers, we need to help our students learn about and practice both individual sounds and the overall musical patterns of English. This chapter takes a closer look at the first two topics related to suprasegmental features: Syllables and word stress.

Syllables

A **syllable** is a rhythmic unit in speech—a chunk of sound that gets one "beat" in a word. As you read in Chapter 2, "Some Basic Concepts of Phonology," each syllable must have a "heart"—usually a vowel, but sometimes a **syllabic consonant.** In English, a syllable can also have one or more consonants before the vowel and one or more consonants after it. Here are some example words with the number of syllables in each (**sound 8.1**):

book	1 syllable
pen•cil	2 syllables
com•put•er	3 syllables
dic•tion•ar•y	4 syllables
con•grat•u•la•tions	5 syllables
re•spon•si•bil•i•ty	6 syllables

It may seem that counting the syllables in a word is a simple thing. We just count the beats, maybe clapping or tapping along with the syllables to help us feel the rhythm better. (See the sidebar "Four Ways to Count Syllables in English" for additional suggestions.) But for learners, counting syllables is not always easy, especially if their native language has different syllable structure patterns than English or a different way of counting syllables. Here are some things that can cause confusion in counting syllables:

- When vowel sounds are spelled with more than one vowel letter or with a final "silent *e*" (*read, beautiful, make*), learners may count the vowel *letters* instead of the vowel *sounds.*

- If a word has two vowel letters together, learners may find it challenging to tell if the sequence of vowel letters represents one syllable or two. For example, *cream* (/kriym/) and *suit* (/suwt/) each have one syllable, but *create* (/kriy•eyt/) and *ruin* (/ru•wın/) each have two, even though they're spelled with the same vowel letters.

- In words with consonant clusters, learners may feel that each consonant in the cluster should have its own syllable, especially if their native language has a strict consonant-vowel syllable structure with few or no clusters. For example, *spring* or *strike* may seem to have more than one syllable to students who cope with unfamiliar consonant clusters by inserting extra vowels between them. Similarly, learners whose languages don't have word-final consonants may add an extra vowel after a consonant at the end of a word and feel that this is an extra syllable.

- Learners may be unsure about when the *-s* and *-ed* endings add an extra syllable and when they don't. (See Chapter 6, "Pronunciation of Some Word Endings.")

- Learners may be fooled by the spelling of words with "disappearing syllables" that are not usually pronounced. (See the next paragraph.)

Four Ways to Count Syllables in English

1. Listen and count
   - Say the word. Count the vowel sounds you hear. That's the number of syllables.
   - Be sure to count the vowel *sounds*, not the vowel *letters*.

2. Touch your chin
   - Put your hand under your chin. Say the word.
   - Count how many times your chin moves down and touches your hand. That's the number of syllables.
   - If the word contains high vowels (/iy/, /ı/, /uw/, /ʊ/), schwa (/ə/), or syllabic consonants /n/, /l/, or /r/, it may be hard to feel your chin move because your mouth doesn't open very far for these sounds.

3. Clap and count
   - Say the word slowly. Clap each time you hear a vowel sound and feel a "beat."
   - The number of claps is the number of syllables.

4. The hardest way
   - Count the number of vowel letters in the word. Also count *y* if it represents a vowel sound.
   - Subtract one for each "disappearing syllable" like *au* in *restaurant* or the second *o* in *chocolate.*
   - Subtract one for each silent vowel letter (like *e* in *horse*).
   - Subtract one for each vowel **digraph** (like *ee* in *tree*).
   - Subtract two for each vowel **trigraph** (like *eau* in *beautiful*).
   - The number you end up with is the number of syllables.

5. The easiest way
   - Check a dictionary. The pronunciation symbols in good dictionaries are divided into syllables and the stress is marked.

Disappearing Syllables

Some words in English are normally pronounced with what might be called "disappearing syllables"—we see letters in the spelling of the word, and if we pronounce the words very slowly and carefully, we *might* hear a syllable, but in normal speaking, a syllable is not pronounced. For exam-

Table 8.1. Some words with disappearing syllables (sound 8.2).

as**pi**rin	**nat**urally
average	**rest**aurant
business	**sep**arate (adjective only)
camera	**temp**erature
chocolate	**veg**etable
comfortable	
de**lib**erate (adjective only)	*-ary (These are just a few examples)*
desperate	ele**ment**ary
different	docu**ment**ary
en**vir**onment	compli**ment**ary
evening	
every	*-ally (These are just a few examples)*
family	**bas**ically
favorable, **fav**orite	**prac**tically
general	acci**dent**ally
interest, **int**eresting	**aw**fully
laboratory	

Note. The syllables written in smaller letters are not normally pronounced. Stressed syllables are in bold.

ple, *chocolate* looks like it should have three syllables: *choc•o•late,* but in normal spoken English, it has only two syllables: /'ʧɑk•lət/. These pronunciations should not be thought of as sloppy or careless; they are normal and acceptable in all types of English. Some other words with similar disappearing syllables are listed in Table 8.1.

Word Stress

If a word in English has more than one syllable (we call these **polysyllabic words**), one of the syllables is **stressed**; that is, it is emphasized more than the others. It's very important for learners to put the stress in the right place. If the wrong syllable is stressed, listeners may not be able to understand what word is being said. This is because we understand words not only from their individual sounds, but also from their pattern of stressed and unstressed syllables. For example,

if we expect the word *conversation* to have a pattern like this: , but someone

pronounces it with a pattern like this: , it will take us longer to realize what the word is and to understand its meaning.

Characteristics of Stressed Syllables

How are stressed syllables different from the other syllables in a word? What characteristics does the stressed syllable need to have to let the listener know that it is being emphasized? In English, a stressed syllable can have any or all of the following qualities:

It's longer in duration than the other syllables:

Illustration 8.1. Longer in duration.

It's louder than the other syllables:

Illustration 8.2. Louder.

It's higher in pitch than the other syllables:

Illustration 8.3: Higher in pitch.

Its vowel sound is more distinct than other syllables. (It's not reduced.):

consənənt

Illustration 8.4: Vowel sound is more distinct.

Not every stressed syllable will have all of these qualities, especially if the speaker is talking quickly, but overall, these are the signs that tell the listener which syllable is stressed. It's important for learners to get used to using these signals to make stressed syllables stand out.

Primary and Secondary Stress

We know that in every polysyllabic word, one syllable has the **main stress**, or **primary stress**. In longer words, there is often another syllable that receives a little stress, but not as much as the main-stressed syllable. We say this syllable has **secondary stress.** For example, the word *congratulations* has five syllables, with the primary stress on the fourth syllable (**sound 8.3**):

con grat u **LA** tions

But we can also hear that the second syllable has some stress; it is pronounced with just a bit more force than the syllables before and after it:

con **grat** u **LA** tions

The other syllables in the word have no stress at all. They are called **unstressed syllables.** *Congratulations* has three unstressed syllables: *con, u,* and *tions.*

Using phonemic symbols and including symbols to mark primary and secondary stress, we can write *congratulations* this way: /kənˌgræʧəˈleyʃənz/. (See the sidebar "Symbols for Indicating Stress.")

It's very important for learners to know where the primary stress in a word should be. For teaching purposes, secondary stress is less critical. As long as the primary stress is in the right place, the stress pattern will sound acceptable to most listeners.

Characteristics of Unstressed Syllables

Unstressed syllables are those that don't receive any stress at all. They tend to be short, weak, and somewhat unclear. In contrast to stressed syllables, unstressed syllables can have some or all of these qualities:

- They're shorter in duration than stressed syllables.
- They're a bit quieter than stressed syllables.
- They're lower in pitch than stressed syllables.
- Their vowel sounds are less distinct than those in stressed syllables and are often (but not always) reduced to /ə/. In fact, in many unstressed syllables it doesn't matter if you say /ə/ or /ɪ/ or a sound in between. The unstressed vowel is just the quick little sound that is made while your tongue is moving from one important sound to another. There may be some variation in what the vowel sounds like without causing misunderstanding. (For example, the vowels in the *-ed* and *-s* endings, described in Chapter 6, "Pronunciation of Some Word Endings," work this way.)

For speech to be easily understood, unstressed syllables must be *much* shorter and weaker than stressed syllables. This helps the listener recognize the whole syllable pattern of the word and begin to identify it. If there's not enough contrast between the stressed and unstressed syllables, listeners' minds may be searching their memory for a word that has the wrong stress pattern and never find the actual word.

> ### Symbols for Indicating Stress
> Textbooks and dictionaries use two main ways of indicating stress in words. (Unstressed syllables are usually not marked.)
>
> - A small vertical line above the line of type at the beginning of a syllable shows primary stress: com‚muni'**cation**.
> - A small vertical line below the line of type at the beginning of a syllable shows secondary stress: com‚**muni**'cation.
> - A slanted accent mark with a positive slope (going uphill) above a vowel shows primary stress: commùnicátion.
> - A slanted accent mark with a negative slope (going downhill) above a vowel shows secondary stress: commùnicátion.
>
> Other ways to indicate primary stress:
>
> - Write the stressed syllable in capital or bold letters (or both): communi**CA**tion.
> - Underline the stressed syllable: communi<u>ca</u>tion.
> - Put a circle, dot, or other mark above the stressed syllable:
>
> ●   ★
> communication, communication

Which Syllable Should Be Stressed?

It sometimes seems that word stress in English is arbitrary—that there's no way to predict which syllable will be stressed in any particular word. Actually, there are rules and generalizations that can often (but not always) predict where word stress will fall. They take into account the historical origin of the word, its prefixes and suffixes, and the word's grammatical function in a sentence. These rules are rather complex, and we will look at only a few of them here. Celce-Murcia et al. (2010, pp. 185–198) has a more complete discussion of factors that help determine word stress in English.

Teachers sometimes wonder if they should require students to memorize detailed rules about word stress. As with many other aspects of pronunciation, it's not a good idea to try to teach *all* the rules to students or to expect them to memorize them, especially with younger learners. It's just too much. In any case, memorizing a rule is seldom the best way to learn to use it well. It's better to guide students to discover some basic generalizations about word stress and give them plenty of practice in using the patterns they find.

Also, when learning new vocabulary, it's very important for students to learn stress patterns along with the pronunciation and meaning of the new words. As they say the words many times through repetition and other practice activities, word stress and syllable patterns will start to feel natural and become a part of students' permanent knowledge about the words.

The next sections describe some of the simpler guidelines about word stress that are easy to understand and teach.

Nouns and Verbs: A General Guideline

There's no rule that works 100% of the time in predicting where the stress will be in words in English. However, there is a somewhat reliable generalization about word stress in nouns and verbs that have two syllables.

Table 8.2. Two-syllable nouns and verbs with predictable stress (sound 8.4).

Two-syllable nouns: Oo			Two-syllable verbs: oO		
woman	pencil	window	receive	become	improve
table	color	apple	appear	begin	express
paper	people	mother	describe	compare	believe

According to Avery and Ehrlich (1992), two-syllable nouns are stressed on the first syllable more than 90% of the time, while two-syllable verbs are stressed on the second syllable more than 60% of the time. In other words, two-syllable nouns are much more likely to have a stress pattern like this: ⬤◯, while two-syllable verbs are more likely to have a stress pattern like this: ◯⬤. Table 8.2 lists some words that follow this pattern.

Noun-Verb Pairs With Different Stress

In keeping with the general rule we've just learned, there are some word pairs consisting of a noun and a verb that are spelled the same way, but the noun is stressed on the first syllable and the verb is stressed on the second syllable. For example, 'permit is a noun, but per'mit is a verb (**sound 8.5**):

You need a 'permit to park here.
Please per'mit me to help you.

Sometimes a change in vowel sounds goes along with this change in word stress because the unstressed vowels are often reduced to /ə/. For example, the first syllable in *contrast* is pronounced as /ɑ/ when it's a noun (and that syllable is stressed) but it's pronounced /ə/ when it's a verb (and that syllable is unstressed). Table 8.3 shows a list of some of the most common noun-verb pairs with different stress patterns.

These pairs often have very closely related meanings. For example, a *'permit* is something that *per'mits* you to do something. However, the meanings are not always so close. For example, the

Table 8.3. Some noun-verb pairs with different stress.

When these words are nouns, they're stressed on the first syllable. When they're verbs, they're stressed on the second.				
addict	contrast	implant	progress	relay
address	converse	import	project	repeat
affect	convert	imprint	protest	reprint
ally	convict	incline	rebel	research
combat	decrease	increase	recall	reset
combine	default	insert	recap	rewrite
commune	defect	insult	record	subject
compact	desert	intern	recount	survey
compound	digest	intrigue	redirect	suspect
compress	discard	misprint	redo	torment
conduct	discharge	object	redress	transfer
confine(s)	discount	offset	refill	transplant
conflict	escort	perfect	refund	transport
console	export	permit	refuse	update
construct	extract	present	rehash	upgrade
contest	finance	proceed(s)	reject	uplift
contract	impact	produce	relapse	upset

verb *com'bine* means "to put things together," while the noun *'combine* means "a big tractor-like machine that harvests grain." Although the meanings came from the same source, the connection isn't obvious now.

It's important to remind students that while some noun-verb pairs follow this pattern, not all do. For example, *travel, practice,* and *answer* can all be used as either nouns or verbs, but they're always stressed on the first syllable. On the other hand, *result, command,* and *attempt* are always stressed on the second syllable, whether they're used as nouns or verbs.

Also, there can be differences among individual speakers in the stress patterns of the words in Table 8.3. For example, some people pronounce the noun *address* with stress on the first syllable and some with stress on the second syllable. This is just another case when language is variable and inconsistent.

It's also important to remember that as time goes by, words in English can easily change from one **part of speech** to another, so a word that is used only as a noun now might become a verb in the future and vice versa. When this happens, the word usually doesn't change its original stress pattern.

Stress in Compound Nouns

English has many **compound nouns**—combinations of two words that together make a new noun, such as *newspaper, motorcycle,* or *post office.* Some compound nouns are written as one word (*textbook, toothpaste, haircut*). Others are written as two words (*high school, parking lot, swimming pool*). A much smaller number of compound nouns are written with a hyphen between the two parts (*T-shirt, dry-cleaner, six-pack*). There is no firm rule to predict whether a particular compound noun will be written as one word, two words, or with a hyphen—we just have to check a dictionary— and even then, different dictionaries often list different spellings.

No matter how a compound noun is written, its stress is in the same place—on the stressed syllable of the *first* element in the word. The second part of the compound is unstressed (**sound 8.6**):

If the second part of the compound is a polysyllabic word that would normally have a stressed syllable, all of its syllables are still unstressed or only very lightly stressed

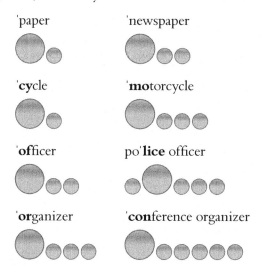

The stress pattern in compound nouns is different from the stress pattern in an ordinary adjective-plus-noun combination. While a compound noun is stressed on the first part, a phrase

made up of an adjective and a noun has some stress on both parts. For example, these compound nouns and phrases have different stress patterns and different meanings (**sound 8.7**):

Compound nouns

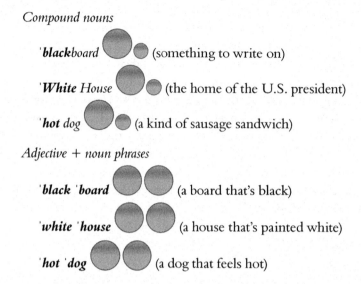

ˈ**black**board (something to write on)

ˈ**White** House (the home of the U.S. president)

ˈ**hot** dog (a kind of sausage sandwich)

Adjective + noun phrases

ˈ**black** ˈ**board** (a board that's black)

ˈ**white** ˈ**house** (a house that's painted white)

ˈ**hot** ˈ**dog** (a dog that feels hot)

If you don't already know, how can you tell if a combination of words is a compound noun or an adjective plus a noun? Here are some guidelines, although they don't always work:

- If it's written as one word or as two words with a hyphen, it's a compound noun.
- If it's written as two words, the more common, well-established phrases are more likely to be compounds. More unusual or unpredictable phrases are probably not, but sometimes it's hard to tell.

For example, Table 8.4 lists some compound nouns beginning with the word *school* and some phrases that use *school* to modify a noun. Overall, the first group contains more common combinations that have been in use for a long time, like *schoolhouse* and *schoolteacher,* and the second group has less common or more recent phrases, like *school psychologist* or *school trip.* Still, it's often hard to predict whether a particular phrase is a compound noun or an adjective plus noun.

So what can students do? When they learn a new compound word, they should learn its stress pattern along with its pronunciation—listen to it when it's modeled, practice saying it correctly, and get used to the whole sound of it. They should also pay attention to the stress patterns of com-

Table 8.4 compound nouns and phrases with "school" (sound 8.8).

Compound nouns (stress on first part)	Not compound nouns (stress on both parts)
school age	school administrator
school board	school classroom
school book	school colors
school boy	school counselor
school bus	school diploma
school child	school festival
school day	school library
school district	school lunch
school girl	school nurse
schoolhouse	school principal
schoolroom	school project
schoolteacher	school psychologist
school work	school transportation
school year	school trip

monly used adjective-noun combinations when they hear them, just as they do when they learn new vocabulary words. Still, learners will probably use incorrect stress from time to time, just as they'll probably make mistakes in pronouncing sounds. This is an inevitable part of learning.

Stress in Phrasal Verbs

English also has many **phrasal verbs,** or **two-word verbs,** such as *put on, get up, turn off,* and *take over.* Phrasal verbs (sometimes called **compound verbs)** are usually written as two separate words, and in sentences, their two parts are sometimes separated by other words. Unlike compound nouns, phrasal verbs are usually stressed on the second part, especially when that part comes at the end of a sentence or thought group (**sound 8.9**).

Please come 'in.   Pick it 'up.   I turned it 'on.

However, when a phrasal verb is followed by a noun that is its object, the stress is different. The first part of the verb receives a little stress, and the primary stress moves to the object of the phrasal verb :

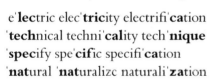

Pick up the 'paper.   I turned on the 'light.

Some of these two-word verbs can also be used as nouns. In this case, they follow the same pattern as the noun-verb pairs that were described earlier (*permit, suspect, progress*). They're stressed on the first part when they're nouns and on the second part when they're verbs. Also, they're typically written as one word when they're nouns, but as two words when they're verbs:

I'll print it 'out. I'll give you a 'printout.
The plane took 'off. It was a smooth 'takeoff.

Suffixes and Stress

Students are sometimes confused by sets of words that come from the same basic root but have their stress on different syllables. At first glance, these changes seem completely random (**sound 8.10**):

e'lectric elec'tricity electrifi'cation
'technical techni'cality tech'nique
'specify spe'cific specifi'cation
'natural 'naturalize naturali'zation

However, there actually is a pattern in the stress placement of these words. All of them have **suffixes** such as *-ic, -ity, -ify,* or *-tion* that have been added to their roots to make a change in meaning. Certain suffixes, especially those that were borrowed from Latin or Greek, cause words to be stressed on a particular syllable. There are several groups of suffixes that affect word stress in different ways:

Group 1. Many suffixes cause the stress to be on the syllable just before the suffix (**sound 8.11**). Table 8.5 shows the most important ones.

congratu'lations   scien'tific   mu'sician

Table 8.5. Suffix Group 1: stress the syllable before the suffix (sound 8.12).

Suffix	Examples
-tion, -sion, -ion	con'dition, ex'tension, o'pinion
-ity, -ety	crea'tivity, i'dentity, elec'tricity, an'xiety
-ic, -ical	scien'tific, e'lectric, i'dentical
-al (sometimes)	depart'mental, inci'dental, adjec'tival
-ial, -cial, -sial, -tial, -ual	fi'nancial, contro'versial, i'nitial, re'sidual
-ian, -cian, -sian, -ia	mu'sician, phy'sician, 'Persian, 'mania
-ous, -ious, -eous, -uous	mys'terious, cou'rageous, am'biguous
-ient, -ience, -iant, -iance	'patient, 'patience, 'radiant, 'radiance
-ify	i'dentify, hu'midify, e'lectrify, 'beautify
-ive, -itive, -ative	pos'sessive, 'positive, 'relative
-itude	'gratitude, 'aptitude, 'latitude, 'attitude
-graphy, -grapher	pho'tography, pho'tographer, bi'ography
-logy, -logist	bi'ology, bi'ologist, soci'ology, soci'ologist

Group 2. A smaller number of suffixes cause the stress to fall *two* syllables before the suffix (**sound 8.13**). Of course, if there is only one syllable before the prefix, that one is stressed, for example: '*donate*. The most important suffix in this group is *-ate* (see Table 8.6).

'**grad**uate   '**dem**onstrate   col'**lab**orate

Table 8.6. Suffix Group 2: stress the second syllable before the suffix (sound 8.14).

Suffix	Examples
-ate	'estimate, pro'crastinate, 'graduate, 'separate

Some words with *-ate* can be either verbs or nouns/adjectives. The stress is the same for both, but the pronunciation of *-ate* changes:

Verbs: *-ate* = /eyt/

He'll *graduate* from college. /'græʤuweyt/
Let's *separate* the truth from the lies. /'sɛpəreyt/

Nouns/adjectives: *-ate* = /ət/

She's a college *graduate*. /'græʤuwət/
That's a *separate* problem. /'sɛpərət/

Group 3. With a few suffixes, we stress the suffix itself (**sound 8.15**). The suffixes in this group have all been borrowed from French, where words tend to be stressed on the last syllable. The most common ones are listed in Table 8.7.

tech'**nique**   kitchen'**ette**   volun'**teer**

Table 8.7. Suffix Group 3: stress the suffix (sound 8.16).

Suffix	Examples
-ee	refe'ree, nomi'nee, refu'gee
-ese	Japan'ese, Chin'ese, bureaucra'tese
-ette	disk'ette, kitchen'ette, cigar'ette
-esque	pictur'esque, gro'tesque, Roman'esque
-ique	u'nique, tech'nique, bou'tique
-aire, -eer	question'naire, volun'teer, engi'neer
-esce, -escent, -escence	coa'lesce, ado'lescent, ado'lescence

Group 4. Finally, many suffixes have no effect on word stress (**sound 8.17**). The stress stays on the same syllable where it was before the suffix was added. Many of these suffixes are of Germanic origin, although -*al*, -*ize* and -*ment* come from Latin. The main suffixes in this group are listed in Table 8.8.

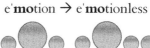

under'**stand** → under'**stand**able   '**beau**ty → '**beau**tiful   e'**motion** → e'**motion**less

Table 8.8. Suffix Group 4: suffix doesn't change the stress (sound 8.18).

Suffix	Examples
-able, -ible	under'standable, 'comfortable, 'possible
-ness	'kindness, 'carefulness, po'liteness
-ful	'careful, 'meaningful, 'beautiful
-less	'careless, 'meaningless, 'thankless
-ish	'selfish, 'yellowish, 'childish
-er, -or, -ess, -ist	'teacher, con'ductor, 'actress, 'dentist
-ly (adjective/adverb)	'manly, 'womanly, 'easily, 'quickly
-en	'threaten, 'tighten, en'lighten
-hood	'brotherhood, 'childhood, 'knighthood
-some	'handsome, 'tiresome, 'loathsome
-dom	'freedom, 'kingdom, 'wisdom
-ward	'homeward, 'seaward, 'forward
-al (sometimes)	oc'casional, 'fictional, 'personal
-ment	'document, en'joyment, enter'tainment
-ize, -ise, -yze	'capitalize, 'realize, 'advertise, 'analyze
Grammatical endings: -s, -ed, -ing, -er, -est	under'stands, 'catches, under'standing, 'catching, 'happier, 'happiest

Exceptions. As with most rules, there are exceptions to these, too. For example, 'television ends in the suffix *-sion,* so we might expect it to be stressed on the second to last syllable, but it's actually stressed on the first. *Cre'ate* might be expected to be stressed earlier because of the suffix *-ate,* but actually the suffix itself is stressed.

There can also be differences in stress among dialects or even between individual speakers. For example, *employ'ee* and *cigar'ette* are predicted to have stress on the last syllable, and they often do, but many people stress them differently: They may stress *em'ployee* on the second syllable and *'cigarette* on the first. In a limited number of words, two stress patterns are acceptable.

Prefixes and Stress

Unlike suffixes, prefixes have little effect on word stress. The prefixes themselves are generally unstressed or weakly stressed, and they don't cause the stress to change in the rest of the word (**sound 8.19**). For example:

> 'cover un'cover dis'cover re'cover
> o'bey diso'bey
> cur'ricular extracur'ricular
> ap'praise reap'praise

Numbers Ending in *–teen* and *–ty*

It's often difficult to hear the difference between pairs of numbers like *fourteen* and *forty* or *nineteen* and *ninety,* even for native speakers of English. When you look at the written forms *fourteen* and *forty,* it seems that it should be easy to tell them apart—just listen for the /n/ at the end of *fourteen.* Unfortunately, though, people don't usually pronounce these numbers clearly enough to hear that last /n/, especially when the next word starts with /n/ or another sound that blends with the /n/. Fortunately, there are other clues that distinguish the *-teen* and *-ty* numbers. Here are two simple clues to help students.

Word stress. The *-ty* numbers are always stressed on the first syllable. The *-teen* numbers are *usually* stressed on the last syllable. (But look at the section on **variable word stress** at the end of Chapter 9, "Rhythm," to see some exceptions. There are always exceptions, aren't there?)

The sound of /t/. Both *forty* and *fourteen* have the phoneme /t/ in the middle, but because of the difference in stress, in American English /t/ sounds different in each word. In *-ty* words, the stress is *before* /t/, so it becomes the **alveolar flap** [ɾ]. It's **voiced**, and it sounds like a quick /d/. In *-teen* words, the stress is *after* /t/, so it doesn't become a flap. It sounds like a normal, **aspirated** /t/. It's voiceless, and it's pronounced with a slight puff of air. (See Chapter 4, "The Consonants of American English," for more details about the **allophones** of /t/.)

In real life, if you're not sure what number you've heard, it's best to just ask for clarification. Everybody does this from time to time, including native speakers, and nobody will mind. Table 8.9 summarizes the pronunciation differences between numbers ending in *-ty* and *-teen.*

Table 8.9 Pronunciation of –ty and –teen numbers (sound 8.20).

Type of number	Stress pattern	Sound of /t/
-ty words (e.g. 40)	O o	Flapped /t/
-teen words (e.g., 14)	o O	Aspirated /t/
Listen: 20 30 40 50 60 70 80 90		
Listen: 13 14 15 16 17 18 19		

Compound Adverbs

Compound adverbs are words made up of two separate parts that function as adverbs. When these words tell location or direction, they are normally stressed on the last part of the word (**sound 8.21**):

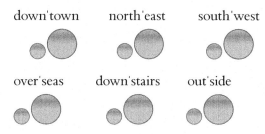

down'town   north'east   south'west

over'seas   down'stairs   out'side

Reflexive Pronouns

Reflexive pronouns are pronouns that refer back to the subject of the sentence. They end in -*self* or -*selves,* and they're stressed on the last syllable (**sound 8.22**):

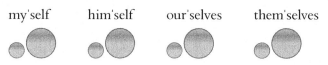

my'self   him'self   our'selves   them'selves

Word Stress in Other Languages

Not all languages have word stress, and even in those that do, it may not work the way it does in English. This can cause problems for speakers of other languages trying to produce the stress patterns of words in English.

In some languages, like Mandarin and Thai, almost all words have just one syllable, so the idea of word stress simply doesn't come up. In other languages that have many polysyllabic words, stressed and unstressed syllables may not sound the way they do in English. For example, in Spanish and Italian, stressed syllables are emphasized and are more forceful and higher in pitch than unstressed syllables, although there is typically a smaller contrast between stressed and unstressed syllables than in English. However, unstressed syllables in these languages are never reduced. That is, the vowels in unstressed syllables still have the same clear sounds as in stressed syllables; they do not become /ə/ as they often do in English.

Japanese is another example of a polysyllabic language that does not use stress in the same way that English does. In Japanese words, one syllable can be higher in pitch than the others, but it is not louder, longer, or stronger because of this, and the lower-pitched syllables are not reduced (Actually, Japanese is said to have **pitch accent** rather than word stress.) To a speaker of English, the higher-pitched syllables may sound like they're stressed, but what's happening is actually somewhat different.

Still other languages, like German and Russian, have word stress that works very much as it does in English. The stressed syllables are emphasized and higher in pitch, and the unstressed syllables may be reduced. Speakers of these languages will probably have less difficulty in getting used to the idea of word stress in English than speakers of languages without word stress. However, some languages with word stress have much more consistent placement of stress than English. For example, in Polish, the primary stress is almost always on the second to last syllable. In Finnish and Hungarian, on the other hand, word stress is almost always on the first syllable, and in French, it tends to be on the last syllable. Speakers of these languages may also have trouble with the more unpredictable word stress of English.

Learners whose native language has a different system of stress or pitch than English will need help getting used to the stress patterns of English. Be sure to make them aware of how word stress is different in English than in their native language. They'll need guidance in noticing and practicing stress in English words—emphasizing stressed syllables and de-emphasizing unstressed syllables.

Teaching Stress Patterns

What can you, as a teacher, do to help students learn the correct stress patterns for the thousands of words they'll need to know in English? Should you ask them to memorize all the rules about how word stress is determined? No, definitely not. Even if students memorize rules, it's hard for them to apply the rules in correctly producing word stress. It works better to help students *notice* the stress of new words and realize that stress is an important and necessary part of each word. Then as learners say and use the new words many times, the stress patterns will become natural and automatic. They'll build up a kind of muscle and sound memory of each word, including the appropriate stress. This is much less frustrating than trying to memorize a list of rules, but it does require that students get plenty of practice using new words in many contexts—something that good language teachers should be helping their students to do anyway.

CHAPTER 9

Rhythm

Just as music has rhythm, every language also has its own rhythm—that is, its own pattern of syllables that are longer or shorter, faster or slower, and more or less emphasized. When we listen to music, we sometimes hear a very regular rhythm, with all the notes lasting about the same time. Other music has a more irregular rhythm, with a mixture of long and short notes.

It's important to remember that rhythm is not the same thing as intonation, in the same way that the rhythm of a song is separate from its melody. Rhythm is about timing; intonation is about how the pitch of the speaker's voice goes up and down.

Types of Rhythm in Language

Phonologists have traditionally divided languages into two groups, based on the type of rhythm they have: **syllable-timed languages** and **stress-timed languages.**

Some languages have a very regular rhythm, with each syllable lasting about the same length of time and receiving about the same emphasis. These are called syllable-timed or syllable-based languages. If we use circles to represent syllables, we can picture the rhythm of a syllable-timed language like this:

Some syllable-timed languages are Spanish, French, Italian, Brazilian Portuguese (and most other Romance languages), Japanese, Korean, Cantonese (and some other varieties of Chinese), Vietnamese, Polish, Farsi, some dialects of Arabic, and Hindi (and related languages).

The rhythm of stress-timed languages is different—it's less uniform, and syllables do not all last the same length of time. Stressed syllables last longer, and unstressed syllables are shorter and quicker. The time between the stresses remains fairly steady, and unstressed syllables have to crowd in between the stressed syllables. We say a language with this type of rhythm is a stress-timed or stress-based language. English is a stress-timed language. We can picture its rhythm like this:

In addition to English, some other stress-timed languages are German, Danish, Norwegian, Swedish (and other Germanic languages), Russian, Czech (and some other Slavic languages), European Portuguese, and some dialects of Arabic.

Although the division into stress-timed and syllable-timed languages is an accepted way of categorizing the rhythm patterns of languages, in reality, the distinctions between these two rhythm types are not always so clear-cut. These rhythm patterns are tendencies, not absolute rules, and they can vary somewhat, depending on the individual speaker and the context (Roach, 1982). There can be differences between the rhythm patterns of different dialects of a language (as in Portuguese and Arabic) and even between different speakers of the same dialect.

In spite of this, we can easily hear and feel that languages have their own characteristic rhythm patterns that set them apart from each other. The rhythm of English is quite different from that of some learners' languages. To be understood easily, students need to be aware that rhythm is an important part of language and try to accurately imitate the rhythm of the language they're learning.

What Makes the Rhythm of English?

In English, as I explained above, not all syllables last the same length of time. In particular, stressed syllables last longer than unstressed ones. These longer, stressed syllables and shorter, unstressed syllables fit together to create the characteristic pattern of English rhythm. For the rhythm to sound natural, the pattern of stressed and unstressed syllables must be right. Stressed syllables need to last longer, and unstressed syllables need to be short and quick so they don't compete with the stressed syllables.

Notice the rhythm of these sentences (**sound 9.1**):

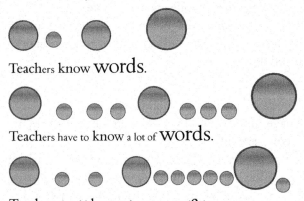

Teachers know words.

Teachers have to know a lot of words.

Teachers should know about pronunciation.

The time between the stressed syllables in each sentence stays fairly constant—not precisely the same, but close—even though there are many more unstressed syllables between some pairs of stressed syllables than others.

Content Words and Function Words

To know which words and syllables in a sentence are stressed or unstressed, you need to know the difference between **content words** and **function words**. I talked earlier about function words—words that have grammatical meaning, such as prepositions, articles, pronouns, and conjunctions. These are words that show the relationship between other words and don't have much meaning in themselves. Table 9.1 gives examples of function words.

Content words, on the other hand, are words that have lexical meaning, not grammatical meaning. That is, they have meaning in themselves; they refer to objects, actions, or ideas in the real world. We can think of them as the words that are most important in conveying the basic

Table 9.1. Function words (sound 9.2).

Category	Examples
Articles	a, an, the
Auxiliary verbs	does, did, has, had, am, is, can
Personal pronouns	I, you, he, she, me, him, her
Possessive adjectives	my, your, his, her, its, their
Demonstrative adjectives	this, that, these, those
Prepositions	in, on, under, with, to, for
Conjunctions	and, or, but, so, because, before, while
Relative pronouns	which, who, whom, whose, that

meaning of a sentence. Table 9.2 gives examples of content words, which include nouns, verbs, adjectives, adverbs, and question words.

In English, content words tend to receive more stress than function words, and therefore, they are usually longer in duration. Function words tend to be unstressed, and so they last a shorter time. This is a basic principle that helps create the rhythm of English.

Reduced Function Words

Look again at this example sentence (**sound 9.3**):

TEACH•ers should **KNOW** a•bout pro•nun•ci•**A**•tion.

There are five unstressed syllables between the last two main stresses (*know* and *a*). How can speakers manage to say so many unstressed syllables so quickly?

You learned in Chapter 5, "The Vowels of American English," that unstressed syllables and function words can have weak, reduced forms. In fact, some reduced forms are even written in a shortened form, especially in product names, like *In-N-Out Burger* (In and Out Burger), McDonald's *Filet-O-Fish* sandwich (Filet of Fish), *Land O'Lakes* dairy products (Land of Lakes), or *Sweet'N Low* artificial sweetener (Sweet and Low).

These reduced forms make syllables shorter and enable them to squeeze in between the stressed syllables. Sometimes sound changes also make it easier for us to say the reduced forms quickly so that regular timing can be maintained. This helps create the "music" of English. If we pronounced each syllable of each word with its full "dictionary" form, or **citation form**, the rhythm would sound unnatural and staccato—we'd be singing an entirely different song.

Table 9.2. Main kinds of content words (sound 9.4).

Category	Examples
Nouns	book, teacher, responsibility
Main verbs	read, eat, study, examine, discuss
Adjectives	big, beautiful, tired, many
Adverbs	often, always, easily, happily
Question words	who, what, where, when, why, how

Here's another example (**sound 9.5**):

I should have **GIV**•en him a **PRES**•ent.

Pronouncing *Can* and *Can't*

The contrast between the words *can* and *can't* is often especially troublesome in American English (**sound 9.6**). Here are some ways to tell them apart.

- *Can't* is usually stressed. It sounds like /kænt/ or /kæn?/, with a clear /æ/ sound. (We may not be able to hear the final /t/.)
  I **CAN'T** go with you. Why **CAN'T** you help me?
- *Can* is usually unstressed. It often sounds like /kən/ or /kn/, with a reduced vowel.
  I **can** go with you. Who **can** help me?
- But when *can* is alone, with no verb after it, it's stressed.
  Can you help me? Yes, I **CAN**.
  Can you help me? I **CAN** tomorrow, but not right now.

This sentence has only two content words: *given* and *present*. All the others are function words, and in normal speech, they're all shortened and reduced so that they fit into the available space. For example, *should have* doesn't sound like its full form of /ˈʃʊdhæv/. Instead, it sounds like /ˈʃʊdə/. Also, *him* sounds like /ɪm/ instead of /hɪm/.

If we say this sentence with full forms of all the function words, the rhythm doesn't sound quite natural, like this:

I SHOULD HAVE **GIV**•EN HIM A **PRES**•ENT.

Categories of Changes in Reduced Function Words

Many common function words are listed in Tables 9.3–9.6 with their citation forms and common reduced forms. In addition to these, other function words also become weaker, quicker, and less distinct when they're unstressed. Some types of changes that can happen when function words are reduced fall into predictable categories such as contractions, loss of consonants, and vowel changes.

Table 9.3. Reduced forms of some function words: prepositions, conjunctions, and articles (sound 9.7).

Word	Citation form	Reduced form	Example
Prepositions			
at	/æt/	/ət/	We're at home. Look at that.
for	/fɔr/	/fɚ/	It's for you. For a long time.
from	/frɑm/	/frəm/	He's from Irvine.
of	/əv/	/ə/ /əv/	(Before consonants) A cup of tea. (Before vowels) A couple of eggs.
to	/tuw/	/tə/ /tuw/	(Before consonants) Go to school. (Before vowels) Go to a movie.
Conjunctions			
and	/ænd/	/ən/, /n/	Up and down. Salt and pepper.
or	/ɔr/	/ɚ/	Soup or salad. Yes or no.
as . . . as	/æz/	/əz/	As fast as you can. Just as good.
because	/biykɔz/ /bəkʌz/	/kəz/ /bəkʌz/	I'm smiling 'cause I'm happy. I'm happy because it's Saturday.
Articles			
a	/ey/, /ə/	/ə/	(Before consonants) A box. A unit.
an	/æn/	/ən/	(Before vowels) An egg. An hour.
the	/ðiy/	/ðə/ /ðiy/	(Before consonants) The children. (Before vowels) The end. The others.

Contractions

When we use shortened forms like *I'm, he's, I'd, isn't,* and *can't,* whole syllables are lost, and the combined form becomes shorter (see sidebar, "Pronouncing *Can* and *Can't*"). For example, in the following sentence, *do not* and *you are* can be changed to the contractions *don't* and *you're* (**sound 9.8**). (More contractions are listed in Chapter 12, "Connected Speech.")

> I am a**FRAID** I do not under**STAND** what you are **SAY**ing.
> → I'm a**FRAID** I don't under**STAND** what you're **SAY**ing.

Loss of Consonants

The following words (pronouns and possessive adjectives) that start with /h/ can lose the /h/ sound in their reduced forms (**sound 9.9**):

> He → /iy/ Did he **TELL** you about it?
> Him → /ɪm/ We **HELPED** him.
> His → /ɪz/ Do you know his **NAME**?
> Her → /ɚ/ Do you know her **NAME**?

The pronoun *them* can also lose its initial /ð/ sound and be pronounced /əm/. (However, /ð/ is *not* lost when we say *they* or *their*—only *them.*)

> Them → /əm/ Did you **TALK** to them?
> They → /ðey/ (not /ey/) What do they **NEED**?

Because of these changes, *him* and *them* often sound very similar. Fortunately, in conversation we can usually tell which word is being said from context.

Table 9.4. Reduced forms of some function words: "be" verb, auxiliary verbs, and modals (sound 9.10).

Word	Citation form	Reduced form	Example
"Be" verb, auxiliary verbs, and modals			
am	/æm/	/əm/, /m/	What am I doing? I'm going.
are	/ɑr/	/ɚ/	What are you doing? You're going.
is	/ɪz/	/ɪz/, /z/, /s/	Is he happy? He's happy. It's hot.
have	/hæv/	/əv/, /v/, /ə/	What have they done? They've finished. You should have studied.
has	/hæz/	/əz/, /z/, /s/	Bob has left. He's told them. It's been a long time.
had	/hæd/	/əd/, /d/	Bob had left. He'd told them.
do	/duw/	/də/	What do you want? Do you want to dance?
does	/dʌz/	/dəz/, /z/	Where does he live? Who does he know?
did	/dɪd/	/əd/, /d/	What did you do? Who did you see?
can	/kæn/	/kən/, /kn/	I can see it. What can you do?
will	/wɪl/	/əl/, /l/	What will you do? I'll go now.
would	/wʊd/	/əd/, /d/	It'd be nice to go. I'd go there.

Table 9.5. Reduced forms of some function words: expressions with *to* and modal + *have* (sound 9.11).

Word	Citation form	Reduced form	Example
Expressions with **to**			
going to	/gowɪŋ tuw/	/gʌnə/ /gɔnə/	I'm going to do my homework. Are you going to eat now?
want to	/wɑnt tuw/	/wɑnə/	I want to go to Disneyland. Do you want to come with me? *But not: *He wanna *He wantsa*
have to	/hæv tuw/	/hæftə/	We have to wait for the bus. Do you have to study?
have/has got to	/hæv gɑt tuw/ /hæz gɑt tuw/	/əvgɑtə/ /əzgɑtə/ /gɑtə/	Students have got to study. The student has got to study. I've got to go. I('ve) got to go.
Modal + **have**			
should have	/ʃʊd hæv/	/ʃʊdə/	You should have waited for me. You shouldn't have forgotten.
could have	/kʊd hæv/	/kʊdə/	We could have tried harder. We couldn't have known that.
would have	/wʊd hæv/	/wʊdə/	He would have helped you. He wouldn't have told the secret.
must have	/mʌst hæv/	/mʌstə/	They must have been hungry. (American English speakers don't really say *mustn't have*.)
might have	/mayt hæv/	/maytə/	I might have known the answer. (*Mightn't have* is also kind of strange.)

★ An asterisk marks something that is incorrect.

Have, has, and *had* often lose their initial /h/ when they're used as auxiliary verbs (**sound 9.12**). As mentioned earlier, sometimes they're reduced even further into contractions.

Have → /əv/ or /v/   What have you **DONE**?
Has → /əz/, /z/, or /s/ What has he **DONE**?
Had → /əd/ or /d/   What had he **DONE**?

However, if these words beginning with /h/—*he, him, his, her, have, has,* and *had*—are at the beginning of a sentence, they do not lose the /h/ sound.

Of and *and* often lose their final consonant sound, especially when they come before a word that starts with a consonant (**sound 9.13**):

Of → /ə/ And → /ən/
I want a **CUP** of **COF**fee with **CREAM** and **SU**gar.

Articles

Students learn very early that the indefinite article has two forms: *a* (usually pronounced /ə/) before consonant sounds and *an* (usually pronounced /ən/) before vowel sounds. In most speakers' pronunciation, the definite article *the* also has two different pronunciations, although they're both spelled the same way. *The* is usually pronounced /ðə/ before consonant sounds and /ðiy/ before vowel sounds. Table 9.7 gives examples.

**Table 9.6. Reduced forms of some function words:
pronouns, possessive adjectives, and miscellaneous words (sound 9.14).**

Word	Citation form	Reduced form	Example
Pronouns and possessive adjectives			
you	/yuw/	/yə/	You did it. Do you want to go?
he	/hiy/	/iy/	Is he here? What did he do?
him	/hɪm/	/ɪm/	Tell him. Give him some time.
her	/hɚ/	/ɚ/	Tell her. What's her name?
them	/ðɛm/	/ðəm/ /əm/	Did you tell them your name? I saw them. Give them a present.
your	/yuwr/	/yɚ/	What's your name? Use your pen.
his	/hɪz/	/ɪz/	What's his name? She's his mother.
our	/awr/	/ɑr/	Our car is big. They're our friends.
Miscellaneous words			
that	/ðæt/	/ðət/	He said that he was ready. The book that I read was good.
than	/ðæn/	/ðən/ /ən/	Elephants are bigger than mice.
kind of	/kayndəv/	/kayndə/	We're kind of late.
sort of	/sɔrtəv/	/sɔrtə/	It's sort of hot today.

It's important to remember that the pronunciation of the articles is based on the *sound* of the word that comes after them, not the spelling; spelling is not always a reliable indication of pronunciation.

Vowel Changes
The vowel in a reduced form of a function word often changes to /ə/ (**sound 9.15**):

You → /yə/
From → /frəm/
To → /tə/
Did you **FLY** from New **YORK** to ChiCAgo?
  /yə/   /frəm/   /tə/

Table 9.7. Pronunciation of definite and indefinite articles (sound 9.16).

	Before a consonant sound		Before a vowel sound	
a/an	A box A child A unit	/ə ˈbɑks/ /ə ˈʧayld/ /ə ˈyuwnət/	An apple An umbrella An hour	/ən ˈæpəl/ /ən əmˈbrɛlə/ /ən awr/
the	The box The child The unit	/ðə ˈbɑks/ /ðə ˈʧayld/ /ðə ˈyuwnət/	The apple The umbrella The hour	/ðiy ˈæpəl/ /ðiy əmˈbrɛlə/ /ðiy ˈawr/

Common Expressions

Some common expressions with **modals** or similar verbs have their own common reduced forms (**sound 9.17**). (More of these are listed in Table 9.5.) For example:

Going to → /ˈɡʌnə/ or /ˈɡɔnə/ (sometimes written *gonna*)
Want to → /ˈwɑnə/ (sometimes written *wanna*)
Have to → /ˈhæftə/ (sometimes written *hafta*)
Have got to → /(əv) ˈɡɑtə/ (sometimes written *gotta*)
Could have → /ˈkʊdə/ (sometimes written *coulda*)
Should have → /ˈʃʊdə/ (sometimes written *shoulda*)

These reduced pronunciations are commonly used in many types of speech in all but very formal situations. However, it's important *not* to use the written forms—*gonna, wanna, hafta,* and so forth—in formal, business, or academic writing. The written forms should only be used in very casual situations, like notes, texts, or emails to a close friend.

When Are Function Words Not Reduced?

There are some situations when function words should *not* be reduced. This usually happens in one of these situations:

- When we want to emphasize the function word.
- When the function word is in a position that needs to be stressed in order to make the rhythm sound right.
- When they're actually main verbs, not auxiliary verbs.

Let's look more closely at each of these situations.

To Give Emphasis

Sometimes a function word is very important to the meaning of a sentence. In this case, we emphasize it by using its full form, not its reduced form (**sound 9.18**). For example:

We **MIGHT** go with you, but we haven't decided.
Put your book **ON** the desk, not **UNDER** it.
A: Would you rather be rich or good-looking?
B: I want to be rich **AND** good-looking!

We'll read more about this type of emphasis in Chapter 10, "Thought Groups and Prominence."

To Maintain Rhythm

We don't reduce *be* verbs, modals, or other auxiliary verbs when there's not another word soon after it that will receive stress, such as a main verb, predicate noun, predicate adjective, or the negative word *not.* Compare these examples (**sound 9.19**):

Can you help me? (*Can* is reduced.)
Yes, I can help you. (*Can* is reduced.)
Yes, I **CAN**. (*Can* is not reduced; there's no verb after it.)
Are you listening to me? (*Are* is reduced.)
Yes, I'm listening. (*Am* is reduced.)
No, I'm not listening. (*Am* is reduced.)
Yes, I **AM**. (*Am* is not reduced; there's no other word after it.)
No I'm not. (*Am* is reduced. *Not* comes after it.)
Is the new student lazy? (*Is* is reduced.)
If he **IS**, we'll soon find out. (*Is* isn't reduced, but *will* is reduced.)

Here's another case when we don't reduce function words because the rhythm requires full forms. Prepositions are usually reduced, but when a preposition is the last word in a sentence or clause, we don't reduce it. In this case, we don't necessarily emphasize the preposition; we just don't reduce it. This sometimes happens in questions or in sentences with adjective clauses or noun clauses (**sound 9.20**).

> What are you listening <u>to</u>?
> Where can I plug my computer <u>in</u>?
> That's the man I wanted to introduce you <u>to</u>.
> The painting I'm looking <u>at</u> is strange.
> I don't know where he's <u>from</u>.

To Show a Word Is Really a Main Verb

Some verbs can be used as either main verbs or auxiliary verbs, like *have, do,* and *be going to.* We reduce these forms when they're auxiliary verbs (helping verbs), but generally not when they're main verbs. For example (**sound 9.21**):

> *I'm going to study* can become *I'm gonna study.*
> But *I'm going to school* cannot become ★*I'm gonna school.*
> *We could have studied* can become *We coulda studied.*
> But *We could have fun* cannot become ★*We coulda fun.*

Changes in Word Stress

We know that in English, every polysyllabic word has one stressed syllable. However, there are times when the position of stress in a word can change if this will help maintain a more comfortable overall rhythm. Having two stressed syllables together makes an awkward rhythm in English; an alternation of stressed and unstressed syllables is more natural sounding. Therefore, the stress sometimes moves to create an alternation of stressed and unstressed syllables (Ladefoged, 2006, p. 115). We can call this process **variable word stress.** Here are some examples of when this stress change can happen.

Numbers

Numbers ending in *-teen* are normally stressed on the last syllable. However, the stress in these numbers can change to the first part in these situations:

> When we're counting, we tend to stress *-teen* numbers on the first syllable (**sound 9.22**):

THIRteen, FOURteen, FIFteen, SIXteen, SEventeen.

Years starting with *-teen* numbers usually have some stress on the first syllable. There is also primary stress on one of the syllables in the last part of the year:

> 1999 → NINEteen ninety-NINE
> 1492 → FOURteen ninety-TWO
> 1812 → EIGHTeen TWELVE

In combinations of a *-teen* number plus a noun, the stress on the *-teen* number often moves to the first syllable:

> 15 years → FIFteen YEARS
> 19 people → NINEteen PEOPle

Numbers between 21 and 99 are also usually stressed on the last part (the "ones" part). However, when they are followed by a noun, the stress can move to the first part of the number:

24 → twenty-FOUR   32 → thirty-TWO
24 hours → TWENty-four HOURS
32 ounces → THIRty-two OUNCes

Other Words With Final Stress

When a word with final stress is followed by a word with initial stress, leading to two stressed syllables in a row, the stress in the first word can move to an earlier syllable, although it doesn't have to. For example, *volun'teer* is normally stressed on the last syllable, but in a phrase like *'volunteer 'teacher,* it can move to an earlier syllable.

Important Points for Teaching Rhythm

To make the rhythm of English sounds natural, the most important thing students need to remember is this: Make the stressed syllables longer and clearer, and the unstressed syllables shorter and less clear.

In learning about reduced forms of words, it's very important for learners to be aware of how those forms sound so that they'll recognize and understand them when they hear them. Even if learners don't always use reduced forms themselves, it's absolutely necessary to understand them for comprehension of natural, spoken English. This is especially true in casual or rapid speech, but also in more formal, careful speech. Native speakers do not normally speak using only full citation forms of function words—not even when they're speaking slowly and formally.

Thought Groups and Prominence

Can you imagine what it would be like if people kept talking steadily without ever pausing? Listeners would have a hard time understanding our speech, and they'd soon get tired of listening to us talk nonstop. Before long, we'd run out of breath and our faces would turn blue. Obviously, we need to pause when we talk.

Pauses give speakers a chance to catch their breath, but they also make our speech easier to understand. Pauses help listeners understand which groups of words belong together grammatically and how the meaning is organized. When we pause, listeners have a little time to absorb the meaning of what we've said, and it's easier for them to follow our ideas.

We need to pause when we talk, but we can't pause just anywhere. It makes more sense to pause in some places than in others. For example, which of these sentences seems more natural (**sound 10.1;** slash marks represent pauses)?

1. Last Thursday / I went to the supermarket / and bought some vegetables. /
2. Last / Thursday I / went to / the supermarket and bought / some / vegetables. /

It's easy to see that the first sentence is divided more naturally. Its pauses break the sentence up into logical parts that each have both a grammatical structure and a chunk of meaning. These groups of words that are divided by pauses are called **thought groups**. In contrast, the parts of the second sentence seem random and just don't make sense.

In reality, not everyone breaks up thought groups in the same way. When people talk faster, they will probably pause less often and use fewer thought groups; slower speech leads to more pauses and more thought groups. In more formal language, such as when someone is giving an important speech, the speaker often uses more pauses. These can be a valuable tool for the speaker to draw the listeners' attention to important points. The speaker's own style and personal preferences can also affect how often he or she pauses.

In spite of these individual differences, we can make some generalizations about thought groups and how they are divided. Thought groups have these characteristics:

- A thought group has pauses or almost-pauses before and after it. We pause between thought groups, but not within them. A pause might not be a complete stopping of sound. Instead, it might just be a slowing or lengthening of the last stressed syllable of the thought group (Murphy, 2013).

- A thought group contains one **prominent** element. This is the word that receives the most emphasis in that thought group. (More information about prominence begins later in this chapter.)
- Each thought group has its own intonation pattern. That is, the speaker's voice goes up and down in a "melody" for that stretch of speech. Because of this, thought groups are sometimes called **intonation units**. (There's more about intonation in Chapter 11, "Intonation.")
- A thought group usually has its own grammatical structure. It's often a phrase, a clause, or a whole sentence—a chunk of language that feels like it has its own structure and expresses a thought or a unit of meaning (Celce-Murcia, Brinton, & Goodwin, 2010).

Punctuation and Thought Groups

In writing, punctuation shows the boundaries of phrases, clauses, and sentences. In spoken language, of course, there is no punctuation to mark these grammatical units. Instead, the listener must pay attention to pauses and intonation patterns. In the following sentences, notice the difference in punctuation, pauses, and intonation, and see how the meaning changes (**sound 10.2**):

"Tom," said the teacher, "is brilliant."

Tom / said the teacher / is brilliant /

Tom said, "The teacher is brilliant."

Tom said / the teacher is brilliant /

Although the words are the same, the meaning is completely different. In the first sentence, the teacher is speaking and Tom is brilliant. In the second, Tom is speaking and the teacher is brilliant. Here's another example (**sound 10.3**):

The students, who study hard, will get good grades.

The students / who study hard / will get good grades /

The students who study hard will get good grades.

The students who study hard / will get good grades /

Again, the words are the same, but in speaking, pauses and intonation change the meaning. In the first sentence, all the students study hard and get good grades. (This is called a nonrestrictive adjective clause—it gives extra information about the students, but doesn't narrow down the number of people that the clause refers to.) In the second, only the students who study hard will get good grades. (This one is a restrictive adjective clause. It changes the meaning of the sentence by restricting the number of people that the clause refers to.) When these pairs of sentences are written, punctuation gives us clues to their meaning, but when they're spoken, only pauses and intonation indicate the difference.

This humorous message was seen in our ESL program office (**sound 10.4**):

Let's eat Grandma.
Let's eat, Grandma.

Punctuation saves lives!

Pauses also save lives. (Or at least they help us communicate our meaning more clearly!)

What Is Prominence?

In every thought group, there is one word that is emphasized more strongly than the rest. This most emphasized word is called the **prominent word,** or the word that has **prominence**. Prominence can also be called **focus** or **sentence stress.** If the prominent word has more than one syllable, only its stressed syllable is emphasized. In some cases, the prominent word is one that is very important for the meaning of the sentence or one that the speaker wants to bring special attention to; however, even if there is no word that needs particular attention, there is still a prominent word that is pronounced more forcefully than the rest.

How is the prominent word different from the others? In some ways, the prominent word in a thought group is like the stressed syllable in a word. Some of the same qualities make it "pop out" at the listener. These are the characteristics that make the prominent word different from the rest of the words in a thought group:

- The prominent word is pronounced more forcefully than the other words, and it may be louder than the others.
- There's a change in pitch on the stressed syllable of the prominent word. It usually has a higher pitch than the words around it, although this may be different if the sentence ends in rising intonation, as in a yes/no question. (There's more about intonation in Chapter 11, "Intonation.")
- The stressed syllable of the prominent word is a bit longer in duration than the other syllables in the thought group.
- The vowel sound in the stressed syllable of the prominent word is clear and distinct. It's not reduced.

Just as with word stress, it's also important to make the other words in the sentence weaker so that the prominent word will stand out in contrast to them.

Which Word Has Prominence?

As we've learned, to make the rhythm of English sound natural, we emphasize content words (the "important" words that carry meaning in themselves) and weaken function words (words that show the grammatical relationships between other words). Tables in the previous chapter list examples of content words and function words.

In a typical thought group, there are both content words and function words, which are made up of stressed and unstressed syllables. All the stressed syllables can receive some emphasis, but only one syllable in one of those words receives prominence. How can we tell which word should receive prominence? There are several guidelines that can help us predict the prominent word.

The "Last Content Word" Rule

In most thought groups, when there's nothing special that the speaker needs to emphasize, the last content word in the thought group receives prominence. All the words in that thought group after the prominent syllable are unstressed and often low-pitched, even if they normally would be stressed. This is the "default" stress pattern for typical sentences (**sound 10.5**).

I've already started to read the TEXTbook.

There's so much useful inforMAtion in it.

I think I'll read it aGAIN.

Do your homework quickly and CAREfully.

Please be QUIet. I'm trying to STUDy.

However, if there are adverbs telling a place or time at the end of a thought group, they are often unstressed and spoken with a low pitch (Lane, 2010, p. 97).

We went to DISneyland yesterday.

I'd like to GO there sometime.

New Information/Old Information

New information usually receives prominence, while old information doesn't. Old information is something that has already been mentioned in the conversation or something that the speaker assumes the listener already knows about. New information is just that—information, facts, or opinions that the speaker wants to tell the listener for the first time. Since new information is usually fresher and more interesting than what we already know, it's easy to see why it is emphasized (**sound 10.6**):

A: Where do you want to go for LUNCH?

B: How about going to that new Italian RESTaurant?

A: Well, I think I'd rather have MEXican food.

In English, new information often comes toward the end of a sentence. The subject usually names the topic—something that we've already been talking about. The verb phrase is the comment—some new information that the speaker wants the listener to know about the subject. Because of this, this rule matches well with the previous one about the last content word.

Emphasis (Emphatic Stress)

If the speaker wants to emphasize or highlight a word or idea, that word can receive prominence (**sound 10.7**):

No, you may NOT play in the street.

A lot of people like CHOColate, but I REALly love it.

A: Thank you for coming to my PARty.

B: Thank YOU for inviting me.

Words that are emphasized in this way are often content words, but function words can also receive prominence if that helps to communicate the meaning of the sentence:

I said you can have a cookie OR some candy. You can't have BOTH.

HE said it; SHE didn't.

A: Finish your HOMEwork!

B: But I HAVE finished my homework.

Contrast (Contrastive Stress)

If it's important for a speaker to show that two words or ideas are different from each other, those words can both receive prominence. This is very similar to emphatic stress. The speaker is emphasizing two words because they contrast with each other (**sound 10.8**):

I ordered COFfee, but the waiter brought me TEA.

A: Oh, I see you bought a new CAR.

B: No, I didn't BUY it. I only RENTed it.

Disagreeing and Correcting

When we want to disagree with someone or correct a mistake that we hear, we can give prominence to the incorrect item and also to the correction. We can think of this as a kind of contrastive stress, emphasizing a difference between the incorrect and correct information or between what you think and what I think (**sound 10.9**):

A: Isn't Los Angeles the capital of CaliFORNia?

B: No, it's not Los ANgeles; it's SacraMENTo.

A: This soup is too HOT!

B: It seems COLD to me.

A: No, I mean SPICy hot, not TEMPerature hot.

These ways of using prominence to show emphasis, contrast, or disagreement are very common in English, but prominence may not be used to mark these things in other languages; word order or grammatical forms may be used instead. Because of this, it's important for students to learn and practice using prominence and intonation to mark words that they want to emphasize when speaking.

Prominence Changes Meaning

If we change the word that has prominence in a sentence, our understanding of the speaker's meaning or intention can change, too. Even though the basic grammar and vocabulary stay the same, the speaker's purpose and the meaning he or she wants to convey can be very different (**sound 10.10**):

Emma said she lost her KEYS again.

(Standard prominence. I'm just reporting a fact.)

EMma said she lost her keys again.

(*Emma* said it, not anyone else.)

Emma SAID she lost her keys again.

(She *said* it, but I'm not sure I believe it.)

Emma said SHE lost her keys again.

(No one else lost them; *she* did it herself.)

Emma said she LOST her keys again.

(She didn't hide them or sell them; she *lost* them.)

Emma said she lost HER keys again.

(Not my keys or your keys, but *her* keys.)

Emma said she lost her keys AGAIN.

(I can't believe she did it *again!*)

Putting prominence in the appropriate place to express our meaning clearly is very important in communicating well in English.

CHAPTER 11

Intonation

Intonation is the "melody" of language—the pattern of higher and lower pitch as we speak. Using intonation appropriately is important in helping us be understood. Intonation can change a statement into a question or a polite request into a rude command. It can make the speaker sound happy, sad, sincere, angry, confused, or defensive.

It's not simple to predict what the intonation will be for any particular bit of language. Intonation is variable and can be affected by many things, such as

- the grammatical form of the sentence;
- the speaker's assumptions about what the listener knows or does not know;
- the speaker's emotions and intentions;
- the speaker's age, occupation, and personality;
- the speaker's intention to keep talking or stop and give someone else a turn;
- the speaker's text source (e.g., reading from a prepared script or speaking freely);
- the situation: formal or informal, serious or silly, at work or at home; and
- many other factors that often seem random and unpredictable (Celce-Murcia, Brinton, & Goodwin, 2010).

No one can describe or analyze all of these factors, and we certainly don't want to confuse our students with too much detailed analysis. The most practical plan is to teach students some basic patterns that they can use reliably—to give them a "starter set" of intonation patterns. As time goes by, we can expose them to more and more patterns through authentic language in movies, TV, and conversations. With listening and practice, these will help them increase their understanding and use of natural intonation.

Typical Intonation Patterns in American English

American English intonation tends to have a wider pitch range, that is, more extreme "ups and downs," than many other languages. (Of course, this also varies from person to person and situation to situation.) This wider pitch range sometimes makes it difficult for learners to get used to using natural sounding intonation patterns in English. For example, if a learner is used to hearing and speaking with a pitch range something like this:

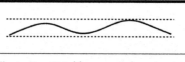

Illustration 11.1. Narrow pitch range.

Then the learner may feel uncomfortable trying to imitate a pitch range like this:

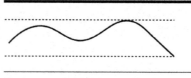

Illustration 11.2. Wider pitch range.

In textbooks, you may see intonation contours drawn in different styles, sometimes very rounded, and sometimes more angular. Both describe the same thing; the difference is mainly a matter of style:

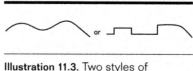

Illustration 11.3. Two styles of intonation contours.

Let's look at some generalizations about intonation that are simple and reliable enough to present to students. We'll look at these from three points of view:

- intonation patterns that are related to **grammar**;
- intonation patterns that are based on the function of the sentence in **discourse** (that is, the purpose it serves in the context of a whole conversation, speech, story, etc.); and
- intonation patterns that convey basic **meanings**

Intonation Patterns Related to Grammar

Sentences of different grammatical types are often used with their own typical intonation patterns. Of course, these are not firm rules that are followed 100% of the time—as I've said, there's a lot of variation in the intonation patterns that speakers use in real life—but they are useful generalizations that help students speak with acceptable intonation patterns.

In matching intonation to the grammar of a sentence, it's the intonation at the end of a thought group or sentence that is the most significant. Is it rising or falling? Does it go all the way up to the highest point in the speaker's pitch range or only part way? Does it fall all the way to the lowest point, or does it stay fairly flat?

In Chapter 10, "Thought Groups and Prominence," we learned that each thought group has a prominent word—often the last content word in the thought group, or sometimes another word that is being emphasized. The highest point in the intonation of a thought group generally coincides with the prominent word. Many thought groups also have a smaller "bump" in intonation near the beginning, often on the subject of the sentence, a question word, or another important word. Let's look at some grammatical patterns and the intonation contours that often go with them.

Statements

Statements usually end in falling intonation. The intonation rises on the prominent word and then stays low after that. The statement ends at the lowest point in the pitch range (**sound 11.1**):

The weather is warm today.

Let's get some ice cream.

Ice cream is cold and delicious.

Commands and Requests

Commands and requests also often end in falling intonation (**sound 11**.2):

Write your name at the top of your paper.

However, the intonation of commands and requests can vary, depending on the situation, the speaker's attitude, and the relationship between the speaker and the listener. For example, a parent telling a child to put away his toys might say it in different ways (**sound 11**.3). Can you feel a difference?

Put away your toys.

Put away your toys.

Put away your toys.

A boss might give instructions to an employee like this:

You need to finish this report.

But if an employee used the same intonation when talking to the boss, there could be trouble.

If a request is in the form of a question, it usually has rising intonation, like a yes/no question (**sound 11**.4):

Can you help me with this?

Questions

Questions do not all have the same intonation. For example, questions that can be answered with *yes* or *no* (**yes/no questions**) generally have different intonation than questions beginning with words like *who, what, where, when, why,* and *how* (called **WH-questions** or **information questions**). Students may not realize this and may use the same intonation with all question types.

Yes/no questions usually end in rising intonation. The prominent syllable is marked by a change in pitch, either higher or lower, depending on the speaker. In either case, the intonation at the end of the sentence goes up to the highest point in the pitch range. You might hear either of these patterns. The first is more commonly represented in textbooks, although the second is closer to the intonation most Americans actually use (**sound 11**.5).

Is this your notebook?

Is this your notebook?

WH-questions usually end in falling intonation. As in statements, the intonation rises on the prominent syllable and then stays low after that, ending at the lowest point in the pitch range (**sound 11**.6):

What's your favorite kind of music?

Where are you going today?

How many brothers and sisters do you have?

Surprise. Rising intonation can be a sign of surprise or disbelief. It can also change a statement into a question (**sound 11**.7):

The meeting is today? I thought it was next week.

What? You won a million dollars?

Sometimes a speaker says something that the listener can't understand or something that sounds strange or unbelievable. In this case, the listener might ask a **clarification** or **repetition question** to get the speaker to repeat or explain what he or she has said. Like expressions of surprise, these questions usually have rising intonation. This is true even if they are WH-questions, which normally have falling intonation. In this kind of question, the question word also receives more emphasis than it normally would (**sound 11**.8):

A: Where did you go on your vacation?

B: I went to Yosemite. It was so beautiful!

A: Where did you go?

B: To Yosemite. Do you know where it is?

A: What's your address?

B: It's 123 Miller Street.

A: What's the name of the street?

B: Miller Street. It's spelled M-I-L-L-E-R.

Tag questions begin with a statement, followed by a short question form at the end, like these:

We're having a quiz today, aren't we?

You've finished your homework, haven't you?

It's not raining now, is it?

Questions like these can be spoken with two different kinds of intonation, each with its own kind of meaning. In both cases, the intonation on the first part goes down, like a statement. However, the last part varies. Sometimes the speaker really wants information and doesn't know what the answer will be. In this case, the final intonation goes up (**sound 11**.9):

We're having a quiz today, aren't we?

  (I really don't remember, and I want to find out.)

You've finished your homework, haven't you?

  (I don't know if you've finished or not.)

It's not raining now, is it?

  (I'm indoors and can't see out the window, so I don't know.)

In other cases, the speaker already knows the answer or assumes that the listener agrees. The speaker isn't really asking for information; he or she is just making conversation or trying to get the listener to express agreement. In this case, the final intonation goes down (**sound 11**.10).

We're having a quiz today, aren't we?

    (I know we're having a quiz; I just want to talk about it.)

You've finished your homework, haven't you?

    (I know you've finished; you always finish it.)

It's not raining now, is it?

    (I can see that the rain has stopped. I just need something to say.)

Questions with *or* that offer a choice between two or more things have intonation patterns like those shown below. The intonation on the choice (or choices) before *or* goes up or sometimes stays rather flat. The intonation at the end of the sentence goes down, like a statement (**sound 11.11**):

Would you rather read a book or watch TV?

Should we have cake, pie, or cookies for dessert?

Would you rather read a book or watch TV?

Should we have cake, pie, or cookies for dessert?

Lists

Lists of three or more things joined by *and* or *or* have intonation similar to that of *or* questions: Up or somewhat flat on the first things in the list and down on the last one (**sound 11.12**).

You'll need your textbook, paper, and a pencil.

You should go home, eat lunch, take a nap, and study.

We'll communicate by phone, text, or email.

You'll need your textbook, paper, and a pencil.

You should go home, eat lunch, take a nap, and study.

We'll communicate by phone, text, or email.

First Clauses or Incomplete Sentences

Sometimes a thought group is not a complete sentence, either because there's another clause coming after it or because the speaker just stops in the middle. In this case, the intonation of the incomplete part is often flat at the end or it falls just a bit, but not as much as at the end of a statement (**sound 11.13**):

I wanted to buy a new car, but I couldn't afford it.

If you think of a good idea, tell me right away.

The answer is . . . Sorry, I don't know.

If you want to get rich, don't become a teacher.

Sometimes these "first clauses" have a very definite rising intonation, almost like a question. This is not a traditional intonation pattern, and you may not see it described in textbooks, but it's become much more common in American English recently (**sound 11.14**):

I wanted to buy a new car, but I couldn't afford it.

If you think of a good idea, tell me right away.

If you want to get rich, don't become a teacher

Intonation Patterns Related to Context

Another way of looking at intonation is to think about the role it can play in **discourse**, that is, in longer conversations, stories, speeches, or other types of connected language, rather than only in single sentences. This view looks at the whole context in which intonation occurs.

Old Information and New Information

By listening to intonation, we can tell which information the speaker and listener both already know (**old information**) and which information the speaker wants to tell the listener for the first time (**new information**).

In Chapter 10, "Thought Groups and Prominence," we learned that new information usually has prominence, while old information does not. The difference in intonation is related to this difference in prominence. New information, which most often comes near the end of a thought group, has a "bump up" in pitch on the prominent word, followed by falling intonation. Some authors refer to this pitch pattern as a **proclaiming tone**; the speaker is proclaiming, or announcing, some new and important information (Brazil, 1997).

Old information within a thought group does not have prominence. In a similar way, thought groups that give old, shared information have intonation that shows that their information is not new—it's just there to remind the listener of the topic the speaker is talking about, as if the speaker is saying, "You're with me on this; you know what I'm talking about; we have something in common."

Thought groups that give old, shared information are often spoken with a rising intonation or a partial fall. This is sometimes called a **referring tone**. The speaker isn't telling something new; he or she is simply referring to something that is already known (Brazil, 1997). In the following example, new information is in bold letters and old information is in normal letters (**sound 11.15**).

My brother Tom—**He's coming to visit.**

(You know my brother. This is news.)

Oh, good! When he's here, **let's take him to the beach.**

(New opinion. I know this now. This is my new suggestion.)

Taking Turns

In a conversation, intonation can also help show whether a speaker wants to continue talking or is finished and ready for the listener to have a turn. Speakers often use a falling intonation pattern when they're finished talking, sometimes with an extra-low ending pitch. If the intonation of a statement is rising or fairly flat, the speaker is probably not finished talking. (Of course, if the speaker is asking a yes/no question, rising intonation is normal, and he or she is probably finished and waiting for an answer.)

Intonation Patterns Related to Meaning

Some linguists have made generalizations about the basic meaning of different types of intonation when they come at the end of a thought group. We might think of these as a sort of summary of the uses of the intonation patterns that we've already looked at. These are the three main intonation patterns that have been described (Celce-Murcia et al., 2010; **sound 11.16**):

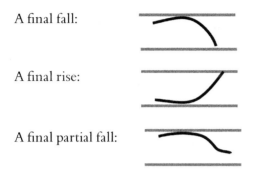

A final fall:

A final rise:

A final partial fall:

A Final Fall

When the speaker's voice falls low at the end of a thought group, it gives a feeling of finality, completion, and certainty. This matches the ideas about grammar and intonation patterns, where falling intonation is connected to statements, commands, the last element of a list, or a tag question when the speaker is sure the listener will agree. It's easy to see that all these express certainty. (WH-questions and *or* questions don't fit quite so neatly; we're asking for information rather than giving it.)

A Final Rise

A final rise in intonation expresses uncertainty, surprise, or lack of information. It's used in yes/no questions, tag questions when the speaker really doesn't know the answer, clarification questions, and requests (usually when the speaker feels uncertain about whether he or she should make the request or doesn't feel confident about the listener's reaction).

A Partial Fall

When the speaker's voice goes down only slightly at the end of a thought group, it's a sign of incompleteness. There may be another clause coming, or the speaker may just stop in the middle of a thought group and not finish the sentence. This can mean, "I'm not finished talking, so don't interrupt me."

Some Intonation Patterns That Convey Meaning by Themselves

There are several intonation patterns that can convey meaning by themselves, even without real words. The sound a speaker makes might be just a hum or a vowel sound, but its "melody" means something. These are almost like separate vocabulary items or intonation "words" that students must learn to understand everyday conversation. For example, if we say /m/ with a quick rising intonation, listeners understand that we mean "What?" even if we haven't actually said the word. Some examples in English are in Table 11.1.

Some of these patterns are the same across many languages. (For example, the rising intonation that means "What?" seems to be almost universal.) But others vary from language to language, so it's good for students to be aware of them. A certain intonation "word" may not mean what they expect it to mean.

Table 11.1. Intonation patterns and meaning (sound 11.17).

Intonation pattern	Meaning	Possible spelling
	Yes.	Mm hmm. Uh huh.
	No.	Huh uh.
	I hear you. I'm thinking about it.	Hmm.
	What? I don't understand.	Huh? Hmm?
	I understand.	Oh!
	I don't know.	(none)

Do All Languages Have Intonation?

Yes, all languages have some kind of intonation. None are spoken in a flat monotone. But of course, not all languages have the same patterns of intonation. Each language has its own characteristic "melody" to fit different purposes in conversation or different kinds of sentences. If you listen to a conversation in your own language, whether that's English or another language, and try to hum along with the rises and falls in pitch as the speakers talk, you'll start to recognize its melody. And if you listen to the speech of someone who is just learning your language, you might notice that their intonation doesn't sound quite natural; they may still be using the intonation of their own language.

Sometimes speakers don't notice the intonation of their own language. It's so familiar that they don't realize it's there, but it is. Hearing the intonation of your own language is like tasting water. We drink water every day, and we're so used to its taste that we might think that it has no taste. But if we go to a new place where the water is a little different, maybe with a different mineral content or more or less chlorine, we immediately notice that the taste is not quite the same. We only notice the taste of our own familiar water in contrast to something a little different. In the same way, we often don't notice familiar intonation patterns until something calls our attention to them.

Sometimes when people hear a language they don't understand, they say that it has a "sing-song" sound—it sounds like music. What's really happening is that they're noticing the melody of the new language because it *is* new and unfamiliar. Their own language may also seem to have a "sing-song" sound to speakers of another language.

Why Do Learners Have Trouble With Intonation?

In a way, it seems that intonation should be the easiest aspect of pronunciation to learn. After all, intonation is accessible. We can easily hear the "melody" of speech, even if we don't understand what's being said, just as we can hum along with a song without understanding the words. But students often do have trouble using intonation naturally. Here are some factors that might stand in their way:

Lack of knowledge. If students haven't been taught about intonation, or if they haven't been exposed to enough "real" English to hear and internalize its typical intonation patterns, they may simply not have the information they need to produce natural sounding intonation. After all, intonation has not always received much attention in many traditional language classes.

Lack of noticing. Even if students have received information about intonation from the teacher or a textbook, they may not have noticed or remembered it. Perhaps they haven't been paying attention to the intonation of the models they've heard, or they might have been daydreaming in class, or for many other reasons, they just don't realize it's important. Being given information is not enough; the learner has to notice and pay attention to the information.

Habits. For language learners, the melody of their own language is such an ingrained part of them that it may not have occurred to them that anything different is possible. It's sometimes hard for learners to realize that the teacher really does want them to speak differently and then to take the steps that are necessary to change. This is especially true for adult learners; their language habits have been with them for a very long time.

Overly careful models. When reading sentences for students to repeat, some teachers are in the habit of saying them extremely slowly and carefully. They may even give each word its own full emphasis with a little rising intonation on each word, as if the sentence were just a list of individual words. Needless to say, this is not a model that will help students use natural sounding intonation.

Feelings. Sometimes students feel self-conscious about using strange, new intonation patterns. Adolescent or young adult learners in particular might feel awkward or embarrassed if they sound different from others around them. Even adult learners can feel hesitant about breaking out of familiar intonation habits to try new and unfamiliar "melodies." For some learners, trying to sound truly different can be as disturbing as being asked to walk around naked. (Well, maybe not quite!)

Too many things to think about. Learners have to think about a lot of things when they speak in addition to pronunciation—word choice, grammatical forms, politeness, meaning—and these things have not yet become automatic. It's hard to have any attention left over for intonation. It's very difficult to concentrate on so many things at once.

Motivation. Some learners just don't care about intonation. Maybe they're not convinced that intonation really is important, and so they don't want to bother with it. Or they might think that if they're not going to be tested on it, they'll save their effort for other things that will be tested. (Is it possible that some teachers also feel this way?)

What Can the Teacher Do?

So what can you, as a teacher, do to help your students overcome all these obstacles?

- Make sure to include intonation practice in your teaching and help students notice it and understand its function and importance in language.
- Give students lots of exposure to authentic English through recordings and videos, and give them chances to analyze and imitate the intonation of the speakers.
- Encourage students to pay attention to the intonation they hear in recordings or videos and to form their own generalizations about what it means and how it's used. This ability to listen and analyze language is a skill that they can use even after they are no longer your students.
- Try to create a warm, unthreatening classroom environment where students can feel comfortable trying out new intonation patterns and new language in general.
- Don't ask students to memorize intonation rules, as memorizing rules is usually *not* the most effective way to teach intonation or other aspects of pronunciation. Help students think about rules as guidelines to help them make appropriate choices, not commands that they have to follow. We can often learn to use a new bit of language even without being able to quote the rule that fits it.

CHAPTER 12

Connected Speech

Language learners often feel that natural, spoken English is fast and hard to understand. They can't hear each word clearly; instead, all the words sound like one long, confusing stream of sound. This is because when people talk normally, their words naturally blend and change in predictable ways. (This happens in all languages, not only in English.) We call this **connected speech**.

Connected speech is not sloppy, uneducated, or rude. It's just normal. It happens when people speak quickly and casually, but also when they speak slowly and formally. Connected speech is not limited to one geographic area or one variety of English. Native speakers of standard North American, British, Australian, and New Zealand English all use connected speech, as do speakers of all regional dialects. In other words, any time people speak, they're using connected speech (Ladefoged, 2006, pp. 109–110).

Why Is There Connected Speech?

When people speak, there are usually two people involved—the speaker and the listener. Both of these want their job to be as easy as possible. The speaker wants to be able to speak easily, and the listener wants to be able to understand easily. But the needs of these two sides are in conflict:

The speaker. The speaker's mouth basically wants to work in the easiest way possible, with the least movement or effort. This leads the speaker's **articulatory system** to take shortcuts—to move from one sound to the next in the shortest and easiest way, to blend sounds together when it can, and to change and sometimes omit sounds. Our mouths are a little bit lazy.

The listener. On the other hand, listeners need to be able to hear the difference between sounds, or they won't be able to distinguish the words that the speaker is saying. For the listener, it would be easiest if all the words were pronounced distinctly and clearly, with not too many sounds omitted or changed. This means that our mouths can't be *too* lazy, or we won't be understood.

When we speak, we unconsciously find a balance between the needs of the speaker and the needs of the listener. The movements of our mouths have to be comfortable and efficient, but not too indistinct to be understood.

Words in connected speech are changed in some predictable ways. (These are changes in the *sounds* of words. Their written forms usually don't change.) These are the three most common types of sound changes, or **phonological processes**, in English:

- **Linking** (sounds blend together)
- **Assimilation** (sounds become more similar)
- **Deletion** (a sound is omitted)

Linking

In normal speech, words within each thought group are not pronounced as separate, individual units. Instead, the last sound of one word is linked to or blended with the first sound of the next word. In other words, the words in a sentence are *not* like a string of beads, where the individual shapes can still be seen as separate objects (Figure 12.1).

Instead, they're like a row of magnets that stick together so strongly that they seem to form one bar. Even though they're actually still individual magnets, it's hard to find the boundaries between them (Figure 12.2).

Figure 12.1. String of beads.

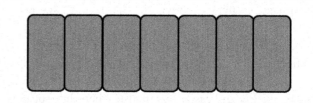

Figure 12.2. Bar of magnets.

This type of "sticking together" happens whenever words are spoken together *within* a thought group. However, it does not happen across the boundaries of thought groups. That is, the last sound in one thought group is not linked to the first sound in the next one because there is typically a short pause between thought groups that prevents linking. A sentence with two thought groups is more like two separate sets of magnets arranged with matching poles together so that they don't attract—there has to be a space between them (Figure 12.3).

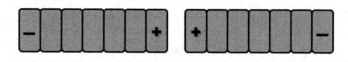

Figure 12.3. Two bars of magnets with matching poles together.

There are several kinds of systematic changes that happen when certain sounds are linked between words. Here are the most common types:

Consonant + Vowel

When a word ending in a consonant sound is followed by a word beginning with a vowel sound, the final consonant sound is linked to the following vowel sound. It sounds like it has become a part of the following word (**sound 12.1**; in the following diagrams, *C* means any consonant sound and *V* means any vowel sound):

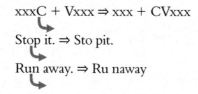

xxxC + Vxxx ⇒ xxx + CVxxx

Stop it. ⇒ Sto pit.

Run away. ⇒ Ru naway

Similarly, when a word ending in a consonant cluster is followed by a word beginning with a vowel sound, the last consonant sound in the cluster is linked to the following vowel (**sound 12.2**):

xxxCC + Vxxx ⇒ xxxC CVxxx

She likes art. ⇒ She like sart.

The world is big. ⇒ The worl dis big.

Vowel + Vowel (Linking with Glides)

This type of linking happens when a vowel sound that ends in a glide (/y/ or /w/) is followed by another vowel sound.

/y/-type vowels. The vowel sounds /iy/, /ey/, /ay/, and /oy/ all end in the /y/ glide. When a word ending in one of these sounds is followed by another vowel sound, we can hear a definite /y/ sound between the two vowels (**sound 12.3**):

/iy/ + V   The tree is big. ⇒ The tree /y/ is big.

/ey/ + V   Say it again. ⇒ Say /y/ it again.

/ay/ + V   He's my uncle. ⇒ He's my /y/ uncle.

/oy/ + V   We enjoy it. ⇒ We enjoy /y/ it.

/w/-type vowels. The vowel sounds /uw/, /ow/, and /aw/ all end in the glide /w/. When a word ending in one of these sounds is followed by another vowel sound, we can hear a definite /w/ sound between them (**sound 12.4**).

/uw/ + V   Who are you? ⇒ Who /w/ are you?

/ow/ + V   Go into the house. ⇒ Go /w/ into the house.

/aw/ + V   How are you? ⇒ How are /w/ you?

Consonant + Consonant

Two identical consonants. When a word ends in a consonant sound and the next word begins with the same sound, we don't pronounce two separate sounds. Instead, two identical consonant sounds blend into one longer consonant. (However, this rule doesn't work with **affricates**. If we say *orange juice* or *rich children,* we hear two separate affricates.)

If the two sounds are **continuants**, they simply blend and continue longer (**sound 12.5**). (Continuants are sounds in which the airstream continues through the vocal tract without being completely blocked off. These are **fricatives**, **nasals**, **liquids**, and **glides**.)

/m/ + /m/ Give him more. ⇒ Give himmore.

/s/ + /s/ Miss Smith ⇒ MissSmith

/l/ + /l/ I feel like singing. ⇒ I feellike singing.

If the sounds are **stops**, the stop is held longer (**sound 12.6**). That is, the tongue or lips block off the airstream and stay in place a bit longer than usual, and then the sound is released. We don't hear two separate stops:

/p/ + /p/ the top part ⇒ the toppart

/d/ + /d/ a good dog ⇒ a gooddog

/g/ + /g/ big grapes ⇒ biggrapes

/k/ + /k/ bake cakes ⇒ bakecakes

Two similar consonants. When a word ends in a stop sound and the next word begins with a stop or affricate, the first stop is not released, and the two sounds blend together (**sound 12.7**). We often don't pronounce them as two separate sounds.

/t/ + /k/ pet cat ⇒ petcat

/g/ + /b/ big building ⇒ bigbuilding

/p/ + /t/ top tier ⇒ toptier

/t/ + /dʒ/ get juice ⇒ getjuice

Linking Within Words

These same types of linking can also happen between sounds in the middle of a word, as well as between words. For example:

Consonant + vowel. A consonant sound joins the following syllable (**sound 12.8**).

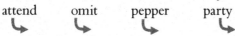
attend   omit   pepper   party

Vowel + vowel. When two vowel sounds come together, a /y/ or /w/ glide can sometimes be heard (**sound 12.9**):

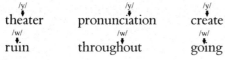
/y/
theater   pronunciation   create
/w/
ruin   throughout   going

Consonant + consonant. Sequences of two identical consonant sounds, or of a stop plus a stop or affricate, are often found in compound words (**sound 12.10**). Then the two sounds blend and become longer.

Same consonant: bookcase   roommate   house-sitter

Stop + stop: hotdog   background

                          seatbelt   eggplant   shopkeeper

Stop + affricate: hatcheck   logjam

Assimilation (Sounds Become Similar)

I talked earlier about speakers' natural tendency to find easier ways to pronounce words—to say sounds using smaller and more efficient movements of the articulators. Because of this tendency, a sound sometimes becomes more similar to a sound that comes before or after it. This process is called assimilation. (It comes from the same root as the word *similar.*) Assimilation makes words easier to pronounce by bringing about easier movements of the tongue, lips, and other articulators from one sound to the next. Every language has some kind of assimilation, although not all languages use assimilation in exactly the same way.

Assimilation often changes the place of articulation of a sound to match a sound next to it. For example, the phoneme /n/ often assimilates to a sound after it. In the following phrases, we can hear differences in the last sound in the preposition *in* (**sound 12.11**):

We're in America. /ɪnəˈmɛrɪkə/

(Before a vowel sound, /n/ doesn't change. There's only normal linking to the following vowel sound.)

We're in Nevada. /ɪnnəˈvædə/

(Before an alveolar sound, /n/ doesn't change. It's already alveolar. The two sounds just blend and become longer.)

We're in Mexico. /ɪmˈmɛksɪkow/

(Before a bilabial sound, /n/ can become /m/. It becomes bilabial too.)

We're in Canada. /ɪŋˈkænədə/

(Before a velar sound, /n/ can become /ŋ/. It becomes velar too.)

We expect *in* to sound like /ɪn/—that's its citation form—but we've seen that this is not always the case. When *in* comes before a bilabial sound, it can also become the bilabial sound /m/. Before a velar sound, it can become the velar sound /ŋ/. (Note: This type of assimilation happens with /n/, but not with /m/. For example, *something* is never pronounced /sʌnθɪŋ/.)

In the previous example, when two sounds came together, the second sound caused the first sound to change. This is the most common situation in assimilation. However, in a smaller number of cases, the first sound causes the second one to change. For example, when we add -*s* and -*ed* endings, the endings are voiced after a voiced sound and voiceless after a voiceless sound. The voicing of the first sound affects the voicing of the following sound. (See Chapter 6, "Pronunciation of Some Word Endings," for more details on these endings.)

Palatalization. In still other cases, two sounds blend together to make a new sound. For example, when we say *Don't you?* it often sounds like *Doncha?* or when we say *Did you?* it sounds like *Didja?* This type of assimilation is called **palatalization** because an alveolar sound (/t/, /d/, /s/, or /z/) becomes a palatal sound (/ʃ/, /ʒ/, /tʃ/, or /dʒ/) when the sound /y/ comes after it. Here are the combinations of sounds that can cause this change (**sound 12.12**):

/t/+/y/ ⇒ /tʃ/ Is that your dog?

/d/+/y/ ⇒ /dʒ/ It made you angry.

/s/+/y/ ⇒ /ʃʒ/ I'll miss you.

/z/+/y/ ⇒ /ʒ/ Is your brother here?

None of these types of assimilation has to happen; people can also pronounce these combinations of sounds without the changes described here. However, assimilation happens constantly in real English, and spoken language sounds much more natural if assimilation takes place.

Deletion (Losing a Sound)

In normal connected speech, sounds may disappear or not be clearly pronounced in certain contexts. This is called **deletion** or **omission** of a sound. It's important to remember, though, that we can't leave out sounds just anywhere. Omitting sounds at random makes language hard to understand. The kind of deletion we're talking about happens only in certain specific situations and in certain sound environments.

Table 12.1. Some common contractions (sound 12.13).

Types of Contractions	Example Words
Be + *not*	isn't, aren't, wasn't, weren't
Do + *not*	doesn't, don't, didn't
Have + *not*	hasn't, haven't, hadn't
Modal + *not*	can't, couldn't, won't, wouldn't, mustn't, shouldn't
Pronoun + *be*	I'm, you're, he's, she's, it's, we're, they're, that's
There + *be*	there's
Question word + *be*	what's, where's, when's, who's, how's
Question word + *will*	what'll, who'll
Pronoun + *will*	I'll, you'll, he'll, she'll, it'll, we'll, they'll
Pronoun + *would*	I'd, you'd, he'd, she'd, it'd, we'd, they'd
Pronoun + *have*	I've, you've, he's, she's, it's, we've, you've

Contractions

The most familiar example of deletion is the shortened forms called **contractions**. These are words like *can't, I'm,* and *we're* that lose a whole syllable when two words are combined. Many of these forms, like the examples just mentioned, are so common and well-accepted that they have standard written forms, using an apostrophe (') to replace the missing parts. Other shortened forms are just as common in speech, but are not often written as contractions. For example, when we shorten *we are,* we say /wiyr/, and it's acceptable to write it as *we're.* However, when we shorten *teachers are,* we can say /ˈtiyʧɚzɚ/, but we don't usually write it as *teachers're.*

Simplification of Consonant Clusters

In Chapter 4, "The Consonants of American English," you already learned about another example of omission: Speakers often simplify clusters of three or more consonant sounds by omitting a middle consonant, but not the first or last consonant. This happens most often when the middle consonant is a stop, /θ/, or /ð/. The remaining consonants can be stretched out to last a little longer (if they're both the same) or linked following the rules described earlier in this section (**sound 12.14**):

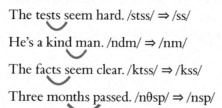

The tests seem hard. /stss/ ⇒ /ss/

He's a kind man. /ndm/ ⇒ /nm/

The facts seem clear. /ktss/ ⇒ /kss/

Three months passed. /nθsp/ ⇒ /nsp/

This type of omission is normal and accepted, although most speakers are not consciously aware that it's happening. It's fine to teach it as a way of coping with difficult consonant clusters, but it's not necessary to force students to follow it.

Loss of /t/ after /n/

When the sounds /nt/ come between syllables and the first syllable is stressed, /t/ is sometimes omitted (**sound 12.15**):

winter ⇒ /wɪnɚ/ (It can sound the same as *winner*)

dentist ⇒ /dɛnɪst/

wanted ⇒ /wɑnəd/

Unlike the changes described in the previous section, some listeners might notice and disapprove of this sound change. It's good to be able to recognize words with the missing /t/, but it's best not to encourage students to use this particular sound change.

Common Expressions

As you saw in Chapter 9, "Rhythm," sounds are deleted in some very common expressions (**sound 12**.16):

Going to → *gonna* /ˈgʌnə/ or /ˈgɔnə/

Want to → *wanna* /ˈwɑnə/

Could have → *coulda* /ˈkʊdə/

Should have → *shoulda* /ˈʃʊdə/

Deleted Sounds and Syllables (sound 12.17)

Chapter 8, "Syllables and Word Stress," mentions some common words that can also have sounds or whole syllables omitted. A few examples are listed here, and there's a longer list of words with "disappearing syllables" in Chapter 8.

governor → /ˈgʌvənɚ/	surprise → /səˈprayz/
chocolate → /ˈtʃɑklət/	vegetable → /ˈvɛdʒtəbəl/
family → /ˈfæmliy/	restaurant → /ˈrɛstrɑnt/
because → 'cause /kəz/	about → 'bout /baut/

Segmentation (Dividing Streams of Sound into Words)

Because of all the linking, blending, and other changes that take place in connected speech, it's sometimes difficult to know where to divide a stream of sound into individual words, but this is a skill that listeners need in order to understand spoken language. The ability to hear spoken language and mentally divide it into understandable words is called **segmentation**.

Learners who hear connected speech may sometimes not understand the words at all, or they may divide the words up incorrectly and misunderstand what was said. An often-heard example is the story of a waiter in a restaurant who asks, "Do you want soup or salad?" and the customer, interpreting it as "Do you want super salad?" answers, "Yes, please."

Differences in segmentation can also be the source of jokes. In the credits at the end of every episode of *Car Talk,* a humorous radio program in which two brothers give callers advice about car repairs, the names of some of the program's (fictitious) staff members are given at the end of each program. If you say the names quickly, they sound like phrases related to their imagined jobs. Can you see how the sounds could be segmented differently to get different meanings (**sound 12**.18)?

- Lighting Expert: Shanda Lear (Chandelier)
- Speechwriter: Audrey Marx (Odd remarks)
- Audience Estimator: Adam Illion (Add a million)
- Chief Benefactor: Myra Chunkle (My rich uncle)
- Weather Forecaster: Windsor Calm (Winds are calm)
- Optometrists: Ike and Zeke Leerly (I can see clearly)

(You can see more *Car Talk* staff credits at http://www.cartalk.com/content/staff-credits.)

How Much Connected Speech Do Learners Need?

When learners listen to authentic English, they'll hear connected speech constantly. If they can't understand connected speech, they won't be able to understand any variety of spoken English. Therefore, it's very important to help students become aware of connected speech in authentic English and practice hearing and understanding it.

It's less urgent for students to learn to produce connected speech themselves. They can usually communicate well even without using all the sound changes we've talked about. But to help students prepare for real-world English, we need to help them understand the changes that take place in connected speech.

CHAPTER 13

Teaching the Musical Aspects of Pronunciation

In teaching students about **suprasegmentals—word stress**, **rhythm**, **thought groups**, **prominence**, **intonation**, and **connected speech**—we often find that the subject matter is less clear and exact than when we teach individual **phonemes**. After all, it's not hard to get teachers to agree on how we produce sounds and what learners need to know about pronouncing them. But with suprasegmentals, the content is harder to define, and in many language classes, it gets very little attention.

Fortunately, there are plenty of ways to use **auditory**, **visual**, and **kinesthetic** methods to practice the musical aspects of pronunciation, and there's plenty of room for imagination and creativity in finding new tools and activities. And some suprasegmentals—especially intonation and rhythm—are actually more accessible to beginners than individual sounds are. It's easy to hear the melody of speech, even if you can't quite catch the sounds and don't understand the words.

In introducing and practicing suprasegmentals, we can still think in terms of the communicative teaching framework described in Chapter 7, "Teaching Consonants and Vowels," with some adjustments to fit the difference in subject matter. The stages of practice in that framework are:

1. Description and analysis (introduction of the feature)
2. Listening discrimination
3. Controlled practice
4. Guided practice
5. Communicative practice (Celce-Murcia, Brinton, & Goodwin, 2010)

In the next sections, we'll look at ways of introducing and practicing each type of suprasegmental feature. We'll see that with some of these features, especially thought groups, prominence, and intonation, context is very important—even more so than with individual sounds. After all, using these features well depends on understanding the situation and the meaning the speaker wants to convey. We often can't predict the best intonation or prominence for a sentence without knowing the whole story of what's happening.

In teaching suprasegmentals, it's important not to forget the first stage, the introduction and explanation of the new features. Students don't intuitively know how these features work. We need to give plenty of examples with some simple, clear explanations to guide students toward noticing and understanding how they work and not rush ahead too soon.

Textbooks or teachers sometimes suggest, for example, eliciting examples of connected speech from students or asking them to predict where the prominent syllable in a sentence will be. However, we can't expect students to come up with these examples on their own too soon. You can't elicit what isn't there yet, and students can't make predictions without some knowledge or experience to guide their guesses. As the teacher, you need to provide a source of information and some general principles before students can be expected to apply what they've learned.

Now let's look at some ways to introduce and practice each of the suprasegmental features. Practice activities are listed roughly in order from simpler to more complex or from more controlled to less controlled.

Syllables and Word Stress

Introducing Syllables and Word Stress

Syllables are hard to define or explain, but easy to illustrate. Say several simple words with two or three syllables, clapping with each syllable. Encourage students to clap or tap their fingers on their desks too. First count the syllables yourself as students count along with you, and then have students try counting syllables on their own. Clapping or making other gestures along with syllables helps students understand what syllables are and count them more accurately.

To introduce the concept of word stress, explain that in English, one syllable in a word is louder, longer, and higher in pitch than the others. That is, one syllable is "bigger" than the others. Say some simple, familiar words, exaggerating the stressed syllable while making a gesture such as nodding, clapping, or waving your hand, and ask students which syllable was stressed. They'll usually be able to recognize it.

To further emphasize the importance of word stress, say a familiar word with the correct stress and then again with incorrect stress so students can hear the difference. For example, say *PENcil*, and then *penCIL*. Ask students which one sounds more like the word they've learned. Point out that with incorrect stress, even words they know can sound odd and unfamiliar. The well-known comment that "You put the emPHAsis on the wrong sylLAble" also helps to point out that words with incorrect stress can be difficult to understand.

Listening to Syllables and Word Stress

Same or different? After learning about syllables and word stress, have students listen to pairs of words and decide if the number of syllables is the same or different. Next, have them listen to pairs of words and decide if they have the same or different syllable patterns, including the number of syllables and the placement of stress.

Listen and mark. Give students a list of familiar words. Have them listen to the words and mark the stressed syllables with circles, accent marks, stars, or some other mark.

Comparing syllables. To build awareness of the difference between syllables in English and their own language, give students a few words that are very similar in English and in their language, but with different numbers of syllables. For example, the English word *chocolate* has two syllables in its most common pronunciation: /ˈʧɑk•lət/, but the equivalent word in German has four: *Scho•ko•la•de*. In French, it has three: *cho•co•lat*. In Spanish it has four: *cho•co•la•te*. In Japanese, it has five: *cho•ko•le•e•to*. Comparing related words like these focuses students' attention on syllables and how they differ between languages.

Practicing Syllables and Word Stress

Physical actions. As students say words, have them do one of the following actions during the stressed syllable:

- Clap their hands, tap the table, snap their fingers, nod their heads, or stomp their feet.
- Open their eyes wider on the stressed syllable.

- Stay sitting during unstressed syllables and stand up on the stressed syllable.
- Stretch a thick rubber band on stressed syllables (but only if you trust your students not to misbehave with rubber bands).

Any of these actions can be done while saying individual words or whole sentences or dialogues. The movements will help students remember to emphasize the stressed syllables.

Pattern matching. Make two sets of cards—one with common stress patterns represented by circles of different sizes (Oo, oO, ooO, oOo, etc.) and the other with categories of meaning (food, plants, jobs, countries, and so forth). Ask students to choose a card from each group and think of as many words as possible with a given stress pattern in a given category within a time limit. This can be done as a pair or group activity or as a competition between teams involving the whole class.

As a variation, make one set of cards with stress patterns and another set with words that the students know. Have students work together to match the patterns with the words.

Syllable scavenger hunt. Ask students to look for and list objects whose names have a certain number of syllables or a certain stress pattern, using real objects in the classroom or outside or objects shown in a detailed picture or photograph from a magazine.

Make syllable models. Use large and small glass or plastic shapes, beads, beans, or Cuisenaire rods to represent stressed and unstressed syllables. To help students feel the difference between the two types of syllables most clearly, choose bigger, heavier, more interesting pieces for stressed syllables and small, smooth, plain pieces for unstressed syllables. Have students arrange the objects to represent the syllable and stress patterns of words.

For example, the words *po'tato, re'peated,* and *sin'cerely* all have the pattern in Figure 13.1.

The words *communi'cation, enthusi'astic,* and *appreci'ation* all have the pattern in Figure 13.2.

Figure 13.3 shows the same two-syllable patterns illustrated using Cuisenaire rods. These don't give the impression of loudness, emphasis, and "weight" as well as glass blobs, but when they're placed horizontally, they help students see that stressed syllables last longer than unstressed syllables. If placed vertically, they emphasize that stressed syllables are higher in pitch.

Throw a ball. Seat students in a circle. Give a very soft ball (not a softball; that's something else entirely) to a student and ask him or her to think of a word with more than one syllable. The student says the word slowly, throwing the ball to another student (who is paying attention and ready to catch the ball) when the stressed syllable begins. The first student must keep saying the stressed syllable until the other student catches the ball. This encourages students to stretch out the stressed syllables and make them

Figure 13.1. Syllable blobs illustrating *potato.*

Figure 13.2. Syllable blobs illustrating *communication.*

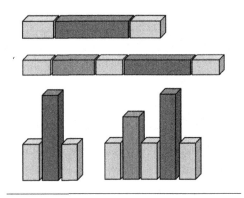

Figure 13.3. Cuisenaire rods showing same stress pattern as syllable blobs.

sound longer than the unstressed syllables. (Of course, you should avoid this activity if throwing things in the classroom is frowned on by your school's administration.)

Matching syllable patterns. Have students work in pairs. One student says a word, and the partner answers with a different word with the same syllable pattern—the same number of syllables and the same position of stress. Partners take turns being first. For example, if the first partner says ˈfather, the other might answer with ˈtable, ˈtextbook, or ˈpaper.

Growing syllables. In a group, the first person says a one-syllable word, the next says a two-syllable word, the next, a three-syllable word, and so forth, until someone can't think of a longer word. Then that person starts again with a one-syllable word. The same activity can be done with phrases instead of single words.

Noun/verb pairs with different stress. Give students a list of sentences or a story containing noun/verb pairs like ˈproduce and proˈduce or ˈrecord and reˈcord and have them practice reading with correct stress. Mix in some words that have the same stress when they're used as both nouns and verbs, like ˈtravel, reˈport, or ˈpressure, to remind students that this noun/verb stress change happens with some, but not all words that can be used as both nouns and verbs.

Suffixes and stress. This activity works best as a competition between small teams. Give the teams some time to prepare first, brainstorming words that can add a suffix to make a new word, for example, *nation* and *national, easy* and *easily,* or *communicate* and *communication*. Tell the teams to be sure they know where the stress should be in each word. After brainstorming, one team says a base word (with correct stress). The other team has to make it into a new word by adding a suffix, and say the new word with correct stress. If the second team can't think of a suffix to add, the first team has to tell them one. For example, if the first team says ˈnation, the second could say ˈnational or nationˈality or ˈnationalize. Points can be given to teams that say a word successfully.

Rhythm

Introducing Rhythm

Squeeze the syllables. The important point in introducing the rhythm of English is to help students hear and feel that some syllables are emphasized and last longer, and other syllables are unstressed and are shortened and reduced so that they squeeze in between the stressed syllables.

Start with a simple sentence with three one-syllable words, such as *Cake tastes good*. Have students repeat, clapping on the stressed words. (In this short sentence, they'll clap on all the words.) Then add extra unstressed syllables, showing how the stressed syllables remain about the same distance apart, and the unstressed words are reduced (**sound 13.1**):

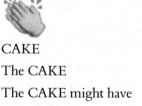

CAKE	TASTES	GOOD.
The CAKE	TASTED	GOOD.
The CAKE might have	TASTED	GOOD.
The CAKE might have	TASTED	deLIcious.
The CAKE shouldn't have	TASTED so	deLIcious.

(Variations of this activity are found in Celce-Murcia et al., 2010; Avery and Ehrlich, 1992; and other sources.)

Syllable symbols. In introducing rhythm, we can use symbols or pictures of various sizes to represent syllables and rhythm patterns and help students visualize rhythm. The two rows of symbols in Figure 13.4 represent the rhythm of the sentence "Everyone studied in the library."

Listening to Rhythm

Move with the rhythm. As students listen to a **chant**, poem, or nursery rhyme, have them clap, tap their fingers, or stomp their feet on the stressed syllables to show the rhythm. Simple musical instruments, such as a xylophone, small drum, or tambourine, can be used in the same way.

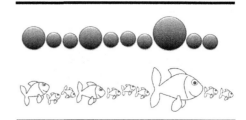

Figure 13.4. Row of circles and row of fish representing the sentence "Everyone studied in the library."

Word and phrase matching. Help students connect the rhythm of a phrase to the rhythm of a familiar word with the same pattern. For example, the sentence *I 'gave it to her* has the same rhythm pattern as the word *re'frigerator*. The process of noticing and recognizing the similarity of patterns helps prepare students to pay attention to the rhythm of language and to imitate it well.

Practicing Rhythm

Walking the rhythm. Have students walk around the room as they read or recite sentences or a dialogue, taking bigger steps on stressed syllables and shorter ones on unstressed syllables. As an alternative, have them take a step only on stressed syllables and stand still on the others (Miller, 2007, p. 82).

Metronome. A metronome is a device that makes clicking sounds at regular intervals. Metronomes are usually used by musicians to help them keep the rhythm of music, but they can also be used to help students feel the rhythm of language. If you set the metronome for a rather slow speed, it's possible to speak so that the stressed syllables coincide with the clicks. If you don't have a metronome, you can find an online version at http://www.metronomeonline.com/.

Use a metronome thoughtfully, however. Not all language is regular enough to speak along with such a perfectly regular beat. You'll need to choose the sentences you say carefully so that they will sound right when spoken with the metronome's beat. (Simple poems and chants are good.) Also, don't set the metronome too fast, or students (and even teachers) won't be able to keep up. Start out slowly and build up a bit more speed after practicing.

Poems and rhymes. Reading or reciting poems or limericks can help students practice rhythm, especially if they clap their hands along with the beat. A limerick is a kind of humorous poem with a particular pattern of rhymes and beats. In this example, the main beats are in *italics* (**sound 13**.2):

Illustration 13.1. Drawing of girl jumping rope.

There *once* was a *fat* old *judge*
Ex*cee*dingly *fond* of *fudge.*
He *grew* so e*nor*mous,
Our *sour*ces in*form* us,
He *now* is not *able* to *budge.*

Nursery rhymes and other children's poems are simple ways to help students practice rhythm. Jump rope rhymes can be especially effective because they are meant to be chanted along with the regular rhythm of jumping rope. If it's not practical to jump rope in class, children can clap their hands while they say the rhymes. Here is a popular jump rope rhyme (**sound 13**.3; see a video of it at http://www.youtube.com/watch?v=V4Cx58njydI):

Teddy bear, teddy bear, turn around.
Teddy bear, teddy bear, touch the ground.
Teddy bear, teddy bear, turn off the light.
Teddy bear, teddy bear, jump out of sight.

Chants. Chants are rhythmic sets of normal English sentences that can be repeated to practice rhythm, stress, and sounds. They have a strong rhythm, but they usually don't rhyme. They give students a chance to repeat new sounds in a way that seems natural and interesting, rather than boringly repetitious. Chants are especially popular with children, who respond well to rhythm and love to repeat favorite lines again and again, especially with gestures and body movements. Chants and rhymes can also be used with adults, but only if the teacher and students feel comfortable with them. If the teacher feels self-conscious or uncomfortable, or if adult students think the activity is too childish, then it's best to choose another form of practice.

Although poems and chants have been used by language teachers for many years, Carolyn Graham, an ESL teacher and jazz singer in New York, created the idea of jazz chants in the 1970s as a way to help her students practice English through the rhythm of jazz.

Here's an example of a simple chant (**sound 13.4**):

What's for dinner?
What's for dinner?
Soup and salad
Bread and butter
Cake and ice cream for dessert.
Set the table!
Set the table!
Plates and glasses
Forks and spoons
Now we're ready. Let's all eat!

When you hear a chant, it sounds like natural, unplanned language, but not all English sentences can be good jazz chants. To write a chant, you have to plan and choose sentences that work. For advice about writing chants, a good resource is Carolyn Graham's book *Creating Chants and Songs* (Graham, 2006).

Thought Groups

Introducing Thought Groups

Fast talker. To show students why thought groups are necessary, take a deep breath and start talking or reading aloud without pausing until you run out of breath. It doesn't matter what you say; just keep talking. Ask the students if it was easy to understand you. Then start speaking again, but a bit more slowly and with normal pauses. Ask the students why the second way was easier to understand. They'll surely remark on the difference that pauses make. This helps students see how difficult it is to understand a speaker who doesn't divide words into thought groups.

Listening to Thought Groups

Mark the pauses. Have students listen to a story, dialogue, or paragraph while following along with a written script. Ask them to draw slash marks or other symbols to show the pauses that divide thought groups. For an easy start, write the story with normal punctuation. (Punctuation often occurs where thought groups are divided.) To make the activity more challenging, print the story without punctuation. Have students listen again and mark the pauses they hear. After some practice, students can be asked to predict on their own where pauses might be. Then check their predictions, and have them read the story aloud with appropriate division into thought groups.

Practicing Thought Groups

Hand gestures. Have students read or recite a dialogue or story, using a "chopping" hand gesture to indicate the pauses that divide sentences into thought groups, or have students wave their hands to show thought groups—up at the beginning of a thought group and down at the end.

Red card, yellow card. Give each student two small cards or pieces of paper, one red and one yellow. Ask them what the colors remind them of. Some students might think of red and yellow traffic lights: Red means stop, and yellow means slow down. Others might think of penalty cards used in soccer games: Yellow for a warning and red when a player is sent out of the game. Either analogy will work. The idea is that the yellow card represents a short pause or not-quite-complete pause (for example, between clauses), and the red one represents a longer pause (usually at the end of a sentence).

As students read a story or dialogue aloud, have them hold up the yellow card to show a partial pause and a red card to show a complete stop. Here's an example of a joke that works well for this (**sound 13**.5):

Patient: Doctor, I have a pain in my eye whenever I drink tea.
Doctor: Next time, take the spoon out of the cup before you drink.

Here's the joke again, with light-colored (yellow) and darker-colored (red) cards marking pauses:

Patient: Doctor ⬜ I have a pain in my eye ⬜ whenever I drink tea ⬛

Doctor: Next time ⬜ take the spoon out of the cup ⬜ before you drink ⬛

Sentence matching. Write or find sentences that can be divided into two or three thought groups. These can be sentences using the language students have been studying, or you can use proverbs or famous quotations. Give students lists of the first and last halves of the sentences in mixed-up order. Have them match the parts to make good sentence. Then practice reading the sentences, pausing between the thought groups (Grant, 2010, p. 107; Figure 13.5).

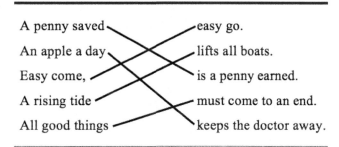

Figure 13.5. Sentence matching.

Prominence

Introducing Prominence

Explain to students that in English one word is emphasized more than the others in every thought group. Give examples of a sentence that could have different meanings or intentions, depending on which word is emphasized. For example, explain and have students think about the difference between these three sentences (**sound 13**.6):

Bob didn't do his HOMEwork.

   (A normal sentence)

BOB didn't do his homework.

   (Someone else did it for him.)

Bob DIDN'T do his homework.

   (You thought he did it, but he really didn't.

Listening to Prominence

Mark it up. Have students listen to short sentences first, and then longer dialogues or stories, following along on a written script. Ask them to notice and mark how the sentences were divided into thought groups. Then ask them to listen again and mark the word in each thought group that was the loudest, highest in pitch, or most emphasized. It's important for students to hear and work with plenty of examples before they're able to predict on their own where prominence should go.

Practicing Prominence

Make models. Many of the methods suggested for word stress can also be adapted to draw attention to prominent syllables. Have students use beads, beans, or glass shapes again, but this time each one will represent a whole word instead of a syllable. Use a larger shape to represent each prominent word. The picture in Figure 13.6 uses large and small magnets to represent the sentence "We're planning a picnic in the park," with one magnet for each word (**sound 13.7**).

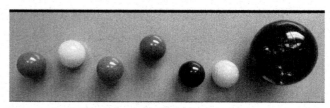

Figure 13.6. Balls used to represent prominence for the sentence, "We're planning a picnic in the park."

For a simpler exercise, have students place a marker only on the prominent word in each thought group in written sentences.

We're planning a *pic*nic in the PARK.

Rubber bands. While saying a sentence, have students stretch a thick rubber band vertically on prominent syllables. This emphasizes that the intonation (usually) goes up on that syllable. If you'd rather not use rubber bands, substitute a different movement, like clapping or raising hands on the prominent syllable.)

Corrections. To practice using contrastive stress in correcting false information, have students work in pairs. One student says a false statement, and the partner gives the correct information, using appropriate contrastive stress (**sound 13.8**):

A: Sydney is in Austria.

B: No, it's not in AUStria. It's in AuSTRALia.

B: There are eight days in a week.

A: No, not EIGHT days. There are only SEVen days in a week.

Find the difference. This is another activity to practice contrastive stress. Find or make two pictures that are almost the same except for some details. The differences should be easy to see—if you look at both pictures, the differences should be obvious. Put students in pairs and give a different picture to each partner. Without looking at their partner's picture, students try to discover the differences between the two pictures by telling each other about their picture and asking each other questions. As they talk about the differences, they should emphasize words that are being contrasted or information that is a correction to a mistake (Celce-Murcia et al., 2010; Figure 13.7).

Here's an example conversation about the two pictures labeled "Picture A" and "Picture B," with prominent syllables in capital letters (**sound 13.9**):

A: I see a SAILboat in my picture.

B: Oh! I see TWO sailboats in my picture. Do you see a bird standing on a SANDcastle?

A: No, I see a SANDcastle, but there's no BIRD on it.

Figure 13.7. Find the differences between pictures A and B.

There are many sources of these pictures in books and on the Internet; search for "find the difference pictures." You can also draw or make your own pictures. The pictures shown here were made with a free iPad app called Doodle Buddy. It includes several backgrounds to choose from and a selection of small pictures to add.

Predicting prominence. After students have had a chance to practice a lot and have a good feel for where prominence falls, you can ask them to predict where they think prominence will occur. Give them a dialogue or story, with or without punctuation, and ask them to mark probable thought groups and prominence. Discussing their choices with a partner can help clarify the reasons for their choices.

It's important to realize that predicting prominence may be difficult if the examples are complicated, so start with simple sentences that obviously fit the patterns students have learned. When you check students' predictions, allow for the possibility that there could really be more than one way to say the sentence and more than one location for prominence.

Intonation

Introducing Intonation

To help students see that intonation is important and can change meaning, say a simple sentence with falling intonation and then with rising intonation (**sound 13**.**10**):

Today is Monday.

Today is Monday?

Ask students if the two sentences have the same meaning. They'll usually realize that they don't; the first is a statement, and the second is a question. You can also say a short sentence, like "I'm going home tomorrow" or even just "hello" with different intonation patterns to show how the same words can sound happy, sad, excited, surprised, or angry. It's OK to exaggerate your intonation during practice to make it easier for students to hear the patterns. They're not likely to carry the exaggerated intonation over into their own speaking.

Listening to Intonation

Marking intonation. Have students listen to a dialogue or story while following along on a written script and mark intonation patterns over the words to show how they hear the speakers' voices rise and fall. Help students notice when the speakers' voices go up or down at the ends of sentences and explain why. Then have students practice and imitate what they've heard.

Intonation blocks. This is another way to practice recognizing intonation patterns. Cut shapes out of thick paper or thin foam sheets to represent chunks of intonation (see an intonation block pattern in Figure 13.8). You can make bigger intonation blocks with magnets attached to use on a whiteboard or blackboard or smaller ones for students to use on their desks. Use the pieces to assemble models of the intonation of sentences, or have students add appropriate blocks above sentences written on the board. See Figure 13.9 to see how the blocks can be used (**sound 13.11**).

Practicing Intonation

Modeling intonation. Give students something long and flexible, like a pipe cleaner, string, or ribbon, and ask them to shape it to match the intonation of sentences. (A pipe cleaner is a piece of wire covered with fuzzy threads. When you bend it, it keeps its shape. Pipe cleaners are sometimes called *chenille stems*.) The shape doesn't have to be exact; the important thing is to have the correct intonation at the end of the sentence or thought group: Rising, falling, or staying fairly flat. This is similar to drawing intonation contours above written sentences, but in three dimensions (**sound 13.12**):

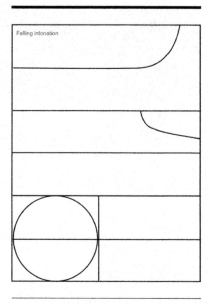

Figure 13.8. Intonation block pattern.

Do you enjoy doing your homework?

Yes, I *love* doing my homework.

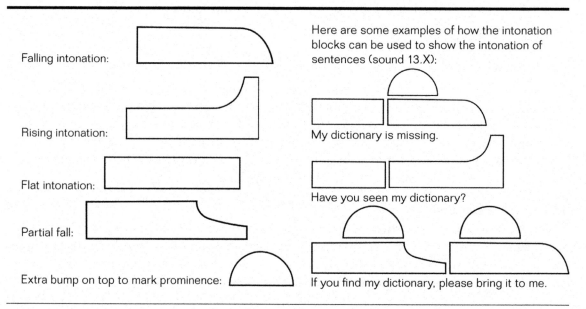

Falling intonation:

Rising intonation:

Flat intonation:

Partial fall:

Extra bump on top to mark prominence:

Here are some examples of how the intonation blocks can be used to show the intonation of sentences (sound 13.X):

My dictionary is missing.

Have you seen my dictionary?

If you find my dictionary, please bring it to me.

Figure 13.9. Examples using intonation blocks.

Conduct an orchestra. Use your hands, a pencil, or any long, thin object as a baton to show intonation as if you were conducting an orchestra. Move the baton up when the intonation rises and down when it falls. The teacher or a student can be the conductor with other students following along as they say sentences, or all the students can be conductors together.

Human intonation model. Choose a sentence and have several students stand in a row, with each person representing one word or one syllable in the sentence. Let the students discuss how the intonation should sound and then have each person stand up tall or crouch down to represent the pitch of his or her word. Figure 13.10 is a representation of the intonation of "How are you today?" with one person representing each syllable (**sound 13.13**).

Figure 13.10. Human intonation model of "How are you today?"

Use a kazoo. A kazoo is a simple musical instrument that is played by putting the larger end in your mouth and humming a melody (**sound 13.14**; Figure 13.11). The kazoo makes the sound of your voice louder and adds a buzzing quality to it. It's different from many instruments because you *hum* into it; you don't blow, as you would with a recorder or flute. Students can easily imitate intonation patterns with a kazoo. The advantage of using a kazoo (rather than repeating actual sentences with the correct intonation) is that the learner can concentrate only on the melody of intonation without having to think about individual sounds, vocabulary, and other details. If kazoos aren't available, students can simply hum.

As a variation, have two students practice and perform a conversation with kazoos or by humming. Ask other students to identify questions and answers and try to guess what they're saying.

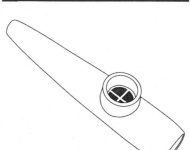

Figure 13.11. Kazoo.

Computer software. There are several software programs that allow you to record your voice and see a diagram showing the intonation pattern of what you've said. These sometimes come as part of a larger pronunciation practice package and can be expensive. However, here are two free software programs that can analyze intonation patterns.

- **Praat** was created by two Dutch phoneticists, Paul Boersma and David Weenink, at the University of Amsterdam, the Netherlands. Praat is useful, but it can take some effort to learn to use. Video and print tutorials are available online. (Google "Praat tutorials" to find them.) You can download the program for free at http://www.fon.hum.uva.nl/praat/ for either Windows or Mac (see screenshot in Figure 13.12).
- **Speech Analyzer** was developed by SIL International (the Summer Institute of Linguistics), and is available only for Windows (see screenshot in Figure 13.13). It can be downloaded at http://www-01.sil.org/computing/sa/index.htm.

When using one of these programs to look at intonation contours, you can see the patterns best with sentences that don't have any stops, fricatives, or affricates, especially voiceless ones. Those sounds result in blank spots in the intonation line. Choose sentences that have lots of **sonorants**:

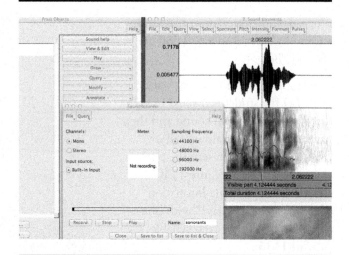

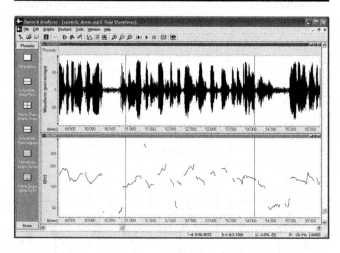

Figure 13.12. Praat screenshot.

Figure 13.13. Speech Analyzer screen shot.

Vowels, nasals, liquids, and glides. Figure 13.14 shows the difference in the intonation lines of two sentences, analyzed using Praat.

Questions and answers. Many simple speaking activities also provide good practice with intonation. For example, give partners a picture and have them ask and answer questions about it, either about what they can see in the picture or about what they imagine the story behind it to be. Remind them that yes/no questions typically have rising intonation, while WH-questions typically have falling intonation.

Dialogues, skits, and shadowing. These provide good practice with intonation because they set up a particular context for language and encourage students to use the intonation that fits that context. More discussion of these techniques is coming later in this chapter.

Predicting intonation. After students have had many chances to hear and practice typical intonation patterns, they can be asked to predict the intonation for a conversation they have seen in writing but haven't heard yet. Predicting intonation can be difficult unless you stick to simple, obvious examples. Don't make the task too challenging at first. If it's not obvious what the intonation for a particular dialogue should be, make sure students have a chance to hear the dialogue before they analyze it.

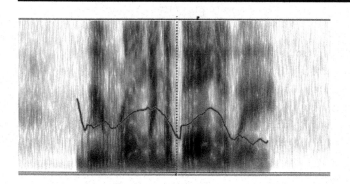

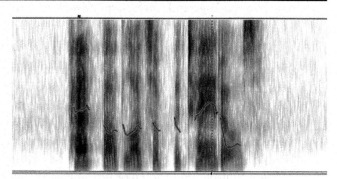

Figure 13.14. Two sentences analyzed using Praat. 1. We're rolling a ball away. *(Only one stop—a voiced one.)* 2. Pat bought lots of potatoes. *(Lots of stops.)*

Connected Speech

Introducing Connected Speech

Make a comparison. A good way to introduce the concept of connected speech is to present a simple sentence and read it very carefully, using the citation form of each word. Ask students if people really talk that way and if it sounds like normal English. (If they're not sure, tell them that this is actually not normal. Real people are not that careful and precise.) Then read the sentence again, using normal connected speech (**sound 13.15**):

I am going to write you a letter.

Carefully: /ay æm gowɪŋ tuw rayt yuw ə lɛtɚ/

Normally: /aymgənərayʧuwəlɛtɚ/

Let students listen to both versions a few times and see if they can point out which sounds are changed or omitted. Reassure them that this is a normal way of speaking, and it isn't considered sloppy, incorrect, or rude. Real people talk this way in all but the most formal and careful speech.

Listening to Connected Speech

Mark the script. As students listen to spoken or recorded sentences, draw attention to sounds that are **linked** and have students draw lines or circles to connect them on a written script. After doing some examples as a group, have students listen and mark linked sounds on their own or with a partner. It's normal to have some disagreement about exactly where linking was heard. At first, try to use sentences that are spoken somewhat slowly, but using connected speech, then gradually speed up to a normal speaking speed. Students might mark sentences in one of these ways (**sound 13.16**):

When did you meet Tom? When did you meet Tom?

I put a bag of chips in my backpack.   I put a bag of chips in my backpack.

Dictations. Dictations are useful for practicing connected speech, just as they are for practicing individual sounds. Prepare several sentences or a short dialogue to highlight the types of connected speech you've been practicing. Have students listen to the sentences spoken with normal reduced forms and "translate" them into their citation forms, writing the full forms of the sentences. Then check what they've written and discuss why certain combinations of sounds were hard to hear or had unexpected sounds. It's very important for the dictated sentences to be spoken with normal connected speech, not overly careful pronunciation (even if the students ask you to speak more slowly and carefully).

Skeleton dictations. Give students a handout showing some sentences that will be dictated, omitting certain words that involve connected speech. (In other words, give them a "skeleton" of the sentences.) Students listen and fill in the blanks with the full forms of the words they heard. Finally, discuss why certain words were hard to hear and how their sounds changed compared to their citation forms (**sound 13.17**):

What do you ____want to____ do today?   /wɑnə/
I ____have to____ do my homework.   /hæftə/

Practicing Connected Speech

Sticky blocks. To show how words "stick together" in connected speech, write words on small wood or plastic blocks. Attach a small magnet to one end of each one and a piece of steel to the other. While saying phrases or sentences with linking, put the blocks together to show that words join together, just like magnets (Figure 13.15; **sound 13.18**). To make the blocks reusable, attach a small piece of slick coated paper or plastic to the side of the block and write words on it with a

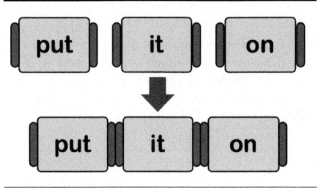

Figure 13.15. Sticky blocks.

dry-erase marker. Velcro can also be attached to the ends of the blocks instead of magnets (Celce-Murcia et al., 2010).

Modeling-clay shapes. In a similar way, you can have students make shapes of modeling clay, such as Plasticine or Play-Doh, to represent individual words. The shapes can be simple balls, or if your students are feeling creative, they could be shaped like the things the words represent. While saying phrases or sentences using linking, students push the clay shapes together to illustrate how words are linked together. (This activity can be a bit messy, though.)

Transparent overlays. Write words in large letters on rectangles of transparent plastic in different colors. Overlap the edges of the words to show how the sounds blend, just as the colors of the pieces blend (Figure 13.16; **sound 13.19**). This is especially good for **palatalization**, which makes a new sound out of two original sounds, just as two colors blend to make a new color. This works especially well on an overhead projector, if you have one available.

Sheets of thin, transparent plastic can be found in many hobby shops. Transparent vinyl in light colors is also sold in some fabric shops to be used as tablecloths or protective covers. File folders, binder dividers, plastic envelopes, or report covers are sometimes also made of a suitable plastic.

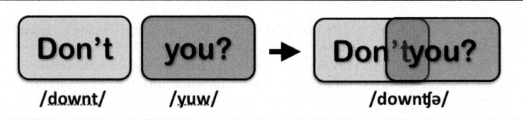

Figure 13.16. Transparent overlays to show palatalization.

Brainstorm words. Ask students to list adjectives and nouns that fit a particular sound pattern, for example, adjectives that end with a consonant sound and nouns that start with a vowel sound (sounds, not letters; Table 13.1). Working in pairs, students choose adjectives and nouns that make sense together and write phrases, adding articles where appropriate. Then they practice saying the phrases with appropriate linking. If students choose the words that they'll practice, the activity can be more interesting and meaningful than if they simply read phrases from a textbook (Hewings, 2004).

Table 13.1. Brainstorm words.

Adjectives ending with consonant sounds			Nouns beginning with vowel sounds		
big	orange	difficult	apples	idea	umbrella
expensive	intelligent	bright	elephant	anteater	eyes

Phrases with linking		
expensive apples	an intelligent anteater	a broken umbrella
bright eyes	a big elephant	The Big Apple

Using Authentic Materials to Practice Suprasegmentals

Written or spoken materials from real life, such as stories, jokes, proverbs, songs, and movies, can provide useful material for practicing suprasegmental features. However, since these authentic materials were not created with the needs of language learners in mind, they need to be chosen and presented carefully so that they won't overwhelm students. Even materials that have great interest in themselves will lead to frustration and boredom if they're far beyond the understanding of a particular group of students. Still, if we choose and use them wisely, authentic materials can be a great addition to pronunciation lessons.

Jokes and riddles can provide good practice material, as long as students "get" the humor. In addition to practicing thought groups, as mentioned earlier in this chapter, humorous materials are also good for practicing intonation, prominence, and linking. Have students practice reading jokes or funny stories aloud and telling them to each other, emphasizing pausing and intonation to make the jokes effective. The biggest challenge here is finding jokes that students will understand and consider funny. Humor in a new language is often hard to understand, so choose carefully.

Proverbs and famous quotations not only provide good pronunciation practice, but let students compare words of wisdom in different languages. Give pairs or small groups of students a list of proverbs or quotations in English. Before practicing pronunciation, ask them to try to guess what they mean and think of proverbs or sayings in their own language that have a similar or opposite meaning. With the whole class, supply the actual meanings of the sayings and see what proverbs they've found in their own language. Now that students understand the meanings of the proverbs, have them practice reading them with appropriate pauses, prominence, and intonation. Finally, give the class a role play situation in which one person has a problem and another chooses an appropriate proverb to offer as advice.

Using Drama and Puppets

Dialogues, short skits, role plays, and puppet shows are simple **drama techniques** that put language in context and make it easier for students to speak with natural intonation, pauses, and connected speech. When students pretend to be someone else in role plays, skits, and puppet shows, it can be easier for them to forget their shyness and try to imitate new intonation patterns.

Puppets are especially useful when teaching children, who enjoy pretending to be another character. Be sure to keep scripted materials at a level that the students can understand, and aim for natural sounding language.

Puppets can be bought in toy stores or teaching supply stores, but it's also easy for teachers and children to make their own puppets. Here are some ways (Figure 13.17):

- **Sock puppets.** Make a face on the toe of a sock using buttons, thread, puffy paint, markers, or bits of cloth or paper. Put the sock over your hand and push the sock between your fingers and thumb to make a moveable mouth.
- **Paper bag puppets.** Draw eyes on the bottom of a paper bag and a mouth lower down on the bag. Put your hand

A sock puppet, a paper bag puppet, and a stick puppet

Figure 13.17. Hand puppets.

inside the bag and move the bottom flap up and down to make the mouth move.

- **Stick puppets**. Draw a picture of a character on thick paper and cut it out. Tape or glue the picture to a craft stick, drinking straw, or other stick-like object.
- **Puppet Pals**. For a more high-tech approach to puppets, use an app like the one for iPad called Puppet Pals. This app lets students choose backgrounds and characters and then record short movies with them. They can make the characters move around and record their own voices to add dialogue. The app is free, but for a small cost you can buy more backgrounds and characters. Other computer programs and websites can also do similar things.

Figure 13.18. Puppet Pals screen shot.

Using Shadowing and Mirroring

Shadowing is one of the most valuable and versatile ways of practicing suprasegmental features. It is an activity in which learners repeatedly listen to and imitate the speakers in a short video clip or sound recording. Then they try to speak the lines of the dialogue with or slightly after the characters in the clip. **Mirroring** is very similar, except that students also try to imitate the gestures and body movements of the speakers. Here's one way to do shadowing:

1. Find a short film clip (less than 2 minutes) with a simple, natural sounding, self-contained conversation. Find or write a transcript for the clip. A list of websites that have video clips is in the Resources section at the end of this book.
2. In class, give the students some background about what's happening in the scene. Don't just jump into the video. Students need to understand what's going on.
3. Play the clip. The first time, the students should just watch and get the general idea of the characters, the situation, and the meaning of the dialogue.
4. Hand out the transcript. Go over any unfamiliar words and expressions. Talk about what's happening, and make sure the students understand the dialogue.
5. Watch the clip again. This time, give students something specific to listen for—pauses, intonation, linking, and so forth—and have them mark that feature on their script. It works best if you give one specific focus; don't expect students to notice everything at once. If there's time, play the clip again.
6. Have students compare their markings with a partner, and then talk as a class about what they found and why it sounded that way. (For example, they might find that a speaker's intonation on a WH-question went up instead of down because she was asking a question for the second time. She didn't hear the man's answer the first time.)
7. Have students practice reading the conversation with a partner. Encourage them to try to say it just the way the characters in the video did, with the same pauses, intonation, emotions, and so forth.

8. Play the clip again. Ask students to try to read the dialogue along with the characters in the film. (This will work best if the characters are speaking slowly.) Do it again if there's time.

9. Review the conversation in a later class by practicing it again.

It's important not to rush the process of shadowing. Students will need to listen to the video clip several times, so short clips work best. Repeatedly watching and listening to the clip gives learners a chance to absorb the sounds and intonation patterns they're hearing and make them a part of their own language use. With repeated listening, they'll notice things that they didn't hear the first time.

Goodwin (2005) describes another series of steps for using short video clips with college-age or adult students to help them focus on intonation, pausing, prominence, and body language:

1. Play the video clip without sound. Ask students to pay attention to the overall situation and to notice the speakers' body language and facial expressions. Then have students guess who the speakers are, what emotions they feel, and what the situation might be.

2. Play the video clip several times with sound. Students check their predictions, figure out the overall situation, and notice any emphasized words that they can hear especially clearly.

3. Hand out a transcript of the conversation. Guide students in predicting pauses, prominence, and intonation.

4. Play each line of the conversation a few times so students can check their predictions. Also point out body movements and facial expressions and have students make notes about these on their transcripts.

5. Have students practice each line of the conversation, repeating after the recording or the teacher's voice. Use gestures or movements to emphasize stress, intonation, and other suprasegmental features.

6. Have students practice the conversation with a partner, imitating the pronunciation, stress, pauses, prominence, intonation, connected speech, and body language of the characters.

7. Make a video of pairs of students performing the conversation.

8. Give the class a role-play prompt of a situation similar to that in the video clip. Make a video of the students' performance of the role play.

9. Have students watch their performance of the scripted and unscripted conversations at home and complete a self-evaluation form.

Goodwin states that one goal of this exercise is to help students become "researchers of real speech" so that they can continue to make their speech seem more natural even after their formal study is over (Goodwin, 2005).

Using Songs and Music

It seems logical that if we're teaching the musical aspects of pronunciation, music should be a good tool. Teaching pronunciation through songs has several advantages:

- Music often tells interesting stories in natural sounding language that contains plenty of linking and other examples of connected speech. If we choose songs carefully, they can also reflect the rhythm of natural speech.

- Songs give us a painless way to do repetition. Saying sentences over and over can become dull, but singing a song many times is much more enjoyable, as long as the students and the teacher like the song.

- Sounds tend to stay in our minds better when we sing them than if we just say them aloud. We've probably all had the experience of having a song stuck in our heads, but spoken sentences just don't have the same staying power.

- Carefully chosen music can help students relax. It can lower the **affective filter** in the classroom, creating a comfortable and nonthreatening classroom atmosphere. This indirectly helps students learn not only pronunciation but language in general.

While songs can certainly be valuable in teaching suprasegmentals, we need to use them carefully. Music has its own characteristics and requirements apart from those of language, and a song is not *always* or necessarily a good model. Here are some points to consider when you're choosing songs to teach pronunciation with music.

Choosing Songs

Choose songs and recordings carefully. Of course, you'll want to look for a song that both you and your students will enjoy listening to and singing, and one that contains the pronunciation feature you want to practice—particular sounds, types of linking, or stress patterns.

The singer in a recording should have clear pronunciation that's easy to hear and understand, and the words should not be drowned out by noisy instruments. Songs with one singer are often easier to understand than songs sung by a group. When more people sing, the sounds are sometimes muffled and hard to distinguish. The more singers, the harder they might be to understand.

Avoid songs that don't provide an appropriate language model. If the singer's pronunciation is strongly nonstandard or hard to understand, the song is probably not a good choice, even though it may be wonderful musically.

Also think about the grammar used in the song. One or two nonstandard or very casual bits of grammar might be all right, but you probably don't want your students to learn to say "You ain't nothin' but a hound dog" after listening to the Elvis Presley song by that name. Of course, also avoid obscene language or topics that are not appropriate for school use.

Choose a song with a simple melody that's easy to sing and remember, especially if you're going to ask students to sing along. Some melodies are more complex than others, and some song styles have so many "wobbles" that their melodies are hard to follow. Choose a melody that students can learn quickly and sing easily, even if music is not their strong point. Keep the pitch range realistic for your students—not too high or too low for their voices.

Activities to Use with Music

Sing along. This is the easiest and most obvious activity. As students sing along with a recording, they'll start to imitate linking and other aspects of connected speech. In effect, it's a very pleasant form of "repeat after me."

Listen and mark. Give students written lyrics and ask them to find and mark examples of the features that they've been studying—linking, contractions, reduced forms, and so forth. Ask them to think about thought groups—do the breaks in the melody match the places where we would expect to find thought group boundaries? Sometimes they do, and sometimes they don't.

Row, row, row your ___boat___

Gently down the stream.

Merrily, merrily, merrily, merrily

Life is but a ___dream___.

Figure 13.19. Cloze listening activity.

Cloze listening. In a cloze listening activity, students try to fill in missing words in printed lyrics as they listen to a song. This is a good way to help students focus on the sounds of connected speech and to "translate" reduced forms into standard spelling. If you use this type of activity, there are some practical aspects to consider: Make sure the words you replace with blanks are ones that can be heard easily.

Spread the blanks out a bit. It takes time to write the missing words, and it's very hard if there are too many blanks too close together. Also, make your blanks long enough so students have plenty of space to write the required words. Figure 13.19 is an example of a cloze activity.

Retell the story. Choose a song that tells an interesting story. Have students listen and go through the meaning, making sure they understand the plot. Ask students to retell the story to a partner, using some of the same phrases, reduced forms, and connected speech forms that they heard in the song.

Find the mistakes. Give students the lyrics to a song, but change some words to incorrect ones with similar sounds. The new words don't have to make sense. For example, "I want to hold your hand" might become "I want a folder hand." Ask students to listen to the song, find the mistakes, and try to write the real words. With more advanced students, ask them to find and analyze examples of connected speech that they heard (Murphey, 1992, p. 70).

Write your own lyrics. Give students the lyrics to a verse of a familiar song—one whose rhythm is like that of natural English. Ask students to change the words or write their own lyrics to express a new meaning, being careful to match the rhythm of the song by choosing words with the right number of syllables and stress patterns (Murphey, 1992, p. 74). For example, the lyrics of "Row, Row, Row Your Boat" could be changed to

> Ride, ride, ride your bike
> Quickly down the street.
> Pedaling home at dinner time
> It's almost time to eat.

But . . . Finally, here's a word of caution: Songs have their own requirements that are often different from what we find in natural language. Sometimes syllables are stretched out in a song, if that works best with its melody and rhythm, even though they wouldn't be emphasized in normal speech. In particular, songs are *not* good for teaching intonation. Songs have their own melody, and it seldom matches the actual intonation of English or any other language. Songs are great for practicing linking, individual sounds, word stress, and sometimes rhythm, but not for intonation.

Pronunciation Software and the Internet

There are many software programs, websites, and series of videos on YouTube for learning about and practicing pronunciation, but be careful! Not all of these are of good quality. Some are amateurish and give inaccurate or misleading information. Some are disguised advertisements that try to get you to buy a more expensive product later. Check and judge materials carefully before you have students use them. If you don't entirely trust a website, use something else.

Recording Pronunciation Practice

Most computers and tablets come with simple programs that allow users to record sound—the details depend on the type of computer. Students can use these to record their pronunciation practice. If you want, they can also submit their recordings to you for comments by email or other means. Check your computer's owner's manual (if it has one) or the manufacturer's website for instructions on recording sound. If your students have cell phones, they can also be used for recording sound and sending it by email or text message.

In addition, some websites provide a more organized way for students to record and listen to their voices and for teachers to leave recorded comments about the practice recordings. Here are two good ones that I've used. Both have free versions.

Figure 13.20. Voxopop screen shot.

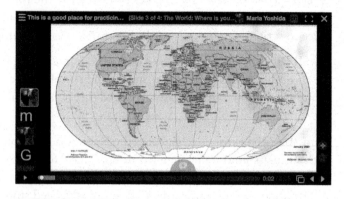

Figure 13.21. Voicethread screen shot.

Voxopop (http://voxopop.com) is a website where people can record their voices in a series of related messages—a kind of spoken discussion forum (see Voxopop screen shot in Figure 13.20). You can use it in several ways:

- Have students record themselves reading a passage for homework practice. You can create a class pronunciation practice page where all the students can leave recordings for you to check and respond to with your own recorded comments and suggestions.
- Create a recorded discussion on a topic related to your class or your students' interests. Students can record their comments and responses to other students' messages for "free-speaking" pronunciation practice.

Voicethread (http://voicethread.com) also allows students to record their voices. Choose a picture that you'd like students to respond to, upload it to a page that you can set up for your class, and it will appear in the middle of the screen (Figure 13.21). Students record or type comments about the picture, and icons appear around the central picture representing all the comments. Users can click the icons to hear or read the comments of others. The teacher can record additional comments about pronunciation or simply respond to the ideas the students have expressed.

Creating Animation or "Talking Heads"

Using websites like **Voki** (http://voki.com), you can make cartoon characters called "avatars," choosing from many different heads, hair styles, facial features, accessories, and backgrounds. The characters can speak in two ways: You can type in words and they'll speak with an artificial voice, or you can record your own voice (better for pronunciation practice). The website has ideas for lesson plans using Voki.

GoAnimate (http://goanimate.com/) is a website that lets you create simple animation, adding your own narration or typing text to be spoken by a digital voice. You choose the background and characters, record the dialogue or narration, add music if you want, and the website produces an animated movie. It's similar to Puppet Pals, but the characters have more ability to move.

Reminders When Using Technology

If you're using any type of technology, have a backup plan. Sooner or later, something will go wrong. Your computer will crash, the website you wanted to use will disappear or be down for repairs, there will be an electrical blackout—anything can happen. Don't rely too much on everything working perfectly. Plan for what you would do in case of a technological disaster, and have a low-tech backup plan ready.

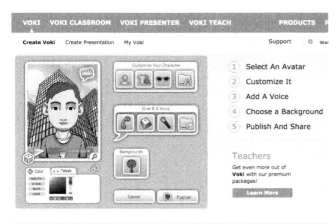

Figure 13.22. Voki screen shot.

Figure 13.23. GoAnimate screen shot.

Even if everything is working fine, remember that technology will never replace a good teacher. Technology is just a tool. Use it well, but don't let it become the main focus of your lesson. A computer program, website, or video can't teach your class for you. Computers are not *necessarily* interesting or fun for students; if they're designed awkwardly or used badly, they can be just as dull as a long-winded lecture. People need human contact, and your human presence and caring are more important to your students than any flashy technology. Use technology; don't let it control you.

Responding to Students' Pronunciation Practice

When students record a sample of their pronunciation or read to you for pronunciation practice during a lesson, how will you respond? Deciding what to say can be difficult, especially if a student is making many mistakes. We want to help students improve, but we don't want them to be discouraged and lose motivation if we criticize too much.

It's best not to try to comment on everything at once. Goodwin (2001) suggests starting by focusing comments only on these categories:

- one or two things that seriously interfere with the speaker's intelligibility;
- just the thing you're practicing now, whether it's a particular sound or a suprasegmental feature;
- things that are easiest to fix, like the pronunciation of a particular word (as opposed to a mistake involving a common sound that occurs many times); and
- mistakes that this student has been making again and again.

When giving comments, be kind and respectful, but honest. Harsh criticism won't help, but neither will empty praise or easy acceptance of everything the student says. When making a correction of a mispronunciation, give a correct example for the student to hear and repeat, or pronounce both the correct and incorrect ways so that the student can hear the contrast. Praise students for specific things that they're doing well, especially if it's an improvement over the past. A dose of honest, specific praise can keep students from feeling that improving their pronunciation is hopeless.

Be Alert for New Ideas

Look around you and try to find spoken or written materials from everyday life that could be useful in teaching suprasegmental features. Use your imagination to find new ways to explain, illustrate, and practice the musical aspects of English pronunciation.

CHAPTER 14

Different Places, Different Learners

Teaching is not like buying a pair of socks. One size does *not* fit all. There isn't just one best way to teach pronunciation—or any other subject, for that matter. We need to ask ourselves: "What's the best way to help *my* students, in their particular situation, to reach their goals and make their pronunciation more intelligible?" Planning and teaching a lesson is a complex task that requires teachers to make lots of choices, and you'll need to consider many factors before deciding what to do in class. Celce-Murcia, Brinton, and Goodwin (2010) suggest considering these things:

- How old are the learners?
- What is their skill level in English overall?
- What language or languages do they speak, other than English?
- What are their goals? What are your goals for them?
- What resources are available in terms of time, textbooks, and equipment?
- What else do you have to fit into your necessarily limited class time to meet the needs of your students and your curriculum? How can you fit pronunciation in with every-thing else?

- What requirements, constraints, or limits are put on your teaching from outside—from the school administration, the local school board, or the national Ministry of Education?
- What is the setting of your teaching? Are you in an English-speaking country where students will need to use English in their daily lives (English as a second language; ESL) or in a country where English is not commonly spoken and your students seldom use English (English as a foreign language; EFL)?

You'll also find that every group of students you teach is a little different, even if they're closely matched in age, skill level, and goals. What works with one group might not work as well with another.

To meet the needs of all the students you might teach, you need to stay flexible and build up a supply of resources, techniques, and activities that you can adapt to fit various teaching situations and groups of learners. Here are some things to think about.

How Old Are the Learners?

Of course, you wouldn't teach 10-year-olds the same way you'd teach 40-year-olds. Learners of different ages require different approaches, methods, and activities.

Children learn best through simple, concrete means—through demonstrations, imitation, movement, and rhythm. Songs with movements and gestures are excellent activities for children. If they like a song, chant, or simple game, they won't mind repeating it again and again. Young children are willing to do things just for fun. The joy of learning and a sense of accomplishment are strong motivators for them.

Young children have an amazing ability to learn a new language, as long as they have plenty of chances to hear it and try using it on their own. But even young children can't learn pronunciation immediately. They also need time and lots of practice to be able to say new sounds with consistent accuracy. In fact, very young children may still be in the process of learning all the sounds of their own language. For example, many native English-speaking children don't master sounds like /r/, /l/, /s/, and /v/ until they are 5 or 6 years old (Sander, 1972).

As children reach middle school or high school age, they are better able to understand verbal explanations and abstract concepts. However, it still works better to keep explanations short, simple, practical, and nontechnical. Most teenagers also enjoy songs and games, as long as they don't seem too childish, and competition can be a strong motivator for them. They can learn well from pair and group work if it's structured, introduced, and conducted carefully.

Adults have a stronger ability to understand explanations and consciously analyze sounds, but this does *not* mean that all we need to do is lecture and analyze. Adults also benefit from learning through demonstrations, models, and pictures, not just verbal explanations and "repeat after me." Gadgets like dental models, listening tubes, feathers, and rubber bands also work well with adults.

Adults learn well in pair- and group-work activities that are geared toward their interests and level of maturity. Many adults also enjoy songs and purposeful games, although it's good to get to know your students' feelings about these before you get in too deep. With any of these activities, however, be sure to present them confidently and explain how they will help your students improve their pronunciation. Most adults accept having fun for the sake of learning, but if they don't see the purpose of an activity, they may feel that their time is being wasted.

What Is the Learners' Skill Level?

Learners of all levels, from beginning to advanced, need continued pronunciation practice. Sometimes teachers are hesitant to teach pronunciation to beginning students for fear that it will make them feel overwhelmed and discouraged. However, beginning learners may be the ones who need pronunciation teaching the most. If we can get beginners started on the path toward clear, understandable pronunciation and help them see that it's important, they'll be more likely to develop good pronunciation as they continue to learn. If we can prevent or at least limit the fossilization of pronunciation habits that lead to unintelligible speech, our students will have an easier time being understood later.

On the other hand, more advanced learners need pronunciation review and remediation too. Some students with good fluency and a very strong knowledge of grammar and vocabulary still have serious pronunciation problems that interfere with **intelligibility**. It's important to keep practicing in appropriate ways that match these students' abilities, interests, and goals.

Students' skill level will also affect the choices we make when finding or writing sentences, dialogues, or other practice materials. The words and grammar used in **minimal pairs**, sentences, dialogues, and activities must fit what the students have learned. Having students repeat words and sentences that they don't yet understand is just an empty tongue exercise; it won't seem like real language. Students need to try using the words and phrases they're practicing in real communication, but if the language is far beyond their understanding, this will be impossible.

What Languages Do the Learners Speak?

A learner's native language has a strong influence on how he or she will learn pronunciation in a new language (see Chapter 1, "Introduction to Teaching Pronunciation"). We can often predict the problems students will have, particularly with individual sounds, if we know what their first language is. It's helpful to understand the sound system of your students' language or languages so you can predict what aspects of English pronunciation are likely to give them trouble. Summaries of "trouble sounds" for speakers of some languages can be found in several books, including Swan and Smith's *Learner English* (2001); Avery and Ehrlich's *Teaching American English Pronunciation* (1992); Lane's *Tips for Teaching Pronunciation: A Practical Approach* (2010); and Kenworthy's *Teaching English Pronunciation* (1987).

To some extent, teaching pronunciation in a monolingual class, in which all the students share the same native language, is simpler than teaching it in a class whose students speak many different languages. It's easy to choose the topics to address, based on the students' common needs.

In a multilingual class, however, we have to face the fact that different people will have different problems. If you choose an activity to address a problem that some students are having, it may be something that other students are already able to do easily. If your students are old enough, talk about this with them. Explain that sometimes the things you practice might seem too easy, but they might be hard for someone else. At other times, the shoe will be on the other foot, and different students will have trouble. Encourage students to be patient and help each other so everyone can learn and improve.

What Are the Learners' Goals?

Different learners have different goals for learning English and for trying to improve their pronunciation. Some are or will be living in an English-speaking country and need to be able to speak clearly to survive and work. Others will be using English in other ways: to travel abroad, to study in an English-language university, or to do business with native or nonnative speakers of English when English is the only language they have in common. Some need to pass a test that includes a speaking component, such as the iBT TOEFL or IELTS. Some just want to pass their English class so they can get on with more important things.

It's important to try to understand the goals of your particular group of learners. Along with more general pronunciation activities, include practice aimed specifically at helping them meet their goals. For example, if your students are adults working in a particular profession, they'll need to learn to pronounce the vocabulary of that field—they can tell you what words they need to use and practice. If they're preparing for a standardized test, they'll need to practice in ways that are similar to the tasks they'll be asked to do on the test. If they're going to give presentations at professional conferences or business meetings, they'll need to pay special attention to appropriate pausing, prominence, and intonation along with individual sounds and pronunciation of specialized vocabulary.

Constraints on Your Teaching

In the real world, we don't always have total freedom to teach the way we want. The factors that put constraints on what and how we teach might include some of the following:

- **Time**. Few teachers have the luxury of teaching a class devoted only to pronunciation; it will usually be just one topic in a broader English class. Class time is limited. How can you find a place for pronunciation along with all the other things you have to teach? (This will be discussed in the next section.)

- **Resources**. Someone else may have already chosen the textbooks and other materials that you will use, and you seldom have control over the technology that's available in the classroom. You need to find the strong points in the resources you have and be creative in using them.
- **Outside forces**. Depending on where you're teaching, school administrators, the local Board of Education, or the national Ministry of Education may specify what is to be taught. Parents and others in the community often have expectations about what will be included and emphasized in teaching. Even standardized achievement or entrance tests can influence what and how you teach.
- **Tradition**. In some teaching situations, the traditional ways of teaching don't emphasize pronunciation, and other teachers may not appreciate it if you try to make changes. They may feel that by trying to do something new you'll undermine their authority or make them look old-fashioned, or they may honestly believe that the traditional way is best. Whatever the reason, trying to change well-established teaching styles can be difficult. Tact and cooperation will usually get better results than lectures and confrontation.

In some cases we may be able to change these limitations by working with school administrators, parents, and others. In other cases, however, we'll just have to learn to accept limitations that we can't change and figure out how to work around them. If computer equipment isn't easily available, we can substitute low-tech methods. If the textbook doesn't include much pronunciation practice, we can supplement with bits of pronunciation practice as a part of reading, listening, speaking, or grammar lessons.

Finding Time for Pronunciation Teaching

Teachers often say, "I don't have time to teach pronunciation. There's too much in the curriculum already!" Teaching pronunciation really is important—too important to ignore just because we're busy. Pronunciation practice doesn't have to take a lot of time if you combine it with other parts of your language lessons. Here are some ideas for fitting pronunciation in with other types of practice.

When Beginning or Ending a Lesson

Do a quick bit of pronunciation practice as a warm-up at the beginning of class, as a closing activity, or for a change of pace between other activities. Many of the activities in Chapter 7, "Teaching Consonants and Vowels" and Chapter 13, "Teaching the Musical Aspects of Pronunciation" can be adapted for a quick pronunciation review:

- Review the pronunciation of some new words by having students say the words in chorus and identify the stressed syllable. Use flash cards or spoken words as a "trigger."
- Do a quick minimal pair practice. Write a minimal pair on the board and label the words "1" and "2." Say one of the words and have students hold up one or two fingers to tell which word they heard. Then have them practice the words with a partner.
- Practice a song, chant, tongue twister, or poem that the students have learned, paying attention to sounds, **rhythm**, **linking**, or other features.
- Show a picture, and have students ask and answer questions about it with a partner. Use a picture that has objects containing sounds you want to practice, or concentrate on **intonation**, rhythm, and **thought groups** in the questions and answers themselves.
- Do a quick dictation of one or two sentences using familiar material containing sounds you've been practicing. For this purpose, keep the sentences short. Dictate and have students write, then show the correct sentences and have students check their own work.

When Teaching Vocabulary

When you introduce new words, make pronunciation a part of your practice. It's not enough for students to recognize the written form of a new word and memorize its meaning; they need to be able to say it correctly and recognize it when it's said by others, especially if it has a common reduced form. Try these ideas:

- Have students repeat the new word several times when they first come across it. This is important at all proficiency levels—for beginners because students are still unfamiliar with sounds and stress patterns and need extra practice, and in more advanced classes because the words they're learning are likely to be longer, more complex, and trickier to pronounce. There might also be interference from similar words in their native language, especially academic or technical words.

- Encourage students to associate the word with its stress pattern—not just with its spelling. Ask them to listen and tell you how many syllables the word has and where the stress is. Have them mark syllables and stress in their notes, flash cards, or other learning materials.

- Help students notice the spelling of new words as it relates to sounds. What vowel and consonant sounds are represented by the letters? What spelling patterns are similar to those in other words? Are there any silent letters or unusual spellings? Are there any related words that have similar spellings but different stress patterns and sounds (*electric/electricity, nation/nationality*)?

- Make sure students hear the word in the context of whole sentences, not only by itself. Give them chances to get used to hearing reduced forms and linked pronunciations. Hearing words in their "natural habitat" will also help give students a deeper understanding of their meaning and use.

- Review the pronunciation of new words often when you come across them in reading, listening, or other activities. Don't assume that hearing a new word once is enough to give students a clear memory of how it sounds or that students will remember how to pronounce a word because they've already been tested on its meaning. On a chart or a corner of the whiteboard or blackboard, keep a list of words whose pronunciation the class has been practicing and review them often. The more often students hear and say the pronunciation, the more likely they'll be to remember and produce it accurately.

When Teaching Reading

When we think of practicing pronunciation during a reading lesson, the first method that comes to mind is undoubtedly reading aloud. It seems like a natural combination—students read a passage aloud, paying attention to how they pronounce words. Many teachers do **round robin reading** or **popcorn reading** in which the teacher calls on students, in seating order or at random, to take turns reading aloud from the textbook. Although this is a common classroom activity, it's often *not* effective for improving either reading skill or pronunciation (Wilson, 2010; Redpath, 2011). Reading aloud requires students to think about many things simultaneously—**decoding** written symbols, producing the pronunciation of words, and understanding the meaning of the text. This is a lot for learners to process all at once. In addition, if only one person is reading, we wonder what the rest of the class is doing. Too often they're daydreaming or looking ahead to see what they'll have to read when their turn comes.

If you want to use reading aloud for pronunciation practice, here are some suggestions to make it more successful:

- Be sure the students understand the vocabulary and meaning of the passage *before* they have to read it aloud. Reading a passage "cold," without preparation, is not very effective pronunciation practice.

- Make sure the difficulty level of the reading is well within the students' reach. To make practice meaningful, students should read familiar material that they don't have to struggle with.
- Keep the reading short—several sentences at most. For pronunciation practice, it's better to read a short passage several times than a long passage just once.

Here are other ways to practice pronunciation during a reading lesson:

- Read the text to the class (or play a recording, if one is available) before you ask students to read aloud. Give them a good model of what it's supposed to sound like.
- Think about **suprasegmentals** as well as individual sounds and words. How should thought groups be divided? What intonation and linking should be used?
- As they listen to a recording or your reading of a passage, have students mark up the text, indicating pauses, intonation, or linking. Give them careful instructions beforehand about what they should be listening for. It's difficult to try to hear everything at once. After they have listened, have students compare their markings with a partner. Knowing that they'll have to check their work with a classmate helps keep students more accountable. Finally, they can practice reading the passage to a partner.
- Have students read aloud to a partner instead of to the whole class. This is less public and much less stressful, and it gives more learners a chance to practice at once.
- Have students read to themselves using listening tubes. These let students hear their own voices while reducing the noise they can hear from the rest of the class. (See Chapter 7, "Teaching Consonants and Vowels" for information about listening tubes.)
- If the class is reading something that includes realistic conversation, such as a play or a story with lots of dialogue, use it as an opportunity for students to act out the play or reenact the conversation from the story. Emphasize not only the pronunciation of individual words, but also the way words are linked, where pauses naturally occur, and what kind of intonation fits the grammar, meaning, and emotion of the conversation.
- Take some time to talk about **phonics**—the systematic relationship between written letters and spoken sounds—when particular spelling patterns or problems come up. Especially in lower-level classes, this can help students make sense of the complex spelling system of English so they can predict the pronunciation of new words better. There's more information about phonics in Chapter 15, "Spelling, Sounds, and Phonics."

When Teaching Speaking

In Chapter 7, "Teaching Consonants and Vowels," we looked at some examples of speaking activities that we can use to practice pronunciation. We can use these same types of activities—information gaps, questions and answers, logic puzzles, role plays, and many more—to practice pronunciation during a speaking lesson. If you plan a practice activity so that it contains vocabulary with particular sounds, words that link together in a particular way, or grammatical patterns that match the intonation you want to practice, students will be practicing pronunciation of those things as they speak. Draw attention to these pronunciation points when you give instructions for the activity so students will notice them as they practice. It's important to emphasize suprasegmentals too, especially pausing in appropriate places, emphasizing key words, and using natural sounding intonation patterns.

During speaking activities, correcting students' pronunciation errors can be awkward and break up the flow of the activity. Instead, you could take notes during speaking practice of pronunciation mistakes made by several people and do some quick practice with these afterward.

Teaching Listening

Learners need to be able to recognize sounds and words when they hear them, especially in everyday language using lots of connected speech. When your class is doing listening practice with recorded materials, take some time to point out examples of **linking**, **deletion**, **assimilation**, and other sound processes, and have students do some practice with them. Here are some ways to do this:

- Before or after listening to a recorded passage, do some practice with new or difficult words in it. In addition to making sure students understand the meaning, have them practice saying the words, counting the syllables, and identifying the stressed syllables.
- In the same way, use some sentences taken from the listening to focus on thought groups, **prominence**, and **intonation**. Have students listen, mark these features on a transcript of the passage, and imitate the chosen sentences. Talk about why certain words are emphasized and why particular intonation patterns are used. What meaning or feeling is conveyed by the intonation?
- When listening to spoken or recorded passages, if students aren't sure what sounds or words they've heard, encourage them to use context to help decide what the words must have been. For example, if they're not sure if they've heard "right" or "light," which one makes sense in the context? Looking at meaning can help students decipher pronunciation, and this is a real-life skill that they'll need in understanding spoken language.
- Find a recorded dialogue and prepare a script with no punctuation—just spaces between thought groups. Play a recording of the dialogue and ask students to use intonation to identify questions and statements or finished and unfinished thoughts and add appropriate punctuation to the script: question marks, periods, and commas. (It's best to avoid less familiar punctuation like colons or semicolons.) To force students to focus on the intonation instead of just grammar, include some questions that have statement word order but rising intonation: *It's raining? You ate twelve hamburgers?*
- Dictations are useful in pronunciation lessons, as we saw in Chapter 7, "Teaching Consonants and Vowels." We can also use dictations during listening practice to make sure students understand sentences similar to those they've already heard and can **segment** a stream of sound into individual written words. We can use dictations to check students' comprehension of sounds, words, and reduced forms.

When Teaching Grammar

Keep the pronunciation of grammatical forms in mind as you teach—both their sounds and the connected intonation patterns—and give students practice in using new grammar with appropriate pronunciation.

- When we think of the connection between grammar and sound, the pronunciation of *-s* and *-ed* endings comes to mind immediately. When you teach these grammatical endings, be sure to emphasize the three sound forms of each and give students plenty of practice in using them in speaking. Don't let students confuse sound patterns with spelling patterns, since they follow separate rules.
- When teaching grammatical structures that have common reduced forms, like *going to* for future time (*gonna*), **modals** followed by *have* (*should have* > *shoulda*, *would have* > *woulda*, *could have* > *coulda*), or expressions with *to* (*want to* > *wanna*, *have to* > *hafta*), be sure students know and practice the sounds of the reduced forms. When giving examples, try not to pronounce them too slowly and precisely; this will only give students a false idea of what the forms will sound like in real life. (See Chapter 9, "Rhythm," for lists of common reduced forms.)

- In teaching the affirmative and negative pair *can* and *can't*, be sure to point out the usual differences in stress and vowel clarity. A similar difference in stress occurs with pairs like *are* and *aren't* and *were* and *weren't*, although the vowels in these don't change.
- When teaching the formation of questions (yes/no, WH-, or tag questions), be sure students know and use appropriate intonation patterns for each type. For commands and requests, illustrate the difference that intonation can make in the tone and feeling of these forms.
- Finally, include some listening practice with the sounds of new grammatical forms. It's not enough for students to learn to produce new grammar—they also need to recognize it when someone else uses it. Practice by letting students listen to sentences using the forms they're learning and identify whether they're present or past tense, affirmative or negative, and so forth.

Teaching Pronunciation in a Large Class

In an ideal world, all language classes would be small, and teachers would have plenty of time to give individual attention to each student's pronunciation. However, this is often not the case. How can we teach pronunciation in a large class of 30, 40, or more students?

- **Choral repetition**. When you have students repeat after a model, do it in different ways—sometimes with the whole class repeating together, sometimes only the left or right half of the class, only the boys, only the girls, only people whose birthdays are in a certain month, or whatever rule you can think of. This makes it a little easier to hear how well the smaller groups are doing, and the variety keeps students more alert.
- **Pair work**. This can range from very simple to more complex activities—reading sentences to a partner, practicing a dialogue together, or doing information gap or communicative activities. (See Chapter 7, "Teaching Consonants and Vowels," and Chapter 13, "Teaching the Musical Aspects of Pronunciation," for examples.) Students can also work in small groups, for example, with two people practicing a dialogue or role play as a third listens and checks on a certain aspect of their pronunciation.
- **Go low-tech**. Use simple tools such as listening tubes during student practice. This helps students hear their own voices while cutting down on the noise they hear from the many students around them. To lower the cost of using these in a big class, have students assemble their own listening tubes from heavy paper. (See Chapter 7, "Teaching Consonants and Vowels," for instructions.)
- **Go high-tech**. Have students record their pronunciation practice for you to listen to and evaluate. Try the following to prevent this from taking an impossible amount of your time:
  — Don't do the whole class at once. Have just some of the students record their practice for each class, eventually getting around to all the students.
  — Keep the recordings short—maybe 30 seconds each.
  — Give your comments efficiently by circling problem areas on a script of the practice passage and adding quick notes. Don't try to respond to every aspect of the recording—just a couple of points that you've told the students to concentrate on or the points that are causing the most problems for that student in being understood.
  — Use a website that collects all the students' recordings in one place where you can easily listen to them, such as Voxopop (http://www.voxopop.com; See Chapter 13, "Teaching the Musical Aspects of Pronunciation"). Just click on the recordings one after another to listen. I've found that this is much less complicated and less time consuming than having students email recordings.

Teaching in an ESL or EFL Context

The location of your teaching—in a country where English is a commonly spoken language or one where it's seldom heard—makes a big difference in your teaching. In ESL classes in countries such as the United States, Canada, Britain, or Australia, students can more easily see the usefulness of having understandable pronunciation. If they're old enough to need to do things on their own, they've probably had the experience of being misunderstood at work, at school, or while shopping. One international student in our ESL program told this story: "The first day I arrived at my host family's house, I asked my host father, 'How can I take a bath?' He answered, 'Where are you going?' He thought I said 'bus' instead of 'bath.'"

Learners who have lived in an English-speaking country for a while, or even for many years, often feel a stronger motivation for improving their pronunciation. They may have experienced problems at work or school because they can't be understood, and adults may even have been told that their pronunciation is preventing them from advancing in their jobs. On the other hand, many others in this situation feel that since they've been able to get by so far with the pronunciation they have, there's no need to change or improve.

Learners in an ESL setting usually have more chances to hear English spoken in daily life than learners in an EFL setting. Even those who mostly speak their native language at home and with friends can't avoid hearing a certain amount of English in the wider world. Assuming they pay attention to what they hear around them, this gives them additional input on what English sounds like.

Learners in an EFL environment have a variety of motivations for improving their pronunciation. Some know that they need to speak English for business, education, or other purposes, and they feel motivated to work toward intelligible pronunciation. Others, however, are learning English only because they are required to and not because they feel any need to master the language. In particular, students in middle school and high school are often very concerned about their grades and future entrance exams for the next level of their education. These tests often have an English component, but pronunciation is seldom a part of it. When students start to focus more strongly on these outward measures of success, they're often less concerned with their overall ability to use English, and their motivation to achieve good pronunciation is lost. When they think about pronunciation, they might ask themselves, "What's in it for me? Will this be on the standardized tests that I have to take?"

Other EFL students in this age group aren't motivated much at all in studying English, either for its own sake or as a tool for their future. Some may even reject the idea of trying to have "nativelike" pronunciation, feeling that it will make them stand out uncomfortably from their peers and seem "stuck up." If we can teach pronunciation in an interesting and engaging way, adapting our material to students' interests, we're more likely to keep these students involved, even if they're not interested in the subject matter for its own sake.

Providing a Pronunciation Model

Choosing the Variety of English to Use as a Model

Many varieties of English are spoken in the world. In addition to such standard varieties as American, British, Australian, Canadian, and New Zealand English, there are many regional or nonstandard varieties of each of these "national Englishes." There are also many well-established ways that nonnative speakers in particular countries speak English. We hope that our students will learn to understand many of these varieties when they hear them, but most teachers will use just one variety as a model in pronunciation teaching. Which kind of English will you use as a model for your students?

- If you're teaching in an English-speaking country, you'll almost certainly use the variety that is an accepted standard in that country. After all, it would seem silly to teach students

American English if they're studying in Australia or British English if they're studying in the United States.

- If you're teaching in a country where English is not widely spoken, these are some paths open to you in choosing a pronunciation model:
  - Use the variety that you can most reliably produce—the one you grew up speaking (if you're a native speaker) or the one you feel most comfortable speaking (if you're not a native speaker).
  - Use the variety that you've been told to use. In reality, many teachers don't have a choice about what variety of English to use as a model. That choice has been made by a school board, national Ministry of Education, or other authority. If you've been assigned particular textbooks, they may include recordings or pronunciation notes based on a particular national variety.
  - Think about the types of English your students will need to understand in the future and choose your model based on your predictions (Celce-Murcia et al., 2010).

Your model might not be a native-speaker variety at all. Some researchers recently have pointed out that since English is used as an international language in business, science, and many other fields, it's not necessary or even desirable to try to get students to sound like native speakers of a standard national variety of English. Walker (2010) suggests that we should concentrate on teaching the **lingua franca core**—those aspects of pronunciation that help the most in increasing intelligibility when nonnative speakers communicate with each other.

Whatever variety you choose, help your students get used to hearing and understanding other accents too, even if you use only one as a model for imitation. The world is a big place, and your students will benefit if they can understand speakers from many parts of it.

Provide a Natural Sounding Model

Whether the pronunciation examples that students hear come from your own voice or from recordings, it's important to give students plenty of opportunities to listen to natural sounding English, including normal connected speech. You're not helping your students if you only let them hear extremely clear, careful pronunciation. This may be all right as a first step in learning a particular point; after all, hearing something slowly helps listeners catch the sounds more accurately. However, it should soon be followed by more natural sounding speech.

I once observed an English class in a Japanese junior high school in which the teacher spoke very slowly, deliberately adding extra vowels after final consonants and within consonant clusters, and intentionally making other changes that Japanese learners typically make. I knew from talking to this teacher earlier that this was not his normal way of speaking; in conversation outside of class his pronunciation was smooth and without these added vowels. I asked him why he spoke that way in class. He told me, "My students can't understand 'real' English. Why shouldn't I speak very slowly and clearly and use the kind of pronunciation they expect? It helps them understand." The simple answer to his question is that this may make it easier for students to understand the teacher now, but it won't help them understand real English outside the classroom. We can't shield students from the real world of language unless we plan to keep them in our own classroom forever.

It's important to note that it's not only nonnative speakers who fall into the trap of speaking too slowly and carefully. Many native-speaker teachers also speak extra clearly (consciously or unconsciously) to try to help their students understand more easily. (I'll have to admit that I sometimes find myself doing this too.) While it's not helpful for the teacher to talk at full speed with a full range of reduced forms unless students are at a very advanced level, we also shouldn't speak with artificial care. All teachers should try to provide a natural, realistic pronunciation model for their students.

Using Technical Language in Explanations

How much technical language should you use in teaching pronunciation? Should you use terms like *fricative* or *aspiration* in your explanations? Is it necessary for students to remember the names of the parts of the articulatory system, manners of articulation, and so forth?

If the students are children, then certainly not; they won't understand technical language, even in their own language. The best advice for introducing sounds to children is "show, don't just tell." For junior high or high school age learners too, technical language is often hard to understand and may bore and discourage learners. If you can give students the knowledge and guidance they need through demonstrations, pictures, and simple explanations, then there's no need for much technical language.

If the students are adults, though, the situation is a little different. Some adults, especially those who enjoy analytical thinking or perhaps have a scientific or medical background, appreciate knowing the official names of things. Others find technical language confusing or burdensome—just one more obstacle that's preventing them from reaching their language learning goals. If you get to know your adult students' backgrounds and preferences, you'll have a better idea of how much technical language to use.

For students of any age, it's more important for them to *feel and understand* what's happening inside their mouths when they pronounce a sound than to remember technical terms. Knowledge about the articulatory system and categories of sounds is a tool to help students reach their pronunciation goals, not a goal in itself.

It's often helpful to introduce and practice some classroom English expressions that you and your students can use in talking about pronunciation:

- How do you pronounce _____?
- How many syllables does _____ have?
- Which syllable has the stress? Which syllable is stressed? Where is the stress?
- Does the intonation go up or down?

If you take the time to introduce and practice expressions like these, students will have an easier time talking about pronunciation during class.

Should You Use Phonemic Symbols in Teaching?

A related question is whether you should use a **phonemic alphabet** in teaching pronunciation. Again, it depends on your students. For some learners it's valuable, but for others it's confusing and intimidating. You'll need to think about your students—their age, expectations, and learning styles—before making this decision. Here are some things to think about.

Age

Young children who are just learning to read and write in their own language will just be confused if we ask them to learn not only the regular English alphabet, but also a set of phonemic symbols. For children, it's better to use other ways of reminding them of sounds, such as gestures, key words for each sound, colors, or pictures of animals or objects that contain the sounds.

Teenagers and adults, on the other hand, are mentally more mature and better able to handle a new system of abstract symbols. Some people have a more analytical mindset than others, and learning to use phonemic symbols will feel natural and comfortable for them. Others might feel threatened by the prospect of having to master a new and unfamiliar system. Get to know your students and base your decision on their needs and preferences.

Expectations

Even among adults, individuals react to a phonemic alphabet in different ways. Many find the symbols reassuring. They seem comfortingly academic and familiar, since many people have seen them before in dictionaries or textbooks. The student thinks, "Ah, good. This is what pronunciation lessons are supposed to look like!" On the other hand, others who have never seen a phonemic alphabet might just feel confused or frustrated.

Learning Styles

People learn new things in different ways—through seeing, through hearing, and through doing. (That is, they use **visual**, **auditory**, and **kinesthetic learning modalities**.) Written symbols are especially valuable for learners whose strength is visual learning. They need to see something to really understand it. People whose strength is auditory learning may not need this visual reinforcement as much. Learners who favor kinesthetic learning might respond better to gestures, hand signals, or other movements than to written symbols for representing sounds.

Requirements

In some teaching situations, you might be required or expected to use phonemic symbols. If so, of course you'll need to follow your school's expectations, but introduce the symbols gradually. Explain why the symbols are useful, and let students see and use them often enough so that they'll be comfortable with them.

Is the Phonemic Alphabet Outdated?

We might wonder if it's still necessary to use a phonemic alphabet in these days of electronic dictionaries, cell phones, tablets, and other devices that can pronounce words for us. Has the phonemic alphabet become obsolete?

I think that there is still great value in using written symbols to represent sounds. Recorded words are helpful, but they slip by quickly and their sounds can be hard to catch, especially if the sound quality from tiny speakers is not clear, if there's background noise, or if the user of the device must keep the volume turned low to avoid disturbing others.

Written symbols are more permanent than sounds. We can take our time to look at them, think about them, and try to say them to ourselves. They give us a lasting record of what we've learned. Phonemic symbols also help learners to pin down the sounds and connect them to a particular phoneme that they've learned. If we only hear a new word, we might think, "What were those sounds? Did I hear this sound or that sound?" Phonemic symbols give us a way to check our hearing.

So should you use phonemic symbols or not? You'll have to make that decision based on your students' needs and abilities. If you think they'll be helpful, give them a try. If you find that they do more harm than good, don't use them.

If you do decide to include a phonemic alphabet in your teaching, don't try to introduce all the symbols at once or make students memorize them all in a day. Introduce unfamiliar symbols little by little as students learn and practice the sounds they represent. Emphasize symbols that represent sounds that don't have a clear, unambiguous spelling in English, like /θ/, /ð/, /ʃ/, or /ŋ/. Vowel symbols are especially useful since the spelling of vowel sounds in English is complex and inconsistent. It's useful to have a consistent way to identify vowel sounds without depending on spelling.

Finally

In planning your pronunciation teaching, you'll need to think about your own students, their specific goals, abilities, and preferences, and other aspects of your teaching situation. All of these will guide you in deciding what methods and activities to use in teaching pronunciation.

CHAPTER 15

Spelling, Sounds, and Phonics

The English spelling system does not have a good reputation. In fact, most learners probably think it's a hopeless mess. Let's look at the facts: The same sound can often be spelled in more than one way in different words: /k/ can be spelled with *c* in *cat,* with *k* in *kitten,* with *cc* in *occur,* with *ck* in *rock,* and with *ch* in *chorus.* On the other hand, some letters can represent more than one pronunciation in different words, like *ough* in *though, through, thought, cough,* and *enough.*

Many words have letters that aren't pronounced at all, like the *k* in *know,* the *e* in *late,* or the *p* in *psychology.* And a few written words can be pronounced in more than one way, even though they're spelled with the same letters, like *read*: /riyd/ when it's present tense and /rɛd/ when it's past, or *bow*: /baw/ if it's a type of greeting or /bow/ if we're talking about archery or hair ornaments. How confusing!

English has an **alphabetic writing system**, which means that, ideally, each letter should represent exactly one phoneme. But this is clearly not the case in English. Some of the kinds of inconsistencies we find in English spelling are listed in Table 15.1. (Not all languages use an alphabetic writing system, though. The sidebar "Types of Writing Systems" lists the most common kinds of writing systems found in the world's languages.)

English Spelling Is Not Quite as Confusing as It Seems

There actually is a regular correspondence between the spelling and the sounds of most English words, although this relationship is sometimes complicated and not always obvious. Kelly (2000) states that

> Surveys of the system have shown that over 80% of English words are spelled according to regular patterns, and that there are fewer than 500 words (out of an estimated total of over half a million words) whose spelling can be considered completely irregular. The fact that some of these words also happen to be amongst the most common ones (e.g., *are, said, come, how, what, could*) gives a distorted impression of irregularity in the system. (p. 123)

The spelling of many words depends on the word parts that they are made up of—their roots, prefixes, and suffixes—as well as on their pronunciation. A **word root** may have the same spelling in two words, even though its pronunciation is different. For example, the words *music* and

Table 15.1. Some English spelling challenges (sound 15.1).

Spelling Situation	Examples	
	Spelling(s)	Sound(s)
One sound, more than one spelling	*f* (*fish*) *ff* (*cuff*) *ph* (*phone*) *gh* (*cough*)	/f/
One spelling, more than one sound	*c*	/k/ *(car)* /s/ *(city)* /ʧ/ *(cello)*
Two letters together represent one sound (a digraph)	*sh* as in *she* *th* as in *think* or *this* *ee* as in *see*	/ʃ/ /θ/ or /ð/ usually /iy/
One letter represents a two-sound combination	*x*	/ks/
A letter represents no sound (a "silent letter")	*k* (*know*) *gh* (*night*) *e* (*nose*)	no sound

musician have the same root, *music,* even though the letter *c* represents a different sound in each of them: /k/ in *music* and /ʃ/ in *musician.* When we spell the root the same way in both words, it's easier for readers to recognize that these words are related.

There are also many consistent, but somewhat complicated, patterns in how vowels and consonants are represented in spelling. The study of these regular spelling patterns is called **phonics**.

What Is Phonics?

Phonics is the study of the relationship between written letters and spoken sounds. The word also refers to a way of teaching people to read that emphasizes the systematic relationship between written letters and spoken sounds.

Phonics is different from pronunciation or phonology. Pronunciation is about the sounds of a language, how we say them, and how they fit together into spoken words and sentences. Phonology is the study of those spoken sounds. On the other hand, phonics is about the relationship between writing and sound.

Some Important Concepts in Phonics

Graphemes

A written symbol or combination of symbols that represents a sound is called a **grapheme**. For example, in English, the letters *f, ff,* and *ph* are all graphemes that can represent the sound /f/ in words like *fix, off,* and *phone.* (This does not mean that these letters *always* represent /f/. For example, in the word *of,* the grapheme *f* represents /v/.)

A grapheme is not the same as a **phoneme**. Graphemes are written symbols, but phonemes are sounds. You can't hear graphemes, and you can't see phonemes—only the symbols that represent them.

Most graphemes can have more than one shape or written form. We can see capital letters and small letters, handwritten letters in printed and cursive versions, letters printed in books or typed on a computer in hundreds of different fonts, old-fashioned versions from different periods in history, and decorative letters that look different just for fun. For example, the grapheme "g" can have any of the forms in Figure 15.1.

Digraphs

A **digraph** is a type of grapheme that is made up of two letters that together represent one sound, either a consonant or a vowel. We can think of it as a two-part grapheme. For example, in English, *sh* is a digraph that represents the sound /ʃ/ in words like *ship* and *fish*, and *ee* is a digraph that can represent the sound /iy/ in words like *see* and *need*. There are also some **trigraphs**, or combinations of three letters that together spell one sound, such as *tch*, which represents /tʃ/ in words like *match*, or *igh*, which represents /ay/ in words like *high*.

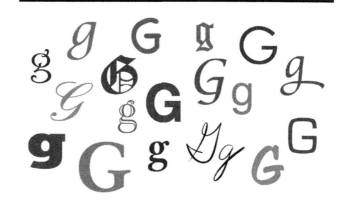

Figure 15.1. The letter *g*.

Consonant Clusters or Consonant Blends

In Chapter 4, "The Consonants of American English," I talked about **consonant clusters** or **consonant blends** as sequences of two or more consonant *sounds*. These terms are also used to talk about combinations of *letters* that represent a sequence of sounds. For example, the letters *str* represent the consonant cluster /str/, and the letters *thr* represent the consonant cluster /θr/. (Notice that consonant clusters or blends are different from digraphs. Digraphs are two letters that together represent a single sound. Consonant clusters or blends are two or more letters that represent two or more sounds.)

English has many consonant clusters, as you saw in Chapter 4. Some have two consonants, such as those at the beginning of these words: *play, true, twin, dry, quick, green, slow, swim, spot, stone, skin,* and *snow*. Some have three consonants, as in *splice, spring, string,* and *scrap* (**sound 15.2**).

Consonant clusters can come at the beginnings of words, as in the examples above. They can also come in the middle of words (*farmer, basket, translate, include, system*) or at the ends of words (*help, ant, lamp, sink, film, earth, arm, ask, soft, against, ends*).

The letter *x* usually represents the consonant cluster /ks/ all by itself, as in *box, index,* or *taxi*. When it comes between vowels, *x* sometimes represents the voiced cluster /gz/, as in *exist* or *exhaust*. The letter *x* seldom comes at the beginning of a word. When it does, it usually represents the sound /z/, as in *xylophone* or *Xerox*.

Some letters are not pronounced at all in particular words. We sometimes call these **silent letters**. For example, the words *talk, listen, climb, knife, night, sign, write,* and *psychology* all contain silent consonant letters. Many of these silent letters represent sounds that used to be pronounced hundreds of years ago. Over time, the pronunciation of English changed and people stopped pronouncing those sounds, but they kept writing the letters. Now these letters are like "ghosts" of dead sounds. We can still see the letters, but the sounds are not really there anymore.

Vowel letters can also be silent. The most common silent vowel letter is *e*, which is often found at the ends of words with tense vowels, like *late, kite, vote, rule,* and *extreme*.

Onset and Rime

Written words (especially one-syllable words) can be thought of as having two parts: The **onset**, or the beginning consonant letter or letters, and the **rime**, or the vowel and any other letters that come after it. (If a word starts with a vowel, like *at, inch,* or *own*, it has no onset—just a rime.) Table 15.2 shows examples of some common words divided in this way. Since we're talking about phonics, not pronunciation, the parts are based on the spelling of the words, not their sounds.

Table 15.2. Examples of onset and rime (sound 15.3).

Word	Onset	Rime	Word	Onset	Rime
cat	c–	–at	may	m–	–ay
bat	b–	–at	tray	tr–	–ay
and	*none*	–and	train	tr–	–ain
sand	s–	–and	trains	tr–	–ains
strand	str–	–and	months	m–	–onths

Word Families

Word families are groups of words that have the same rime with the same pronunciation and therefore are often taught together when children are learning to read. For example, *dog, frog, fog,* and *log* are in the same word family. (In phonics, word families are based on spelling, not on sound alone. So *ate, late, plate,* and *crate* are in the same word family, but *great* is not, even though it sounds the same.)

Homonyms

Homonyms or **homophones** are words that sound alike but are spelled differently, such as *meet* and *meat* or *write, right,* and *rite.* English has many homonyms. Often these are words that were once pronounced differently, and so they were spelled differently. However, over the years their pronunciation has changed so that they now sound alike, but they still have their older, separate spellings. Homonyms can be a particular challenge in learning to read and write, for both native speakers of English and second language learners.

Letter-Sound Relationships: Consonants

Consonant spellings are usually easier to learn than vowel spellings because they represent sounds more consistently. Many consonant letters normally represent just one sound. Table 15.3 lists some very reliable letter-sound correspondences, though even these can have exceptions.

Other consonant letters can represent more than one sound in different words. In some cases there are generalizations that can predict how the letter will be pronounced (see Table 15.4). (Of course, all of these rules have exceptions!)

Consonant Digraphs

We saw earlier that some two-letter combinations, or digraphs, can represent a single sound. In learning to spell in English, students need to learn these digraphs and recognize that they represent sounds that are different from the sounds of the individual letters. Table 15.5 contains common consonant digraphs and the sounds they usually represent.

Table 15.3. Reliable letter-sound correspondences (sound 15.4).

Letter	*b*	*d*	*f*	*h*	*j*	*k*	*l*	*m*	*n*	*p*	*r*	*t*	*v*	*w*	*z*
Sound	b	d	f	h	dʒ	k	l	m	n	p	r	t	v	w	z

Table 15.4. Variable letter-sound correspondences (sound 15.5).

Letter		Possible Pronunciations
c	/k/	Before the letters *a, o, u,* or a consonant: *cat, color, cut, cry, clean*
	/s/	Before the letters *e, i,* or *y: cent, city, cinema, cycle*
	/ʃ/	Before some suffixes beginning with *i★: delicious, special, optician*
g	/g/	Before the letters *a, o, u,* or a consonant: *gas, got, gum, green, glass*
	/dʒ/	Before *e, i,* or *y: gentle, giant, gym, refrigerator* (Some exceptions: *get, give, girl, gigabyte*); also before suffixes beginning with *i: religious, tragic*
	/ʒ/	In some borrowed words: *genre, prestige, mirage*
s	/s/	The most common pronunciation: *sun, since, sleep, kiss*
	/z/	(Sometimes) between two vowels: *present, residence, laser, reason*
	/ʃ/	(Sometimes) before some suffixes beginning with *i★: mansion, tension*
	/ʒ/	(Sometimes) between two vowels: *measure, vision*
		Also check the rules for *-s* endings in Chapter 6, "Pronunciation of Some Word Endings."
t	/t/	The most common pronunciation: *top, tree, cat*
	/ʃ/	Before some suffixes beginning with *i★: nation, ambitious, spatial*
	/tʃ/	After a consonant and before some suffixes beginning with *i★* and also before the suffixes *-ure* or *-uous: attention, combustion, picture, furniture, mature, tempestuous*
x	/ks/	The most common pronunciation: *mix, taxi, fixture*
	/gz/	Sometimes between vowels: *exam, exact, exaggerate*
	/z/	At the beginning of words: *xylophone, xenophobia*
y	/y/	When it's used as a consonant at the beginning of words or syllables: *yes, young, year, beyond, lawyer* Vowel pronunciations of *y* are described in the next section.

★Some suffixes beginning with *i:* The suffixes in this group include *-ion, -ious, -eous, -ial, -ian, -ient,* and *-ience.* They all begin with *i* or *e,* followed by another vowel, and were originally pronounced with a /y/ sound at the beginning.

Table 15.5. Consonant digraphs in English (sound 15.6).

Digraph	Usual sound	Examples
sh	/ʃ/	ship, rush
ch	Usually /tʃ/ Sometimes /ʃ/ Sometimes /k/	chip, chalk, much machine, chagrin, chalet chorus, character
th	/θ/ /ð/	thick, bath, nothing then, smooth, mother
ph	/f/	phone, photograph
wh	/w/ (or /hw/)	when, whether
ck	/k/	neck, sock, tackle
ng	/ŋ/	long, something, singer
gh	Sometimes /f/ Sometimes /g/ Often silent	cough, laugh ghost, ghetto through, night, eight
qu	Usually /kw/ Sometimes /k/	quick, request technique, quiche
Double letters: ss, *tt, gg, mm, ll,* etc.	Double letters usually have the same sound as a single letter. (The vowel before a double consonant is usually "short.")	mess, butter, biggest, swimming, hill

Letter-Sound Relationships: Vowels

In English, the spelling of vowels is much more complicated than that of consonants. American English has 14 to 15 vowel *sounds* (including diphthongs and /ɚ/). However, there are only five vowel *letters* (or six, if we include *y*)—not nearly enough to give each sound its own letter. Because of this, all the vowel letters are used to represent more than one vowel sound, either alone or in combinations. For example, the letter *a* can represent at least five different phonemes (**sound 15.7**):

- /æ/ as in *cat,*
- /ey/ as in *cape,*
- /ɑ/ as in *car,*
- /ɛ/ as in *care,* and
- /ə/ as in *around.*

In phonics instruction, teachers often talk about **long vowels** and **short vowels**. Each vowel letter is said to have a "long sound" and a "short sound." However, it's important to remember that the "short" vowels are *not* really shorter in duration than the "long" vowels. These are just names for two groups of sounds, not physical descriptions of their duration.

Small marks or **diacritics** are sometimes written over the vowel letters to distinguish the long and short sounds: A straight line indicates a long vowel (ā, ē, ī, ō, ū), and short vowels are marked by a curved line (ă, ĕ, ĭ, ŏ, ŭ) or no diacritic at all (a, e, i, o, u).

In phonics, the "long sounds" for each vowel letter are (**sound 15.8**)

- ā = /ey/ as in *came,*
- ē = /iy/ as in *need,*
- ī = /ay/ as in *bite,*
- ō = /ow/ as in *soap,* and
- ū = /uw/ as in *cool* or /yuw/ as in *use.*

Sometimes phonics teachers say that the long vowel sounds "say the vowel's name." The "short sounds" for each vowel letter are (**sound 15.9**)

- ă = /æ/ as in *cap,*
- ĕ = /ɛ/ as in *bed,*
- ĭ = /ɪ/ as in *big,*
- ŏ = /ɑ/ as in *top,* and
- ŭ = /ʌ/ as in *cup.*

The short and long vowel lists together contain only 10 sounds, while English has 14 or 15 vowel sounds. This shows one problem with the phonics categories of short vowels and long vowels. They don't include these sounds at all (**sound 15.10**):

- /ʊ/ as in *book,*
- /ɔ/ as in *caught,*
- /aw/ as in *cow,* and
- /oy/ as in *boy.*

Some generalizations about how vowel sounds are represented in English spelling are described below. (Of course, all have exceptions. A few of the common ones are noted, but there are others.)

- In one-syllable words, if there's only **one vowel letter**, it usually represents a short vowel sound: *man, bed, big, dog, must.*
    Exceptions include *most, both, do* (one vowel letter = long sound).

- When there are **two vowel letters** (a vowel digraph), the vowel is usually the long sound of the first vowel in the sequence ("The first vowel says its name."): *main, bead, seed, lie, coat, due.*

   Exceptions include *said, head, bread, broad* (two vowel letters = short sound).

- **Silent *e*.** When a word has one vowel letter in the middle and ends in the letter *e*, the word usually has a long vowel sound, and the final *e* is not pronounced: *came, eve, mine, home, cute.*

   The exceptions include some very common words: *have, here, there, were, where, give, come, done, one, some, none, move, gone, love, lose.*

- **The vowel digraph *oo*** regularly represents two different sounds: /uw/ and /ʊ/. In most words, we can't predict which sound *oo* will represent.
   — **Sometimes *oo* represents /uw/**: *food, soon, pool, boom, moon, root, tooth, proof.*
   — **Sometimes *oo* represents /ʊ/**: *foot, book, good, look, cook, stood, wood, hook.*
   — **At the end of a word**, *oo* represents only /uw/, and not /ʊ/: *zoo, too, bamboo.*

   Unfortunately, there are exceptions here too, when *oo* doesn't spell either /uw/ or /ʊ/: *door, floor, blood, flood.*

- **One vowel letter before a double consonant letter** usually represents a short vowel. Compare the words in Table 15.6. They all have one vowel, followed by one or two consonants. (Not all of them are exact minimal pairs.)

Table 15.6. Vowels followed by one or two consonants (sound 15.11).

Two consonants		One consonant	
tinny	/ˈtɪniy/	tiny	/ˈtayniy/
matted	/ˈmætəd/	mated	/ˈmeytəd/
bitter	/ˈbɪtɚ/	biter	/ˈbaytɚ/
lopping	/ˈlɑpɪŋ/	loping	/ˈlowpɪŋ/
written	/ˈrɪtən/	writing	/ˈraytɪŋ/

As you remember, American English has three **diphthong** phonemes, or combinations of two vowel sounds that work together as one vowel. (Be sure not to confuse diphthongs with digraphs. Diphthongs are two vowel sounds that together function as one vowel sound: /ay/, /oy/, and /aw/. Digraphs are two written symbols that together represent one sound, like *ie* in *pie*.) Table 15.7 lists the most common spelling patterns for diphthongs in English (**sound 15.12**).

- **Vowels followed by *r*.** If there's a letter *r* after a vowel letter, the sound of the vowel sometimes changes. These vowels are called *r*-colored vowels. Here are some common patterns in American English (**sound 15.13**):

   — In a stressed syllable, the letters *ar* often represent /ɑr/: *car, hard, harbor, apart.*
   — In a stressed syllable, the letters *or* often represent /ɔr/: *or, fork, corner, report, store.*
   — Words spelled with *er, ir,* or *ur* in a stressed syllable often have the sound /ɚ/ (/ər/): *serve, herd, bird, shirt, turn, nurse.*
   — In unstressed syllables, *ar, er, ir, or,* and *ur* often represent /ɚ/: *collar, teacher, doctor, inspiration, refrigerator, natural.*

- **Vowels followed by *l*.** The letter *l* after a vowel also influences the sound that the vowel represents. We call these *l*-colored vowels (**sound 15.14**).

   — In stressed syllables, the spellings *al* and *all* are often pronounced /ɔl/ (or /ɑl/, if you're from the western United States): *salt, fall, ball, tall, install.* This happens in words like *talk* and *walk* too, even though the *l* is silent.

Table 15.7. Common spellings representing diphthongs.

Sound	Not at the end of a word	At the end of a word
/ay/	*i* + (consonant) + *e*: bite, mine, quite, rise, arrive *igh*: right, sight, frighten	*y*: by, try, my, shy, reply *ie*: lie, tie, die *igh*: high, sigh
/aw/	*ow*: owl, town, brown *ou*: out, loud, found, south	*ow*: cow, now, eyebrow
/oy/	*oi*: oil, coin, noise, moist	*oy*: boy, joy, employ, annoy

— In unstressed syllables, *al, el, le, il,* and *ol* often represent /əl/ or a syllabic /l/: *postal, label, table, ventilate, capitol.*

- **The letter *y*** sometimes represents a consonant sound and sometimes a vowel sound. As a vowel, it can stand for these sounds (**sound 15.15**):
  — Between consonants, as a main vowel, it usually stands for /ɪ/: *gym, myth.*
  — In one-syllable words, as a main vowel with no consonant after it, it stands for /ay/: *cry, try, by.*
  — In stressed final syllables (*apply, deny*) and in words ending in -fy (*satisfy, beautify*) it represents /ay/.
  — In unstressed final syllables, it stands for /iy/: *city, happy, busy, regularly, complimentary.*
  — We also see *y* in vowel combinations: *boy, bay, buy, they.*

- **"I" before "E"**. This spelling rule is well-known to most English speakers: "I" before "E" except after "C," and when the sound is "A" as in "neighbor" and "weigh " (**sound 15.16**):
  — *i* is usually before *e*: *piece, friend, believe, tie.*
  — But not if it follows *c*: *ceiling, receive, perceive.*
  — And not when the sound is /ey/: *neighbor, weigh, eight.*
  — However, there are exceptions: *their, weird, either, neither, seize, foreign, beige, species,* and others.

- **Vowel digraphs**. Table 15.8 shows some common two-letter vowel combinations and the sounds they most commonly represent. Of course, there are many exceptions that are not shown in the chart.

Table 15.8. Vowel digraphs (sound 15.17).

Digraph	Most common sounds (There are exceptions!)	Examples
ea, ee	/iy/	seat, sea, see
ai, ay	/ey/	raise, aid, say
oa, ow, oe	/ow/	boat, low, toe
ue, ew, ui	/uw/, /yuw/	clue, few, juice
oy, oi	/oy/	boy, coin
ow, ou	/aw/	cow, out

Learning to Read in English

English has an **alphabetic writing system**. That is, each letter in the alphabet was originally intended to represent one sound. (Of course, we know that this correspondence is not at all perfect today.) To learn to read and write using an alphabetic system, learners first need to understand the **alphabetic principle**: Written words are composed of letters, and the letters represent the sounds of spoken words.

Students who have already learned to read and write in their own language generally have little trouble with this concept, although it may take some adjustment if their native language is written with a **syllabic** or **logographic writing system**. (See sidebar "Types of Writing Systems" for descriptions and examples of the different types of writing systems.) For very young learners who do not know how to read (both native speakers and nonnative speakers of English), this concept does not always come naturally, and it may take them some time to get used to the idea.

As they learn to read and write in English, students also need to develop a related concept called **phonemic awareness**, or the understanding that words are made up of individual sounds that can be separated, counted, and rearranged.

Skills That Readers Need

As we've seen, the English spelling system has some fairly reliable patterns for representing sounds, but these patterns do not always work consistently. To get used to reading both predictable and unpredictable words, learners need to develop two kinds of skills:

- Readers need **decoding skills** for reading words that follow expected patterns. They learn to "sound out" predictable words or put together individual sounds to figure out the whole word.
- Readers also need **knowledge of sight words**—words whose spellings don't follow predictable patterns. They need to memorize the spelling of words like *eye, give, school, love,* and many more that aren't spelled in the expected way.

> **Types of Writing Systems**
>
> In the earliest writing systems, people simply drew pictures of the things they wanted to talk about. Over the years, the pictures were simplified and became standardized symbols for whole words or word parts as part of a **logographic** or **ideographic writing system**. The pictures below show how the Chinese characters for "mountain" and "river" developed from pictures to logographs.
>
> In **syllabic writing systems**, each symbol stands for a whole syllable—either a vowel alone or a vowel plus one or more consonants. You can't separate the symbols into parts representing individual sounds. The set of symbols in this type of writing system is called a **syllabary**. The symbols below are from the Japanese *hiragana* syllabary.
>
> か き く け こ
> ka ki ku ke ko
>
> In **alphabetic writing systems**, ideally, each symbol represents one phoneme. Here are some letters from the Russian alphabet:
>
>
>
> а б в г д ж ф л с
> /a/ /b/ /v/ /g/ /d/ /ʒ/ /f/ /l/ /s/

In learning to read longer words, dividing them up into smaller chunks is a useful strategy that can make the words easier to read. The chunks might be syllables:

strategy → stra•te•gy
refrigerator → re•fri•ge•ra•tor

The chunks might also be **morphemes**—words or parts of words that have their own unit of meaning. For example, *baseball* contains two morphemes: *base* and *ball. Dogs* also has two morphemes: *dog* and the plural ending -s. On the other hand, *alligator* has only one morpheme, even though it's a longer word. It can't be broken up into smaller, meaningful units. Recognizing familiar morphemes in a longer word can be helpful in reading the word.

Some sequences of letters occur again and again in English words with consistent, but odd pronunciation. For example, many words end in -*tion*. We can't predict the sound of this ending by combining the sounds of each letter. (If we could, we might expect it to be pronounced /tiyon/.) But once learners realize that these letters represent /ʃən/, it's easier for them to pronounce the ending again when they see it in a new word. Becoming aware of these common "chunks" of letters is an important step in learning to read new words.

Teaching Phonics

It's useful to teach and practice spelling patterns that students will see in many words. However, if we try to teach too much detail in phonics (or any other subject, for that matter), we risk over-whelming students with too much information, and they'll have a hard time remembering any of it. We can't possibly teach every possible spelling pattern. It's best to choose and teach the patterns that are found in many common words. These will be the most useful for students.

Also, we can't teach phonics to all students in the same way. For example, teaching phonics to middle school English as a foreign language (EFL) learners who can already read well in their first language but are just beginning to learn English is very different from teaching it to elementary school native speakers who are just learning to read, even though they speak English fluently. Many phonics materials in textbooks, workbooks, or on the Internet are aimed at younger, native-speaker learners. If you use materials from these sources, think about whether they fit your students' needs and how you might want to adapt them to fit your own situation better. If you teach older students, you may need to make the topics and illustrations less childish. With any students, try to limit the vocabulary to words your students are familiar with. These may be very different from the words a native English-speaking child is familiar with.

Challenges in Learning to Read in English

In addition to the complexity of letter-sound relationships in English, students who already know how to read in their native language face other challenges. If beginning students speak a language that is written with the Latin alphabet, they often confuse the sounds represented by letters in their own language with the sounds represented by the same letters in English. For example, in English, the letter *w* usually represents the sound /w/ and the letter *v* represents the sound /v/. However, in German, *w* represents /v/ and *v* represents /f/. As another example, the letter *h* most often represents /h/ in English (when it's not in combinations like *ch, sh,* or *th*), but in French and Spanish it is not pronounced at all. And of course, the sounds represented by vowel letters and vowel letter combinations vary greatly between languages.

Students whose native language is written with an alphabet that has letter shapes somewhat similar to those of English, like Russian and Greek, can also be confused by similar-looking letters. For example, the letter *p* in English represents /p/, but the similar-looking letter *p* in Russian represents /r/. (The sound /p/ is represented by the letter π in Russian.)

If the student's native language uses a completely different writing system than English, learning to read in English is even more of a challenge—a much different experience than learning to reinterpret familiar symbols. The unfamiliar English letters may at first seem like random, meaningless squiggles, and the many shapes that each letter can take (like the examples of different shapes of the letter *g* earlier in this chapter) can add to the confusion. If the Latin alphabet is the only one you (the teacher) are familiar with, try looking at something written in Chinese, Hindi, Arabic, or any language with a completely different writing system. It may be hard to tell one symbol from another or even to know where one symbol ends and the next one begins. That's how it feels for students who are used to one of these languages to begin to learn to read and write in English. It's not easy.

As an added complication, if students have already learned the Latin alphabet as an alternative way of representing words in their own language (like *Romaji* in Japanese), they've already gotten used to one way of interpreting the letters. Now, when they learn to use the same letters to write in English, they have to master another system of interpretation that is often quite different. For example, the letters *take* are pronounced /teyk/ if they're an English word, but /tɑke/, with two syllables, if they represent the Japanese word meaning "bamboo." The situation becomes even more complicated if the students are also learning phonemic symbols to represent pronunciation!

Another problem comes from spelling pronunciations. These are cases when someone mistakenly pronounces a word as it's spelled, when it actually has an irregular and unexpected pronunciation. This happens most often with new and unfamiliar words or with words that a learner has seen in writing but isn't used to hearing in spoken language. For example, someone might see the word *choir* and pronounce it /tʃoyr/ instead of the correct pronunciation, /kwayr/. Or they might assume that *recipe* is pronounced /rəˈsayp/, similar to *recite,* when it's actually pronounced /ˈrɛsəpiy/.

At first glance, this may seem like a relatively limited problem, but some researchers claim that these spelling pronunciations of particular words are a more serious barrier to intelligibility than more widespread mistakes in pronouncing individual phonemes. For example, if a student pronounces *foreign* as /fɔreyn/ or *lettuce* as /lɛtyuws/, it may be harder to understand than if the speaker had pronounced the /f/ or /l/ sounds inaccurately (Szpyra-Kozłowska, 2015).

Spelling pronunciations sometimes affect native speakers too. For example, until recently almost everyone pronounced the word *often* as /ˈɑfən/, with no /t/ in the middle, following the same pattern as *soften, fasten,* and *listen* (**sound 15.18**). However, in the last few decades, many people have started to pronounce this word /ˈɑftən/, including a /t/ sound for the letter *t*. At first, most teachers, dictionary writers, and scholars rejected the pronunciation with /t/ as incorrect, but more people began to say it that way anyway. (Why? No one really knows.) Now both pronunciations—/ˈɑfən/ and /ˈɑftən/—are generally accepted. (I still say /ˈɑfən/.)

Over the years, many words have come into English from other languages. These are called **borrowed words**. Some of these have kept a pronunciation that's somewhat similar to the way they were said in the original language. The sounds might make sense according to the spelling rules of the original language, but in English they're unpredictable. The spellings make it harder to read and write those words. Here are some examples with their current English pronunciations (**sound 15.19**):

rendezvous	/ˈrɑndəvuw/	(from French)
genre	/ˈʒɑnrə/	(from French)
hors d'oeuvre	/ɔrˈdɚv/	(from French)
psyche	/ˈsaykiy/	(from Greek)
rhythm	/ˈrɪðəm/	(from Greek)
spaghetti	/spəˈgɛtiy/	(from Italian)
cello	/ˈtʃɛlow/	(from Italian)
pizza	/ˈpiytsə/	(from Italian)

We can't deny that the English spelling system is complicated and sometimes inconsistent. Learners of English, just like children whose native language is English, will always have to memorize the spellings of many sight words with irregular spellings. Still, if we look at some of the principles behind the spelling system, it becomes a little less intimidating.

Final Thoughts: Continuing to Develop as a Pronunciation Teacher

You have a great deal of knowledge about pronunciation—the sounds of English, the musical aspects of its pronunciation, and an array of tools and activities you can use to teach it. How can you continue to develop your skill and effectiveness in teaching pronunciation? Here are some suggestions:

- **Keep increasing your knowledge about pronunciation, and don't rely completely on your intuition about how English works.** Back up your instincts with solid knowledge about phonology and pronunciation. Read, talk to other teachers, attend workshops, and check reputable websites for new teaching ideas. No matter how long you've been teaching, you can't expect to have all the answers, but you owe it to your students to keep learning as much as you can. The longer you teach pronunciation, the more you'll notice and learn about it, and the more effective you can be as a teacher.

- **Learn from your students.** Pay attention to their pronunciation difficulties and misunderstandings to build your ability to predict what points will cause them problems. Put yourself in their shoes to try to see English pronunciation from their point of view.

- **Don't forget what it's like to be a beginner.** Think back on your own experience in learning a new language, whether that language was English or another, and remember that pronunciation is often harder than it seems. If English is the only language you know, learn a new language, preferably one that's very different from English. If English is your second language, draw on your own experience as a successful learner of English to set a good example as an enthusiastic, continuing language learner.

- **Remember that you are not alone.** Thousands and thousands of other teachers face the same questions and problems you do. Share your knowledge and experience with others and learn from them in return, and everyone will benefit. Teaching pronunciation isn't always easy, but you can do it.

Resources

Further Reading

If you want to read more about pronunciation teaching, try some of the books in this section. The order of books in this list is roughly from more general to more specific in topic and, within each type, in order of my personal preference.

Teaching Pronunciation: *A Course Book and Reference Guide* (2nd ed.), Marianne Celce-Murcia, Donna M. Brinton, and Janet M. Goodwin, with Barry Griner. Cambridge University Press, 2010. ISBN #978-0521729765. This book is very detailed and has many, many good ideas for teaching activities. There are thorough explanations of the pronunciation of individual sounds and of suprasegmental features. It makes a wonderful resource and includes two CDs of examples and exercises. Based on American English pronunciation.

Tips for Teaching Pronunciation: *A Practical Approach,* Linda Lane, Pearson Longman, 2010. ISBN #978-0-13-813629-1. Simple, clear explanations about the main points of many facets of pronunciation. It includes a CD of examples and has a chapter on typical pronunciation problems of particular language groups. Based on American English pronunciation.

Teaching American English Pronunciation, Peter Avery and Susan Ehrlich, Oxford University Press, 1992. ISBN #0-19-432815-5. This book is compact and explains concepts well, but has fewer example teaching activities than some others. It has a chapter on typical pronunciation problems of particular language groups. Based on American English pronunciation.

How to Teach Pronunciation, Gerald Kelly, Pearson Longman, 2000. ISBN #0-582429-75-7. A short, simple book, with only a few ideas for teaching activities. Includes a CD with examples from the book. Based on British English pronunciation.

Pronunciation, Clement Laroy, Oxford University Press, 1995. ISBN #0-194370-87-9. Lots of ideas about using psychology, drama, and similar techniques in teaching pronunciation. The techniques apply equally to American or British pronunciation.

Teaching Pronunciation, John Murphy, TESOL, 2013. A short, easy-to-read book, concentrating mainly on thought groups and prominence. It contains some good ideas for teaching those topics.

The Book of Pronunciation, Jonathan Marks and Tim Bowen, Delta Publishing Company, 2012. Includes many examples of activities for raising students' awareness of aspects of pronunciation, with a very heavy reliance on the use of phonemic transcription. Based on British English pronunciation.

English Phonology and Pronunciation Teaching, Pamela Rogerson-Revell, Continuum International Publishing Group, 2011. ISBN #978-0-8264-2403-7. The main emphasis is on teaching pronunciation for the purposes of **English as an international language** (EIL). It doesn't offer many ideas on how to teach pronunciation—it's more about the content of teaching than methods for teaching. It has a chapter on problems of particular language groups, but few languages are represented. No CD, but there's a companion website with audio files and an answer key. Based on British English pronunciation.

Perspectives on Teaching Connected Speech to Second Language Speakers, James Dean Brown and Kimi Kondo-Brown, University of Hawai'i, National Foreign Language Resource Center, 2006. ISBN #978-0-8248-3136-3. The chapters cover research and methods of teaching and testing connected speech (linking, stress, rhythm, reductions, etc.), especially related to the teaching of English and Japanese. Some chapters are very theoretical, but others offer more practical suggestions.

Teaching the Pronunciation of English as a Lingua Franca, Robin Walker, Oxford University Press, 2010. ISBN #978-0-19-442200-0. This book takes a different approach than the others. It suggests that since English has become an international language, students shouldn't be expected to imitate any one national variety of English as their target (standard American English, standard British English, etc.) Instead, the author suggests a "lingua franca core" of pronunciation features that are most necessary in producing speech that is said to be intelligible to the widest range of native and nonnative speakers of English, and not worrying much about the rest. It's an interesting approach, though it may not be easily accepted by most teachers, Boards of Education, parents, and others. Not based on either American or British English pronunciation, of course.

Pronunciation Contrasts in English, Second Edition, Don L. F. Nilsen and Aileen Pace Nilsen, Waveland Press, 2010. The purpose of this book is very narrow and specific, but if you're looking for minimal pairs, this is a fantastic resource. The authors have collected lists of minimal pairs for every imaginable sound contrast in English. This is a big time-saver if you're making practice activities that require minimal pairs.

Books of Activities for Teaching Pronunciation

These are books of activity and game ideas for teachers, not textbooks that would be used directly by students. They're in alphabetical order by title.

New Ways in Teaching Connected Speech, James Dean Brown, editor, TESOL Press, 2012. Lots of suggestions for teaching linking, assimilation, and other aspects of connected speech.

New Ways in Teaching Speaking, Kathleen M. Bailey and Lance Savage, editors, TESOL, 1994. It has a chapter about pronunciation practice activities.

Primary Pronunciation Box, Caroline Nixon and Michael Tomlinson, Cambridge University Press, 2005. Aimed at younger learners. Comes with a CD. Based on British English pronunciation.

Pronunciation Games, Mark Hancock, Cambridge University Press, 1995. Lots of games with pages that can be copied, mainly at a beginning to intermediate level. Based on British English pronunciation.

Pronunciation Practice Activities, Martin Hewings, Cambridge University Press, 2004. Comes with a CD of exercises. Based on British English pronunciation.

Books about Phonetics and Phonology

These are more theoretical books about phonology in general and the sounds of many languages in addition to English (alphabetical by title).

Applied English Phonology, 2nd Ed., Mehmet Yavaş, Wiley-Blackwell, 2011. Based mainly on American English.

A Course in Phonetics (5th ed.), Peter Ladefoged, Thomson Wadsworth, 2006. Discusses both American and British English.

English Phonetics and Phonology: *A Practical Course* (3rd ed.), Peter Roach, Cambridge University Press, 2000. Based mainly on British English.

Vowels and Consonants (2nd ed.), Peter Ladefoged, Blackwell Publishing, 2005. Discusses both American and British English.

Other Books and Articles of Interest

Bear, D. R., Invernizzi, M., Templeton, S., & Johnston, F. (2011). *Words their way: Word study for phonics, vocabulary, and spelling instruction.* Boston, MA: Pearson.

Beck, I. (2006). *Making sense of phonics.* New York, NY: Guilford Press.

Braine, G. (2010). *Nonnative speaker English teachers: Research, pedagogy, and professional growth.* New York, NY: Routledge.

Brown, G. (1990). *Listening to spoken English* (2nd ed.). London, UK: Longman.

Celce-Murcia, M. (1987). Teaching pronunciation as communication. In J. Morley (Ed.), *Current perspectives on pronunciation* (pp. 5–12). Washington, DC: TESOL.

Chela-Flores, B., & Chela-Flores, G. (2001). *Fundamentals in teaching pronunciation: The rhythm and intonation of English.* McHenry, IL: Delta.

Cunningham, P. M. (1995). *Phonics they use: Words for reading and writing.* New York, NY: HarperCollins College.

Dalton, C., & Seidlhofer, B. (1994). *Pronunciation.* Oxford, UK: Oxford University Press.

De Oliveira, L. C. (2011). Strategies for nonnative-English-speaking teachers' continued development as professionals. *TESOL Journal 2*(2), 229–238.

Derwing, T. M. (2010). Utopian goals for pronunciation teaching. In J. Levis & K. LeVelle (Eds.), *Proceedings of the 1st Pronunciation in Second Language Learning and Teaching Conference,* Iowa State University, Sept. 2009 (pp. 24–37). Ames, IA: Iowa State University.

Gilbert, J. (1978, Winter). Gadgets: Some non-verbal tools for teaching pronunciation. *TESL Reporter* (pp. 6–13).

Grant, L. (Ed.). (2014). *Pronunciation myths: Applying second language research to classroom teaching.* Ann Arbor, MI: University of Michigan Press.

Heilman, A. W. (2002). *Phonics in proper perspective.* Upper Saddle River, NJ: Merrill Prentice Hall.

Internet Links

This is not intended to be an exhaustive list—just a few useful websites.

Color Vowel Chart. Developed by Karen Taylor and Shirley Thompson, this website explains a way to use colors to represent the vowel sounds of English. http://clts.solutions/color-vowel-chart/

English Central. A very useful website with a collection of short video clips for students to watch and imitate. Users can record their voices and see how their pronunciation compares with the original. A free version is available, and the paid version also has many pronunciation and vocabulary practice lessons. Teachers can use the website's tools to track their students' work. http://englishcentral.com

English Pronunciation Lessons with Jennifer ESL. A series of videos on YouTube to help students improve their pronunciation. http://www.youtube.com/watch?v=yTPfN_Q1G-I&list =PL81BCA0A2CB139CB7

Phonetics Flash Animation Project of the University of Iowa. Includes videos and animated sagittal section diagrams for each of the phonemes of American English, German, and Spanish: http:// www.uiowa.edu/~acadtech/phonetics/

Praat: Doing Phonetics by Computer. Download free software to record and analyze speech (for Mac and Windows). http://www.fon.hum.uva.nl/praat/

The Pronunciation Doctor. A series of humorous videos on YouTube about pronunciation, made by Marsha Chan. Aimed more at students than teachers. http://www.youtube.com/user /PronunciationDoctor

Rachel's English: Another series of videos about sounds and other aspects of pronunciation to help students. http://rachelsenglish.com/

Speech Analyzer by SIL International. Download free software to record and analyze speech (Windows only). http://www-01.sil.org/computing/sa/index.htm

Using Your Hands to Teach Pronunciation, a teacher training video by Marsha Chan from Sunburst Media. See a short demo video at http://www.sunburstmedia.com/UsgHands-demo.html

Website of recordings to go with Peter Ladefoged's book about phonetics and phonology, *Vowels and Consonants*: http://www.phonetics.ucla.edu/vowels/contents.html

World Atlas of Language Structures Online. An extensive database of information about sounds, words, and grammar of the world's languages. http://wals.info/

A Few Useful Apps

Sounds of Speech: The app version of the University of Iowa's Phonetics Flash Animation Project. Available for Android, iPhone, and iPad.

Sounds Right: An app made by the British Council. When you touch a phonemic symbol in a chart, you can hear the sound and a few words that start with it. British English. Available for iPad.

Sounds: The Pronunciation App: An app made by Macmillan Publishers. Similar to Sounds Right, with the addition of practice quizzes. It has settings for both British and American English. Available for iPad, iPhone, and Android devices.

The Phonetics: An app by Fuminori Homma at the Tokyo University of Foreign Studies. Users can see animated sagittal section diagrams of the pronunciation of English sounds and hear example words at normal or slow speeds, in male or female voices. American English. Available for iPhone and iPad.

Sources of Pronunciation Teaching Tools

Dental models

The most reliable source at a reasonable price is Lakeshore Learning: http://lakeshorelearning.com. You can also search on http://www.amazon.com or other shopping sites, but the available products and prices change often. Dental models are also available from websites that sell supplies to dentists, but these are usually much more expensive. Be sure to get a model that has an open space at the back so you can reach through to use your hand as a "tongue."

Listening tubes

Hear Myself Sound Phone: http://www.lakeshorelearning.com/ (search for "Hear Myself Sound Phone")

Whispy Reader: http://www.imaginativelearningtools.com/shop/customer/home.php

Toobaloo: http://www.toobaloo.com/

Webber Phone: http://www.superduperinc.com/WXYZ_pages/wf22_44.html

Elephone: http://www.superduperinc.com/products/view.aspx?pid=ELE350

WhisperPhone/WhisperPhone Element: http://www.whisperphone.com/

Phonics Phone: http://www.crystalspringsbooks.com/phonics-phone-mo.html

Sources of Video Clips

Here are some Internet sources of video clips to use in practicing pronunciation. Not all clips in these sites are appropriate for pronunciation practice; choose carefully to fit your needs.

English Central: http://www.englishcentral.com

Teacher Tube: http://www.teachertube.com/

School Tube: http://www.schooltube.com/

YouTube: http://www.youtube.com/

YouTube Teachers: http://www.youtube.com/teachers

ESL Video: http://www.eslvideo.com/

Neo K12: http://www.neok12.com/

Learn English Feel Good: http://www.learnenglishfeelgood.com/eslvideo/

Dotsub (Videos with subtitles in many languages): http://dotsub.com/view/

Glossary

accuracy. Correctness in pronunciation; the degree to which someone's pronunciation matches an accepted norm.

affective filter. A negative effect that feelings like nervousness, fear, anger, or boredom can have on learning a language, according to the ideas of linguist Stephen Krashen (Krashen, 2003). We often say that certain activities or methods can "lower the affective filter," in other words, they can make the classroom atmosphere more relaxed and comfortable so that students can learn more effectively.

affricate. A type of sound that is a combination of a stop followed by a **fricative**—an explosion with a slower release. The affricates in English are /tʃ/ and /dʒ/. Affricate is one of the **manners of articulation**.

allophones. Variations of a **phoneme** that are still thought of as being the same sound are called *allophones* of the same phoneme. They're different sounds that function as the same sound. Changing from one allophone to another doesn't change meaning, although it may make a word sound strange.

alphabetic principle. The understanding that written words are composed of letters, and the letters represent the sounds of spoken words.

alphabetic writing system. A system of writing in which each letter in the alphabet represents (or should represent) one sound.

alveolar. A **place of articulation** that describes sounds pronounced with the tip of the tongue touching or almost touching the alveolar ridge.

alveolar flap or tap. A sound made when the tongue taps the **alveolar ridge** very quickly, so that it sounds like a quick /d/. This sound is represented by this symbol: [ɾ]. It's a voiced sound. In American English, this sound is often found as an allophone of /t/ or /d/ between vowels in words like *city, water,* and *ladder.*

alveolar ridge. The rough area in the roof of the mouth, just behind the top teeth. It can also be called the tooth ridge or the gum ridge. Part of the **articulatory system**.

alveopalatal. See **palatal**.

articulation. The way of pronouncing sounds; how we move our tongue, lips, and jaw in pronouncing sounds.

articulators. The parts of the vocal tract that move in various ways to change the size and shape of the open part of the vocal tract and produce all the sounds of a language. They include the lips, teeth, and tongue.

articulatory system. The parts of the body that are used in producing sounds. Includes the **vocal cords, lips, teeth, alveolar ridge, hard palate, soft palate, tongue, jaw,** and **nasal cavity**.

aspiration (noun), aspirated (adjective). The puff of air that is produced with some sounds. In English, **voiceless stops** are aspirated at the beginnings of words.

- Sounds that are pronounced with this puff of air are called *aspirated sounds*.
- Sounds that are pronounced without this puff of air are called **unaspirated sounds**.

assimilation. A sound change in which one sound becomes more similar to a sound that comes before or after it. This makes the words easier to pronounce.

assimilative motivation. See **motivation**.

auditory. See **learning modalities**.

authentic materials. Materials that were created for "real-life" purposes, not for teaching, such as newspapers, magazines, TV or radio programs, movies, advertisements, and poems.

bilabial. A **place of articulation** that describes sounds pronounced with the lips touching or almost touching each other.

borrowed words. Words that have come into one language from another and become a part of the new language. *Spaghetti, bouquet,* and *tsunami* are borrowed words in English.

chant. A set of rhythmic lines that are meant to be repeated over and over, such as *jazz chants,* made popular by Carolyn Graham. A chant might rhyme, or it might not. (A chant is different from a song. A song has a melody, but a chant doesn't.)

choral repetition. Pronunciation practice in which a group of students repeats after a model, all speaking together. The traditional "repeat after me" practice is a form of choral repetition.

citation form of a word. The pronunciation of a word when it is said carefully and usually alone. For example, the citation form of *and* is /ænd/, and the citation form of *to* is /tuw/. In contrast, the **reduced form of a word** is its pronunciation when it is said in normal speech at a normal speed, and it is not being stressed. For example, the reduced form of *and* is /ən/ or /n/, and the reduced form of *to* is /tə/.

clarification or repetition question. A question that is asked to get a speaker to repeat or explain something that was just said. This happens when a listener didn't understand what was said the first time.

closed syllable. A syllable that ends in a consonant sound, like *sun, bat, made,* or the last syllable in *return.*

cloze listening. A practice activity or test in which learners are asked to fill in missing words in a written text. For example, students might listen to a song and try to fill in missing words in written lyrics.

communicative language teaching. An approach to language teaching that emphasizes these principles:

- Students learn a language best through using it, not just by learning about it and memorizing grammar rules and vocabulary.
- In the classroom, students should participate in real communication about their own interests and experiences by using the target language.
- Language learning should be linked to the kinds of communication students will need to do outside the classroom.

- Teachers should use authentic texts and real-life language as much as possible.
- It's all right to take chances and make mistakes. That's how we learn.

complementary distribution. When we don't have a choice of which **allophone** of a **phoneme** to use in a particular situation, we say the two allophones are in complementary distribution. The environment of the sound—the sounds around it—determines which allophone will be used.

compound noun. A combination of two words that together make a new noun, such as *newspaper, motorcycle,* or *post office.* (Sometimes compound nouns are written as one word, and sometimes as two.)

compound verb. A combination of two words that together make a new verb, such as *put on, print out,* or *get on.* Many compound verbs are also called *two-word verbs* or *phrasal verbs.* (Most compound verbs are written as two words.)

connected speech. Changes in pronunciation that happen when words come together and are linked to the words around them.

consonant. A sound in which the airstream meets some obstacles in the mouth on its way up from the lungs. Words like *big, map,* and *see* begin with consonants. Also see **consonant clusters or consonant blends**.

consonant chart. A table that shows all the consonants of a language, categorizing them by **place of articulation**, **manner of articulation**, and **voicing**. A consonant chart for English can be found in Chapter 4, "The Consonants of American English."

consonant clusters or consonant blends. These terms are used to describe both sequences of two or more consonant *sounds* and sequences of two or more consonant *letters*, depending on whether we're talking about pronunciation or phonics. They can refer to:

1. Combinations of two or more consonant *sounds* occurring together, such as the sounds /str/ in *street* or /mp/ in *lamp.*
2. Combinations of consonant *letters* that represent a sequence of sounds, such as the letters *str* in *street* or *mp* in *lamp.*

content words. Words that have lexical meaning rather than grammatical meaning, such as nouns, verbs, adjectives, adverbs, and question words.

continuants. Consonant sounds that continue to come out of the vocal tract without being completely blocked off: **fricatives**, **nasals**, **liquids**, and **glides**. (In other words, all the consonants except **stops** and **affricates** are continuants.)

contractions or blends. Two words that blend together to make a shorter word. Sometimes the two-word combination is written as one word with an apostrophe, such as *isn't, that's,* or *I'm.* In other cases, the combination is not commonly written as one word, such as the pronunciation /wɑtəl/ for *what will* (usually *not* written *what'll*).

contrastive stress. This occurs when prominence is given to two words that are **in contrast** in order to bring attention to the difference between them. For example:

Hamburgers TASTE good, but they're not nuTRItious.

The students in the FRONT of the room were paying attention, but the ones in the BACK were half asleep.

critical period for language acquisition. A theory in linguistics suggests that there is an ideal time for children to learn language lasting up to the age of about 12 to 14. This time is called the *critical period for language acquisition.* Children learn the sounds of language more naturally than adults during this time and can approach native speaker pronunciation if they are surrounded by the language and have many chances to hear and practice its pronunciation.

Cuisenaire rods. Rectangular rods of various lengths and colors. They are often used to teach math to children, but they can also be useful in teaching languages. They're usually made of wood or plastic, and come in lengths from one to ten units long, with each length a different color.

decoding skills. The ability to recognize written words that follow predictable spelling patterns—to "sound out" words by putting together the sounds represented by their letters.

deductive teaching. A teaching approach in which the teacher explains a rule, pattern, or generalization, and then students practice using what they've learned.

Rule → Examples and practice

The opposite approach is called **inductive teaching**.

deletion. A sound change in normal connected speech in which a sound may disappear or not be clearly pronounced in certain contexts. Deletion is also called **omission**, *elision*, or *ellipsis*.

dental or interdental. A **place of articulation** that describes sounds pronounced with the tip of the tongue touching the back or bottom edge of the top teeth.

dental model. A model of the teeth like those used by dentists to teach children how to brush their teeth. This is a very useful tool in showing students the parts of the mouth and the position of the tongue in producing some sounds.

descriptive rules. Language rules that are written to describe how people talk and to make generalizations about how language works. Descriptive rules don't tell us what a language *should* be like; they're a summary of what it *is* like.

diacritics or diacritical marks. Small marks written over or under letters to give more information about the sound. For example, in phonics teaching, straight or curved lines can be written over vowel letters to distinguish the "long" and "short" sounds.

dialect or variety of a language. A form of a language that is associated with a particular place or social group. A dialect can have its own pronunciation, vocabulary, and grammar. When linguists use the term "dialect," it does not necessarily mean an unusual or "lower" way of speaking. A language can have both standard and nonstandard dialects.

digraph. A combination of two letters that together represent one sound. In English, *sh* is a digraph that represents /ʃ/.

diphthong. A vowel sound in which the tongue position changes a lot, so it sounds like two separate vowels combined. In American English, /ay/, /aw/, and /oy/ are diphthongs.

discourse. A connected set of sentences or utterances, such as a conversation, a speech, an essay, or a story. We can use the term *discourse* in talking about either spoken or written language.

drama techniques. Teaching techniques borrowed from acting, such as breathing practice exercises, voice warm-ups, role plays, and skits.

duration. The length of time that a sound lasts.

emphatic stress. When prominence is given to a word to emphasize its importance. For example: *You have to believe me. I DIDN'T forget my homework.*

English as a foreign language (EFL). English is being taught to learners who don't already speak it in a country where English is not commonly spoken.

English as an international language (EIL). English instruction designed for learners who will need to communicate with people from many different backgrounds, both native and nonnative speakers, possibly in many different places.

English as a second language (ESL). English is being taught to people who don't already speak it in a country where English is the most common language.

environment. The sounds that occur around a given phoneme and sometimes affect how it sounds.

feedback. Information and advice given to learners by a teacher or other source about what they're doing right or wrong so that they can improve. Feedback can be either spoken or written.

flap. See **alveolar flap**.

fluency. The ability to produce language and pronounce sounds smoothly and easily, even if it might not always be accurate.

focus. See **prominence**.

fossilization. A process that occurs when a language learner progresses to a certain point but then has a hard time making further progress on a particular point. The learner keeps making the same mistake again and again. The mistakes seem frozen in time, like a fossil of an ancient animal.

free variation. When we have a free choice of which **allophone** of a **phoneme** to use in a particular situation, we say the two allophones are in free variation. It's fine to use either allophone.

fricative. Sounds in which the airstream is compressed and passes through a small opening in the mouth, creating friction—a hissing sound. The airstream is never completely blocked, so the sound can continue. The fricatives in English are /f/, /v/, /θ/, /ð/, /s/, /z/, / ʃ/, / ʒ/, and /h/. *Fricative* is one of the **manners of articulation**.

function words. Words that have grammatical meaning rather than lexical meaning, such as prepositions, articles, pronouns, and conjunctions. They don't have much meaning in themselves; instead, they show the relationship between other words.

glide. A sound that is like a **vowel**, but shorter. The glides in English are /y/ and /w/. They can be used as consonants, as in *yes* /yɛs/, *beyond* /biyɑnd/, *well* /wɛl/, or *away* /əwey/; or as the last part of a glided vowel or a diphthong, as in *see* /siy/, *say* /sey/, *by* /bay/, *boy* /boy/, *too* /tuw/, *toe* /tow/, or *cow* /caw/. Glides are also called semivowels, or "half-vowels." *Glide* is one of the **manners of articulation**.

glided vowel. A category of vowel sounds in which the tongue position changes just a little during the vowel. The glided vowels in American English are /ey/, /iy/, /uw/, and /ow/.

glottal. A **place of articulation** that describes a sound produced with friction in the **glottis** (the space between the vocal cords). The only **phoneme** in this group in English is /h/. (The **glottal stop** is also pronounced in this area, but it's not a separate phoneme in English.)

glottal stop. A sound produced by closing the **vocal cords** tightly and releasing them quickly, like the beginning of a small cough or the middle sound when we say "huh-uh" to mean "no." It's represented by this symbol: [ʔ].

glottis. The opening between the **vocal cords**.

grammar. The system of how words are put together into sentences to express meaning. The word *grammar* also refers to a set of rules that are written to describe how language works.

grammatical meaning. A word that has grammatical meaning can show the grammatical relationship between other words in a sentence. It doesn't have a lot of meaning in itself.

grapheme. A written symbol that represents a sound. In English, the letters of the alphabet are graphemes.

hard palate. The hard part of the top of the mouth, beginning just behind the **alveolar ridge**. It can also be called the **roof of the mouth**.

heart, peak, or nucleus of a syllable. The central part of a **syllable**. It's usually a vowel, but it could also be a syllabic consonant. For example, in the one-syllable word *cat,* the heart of the syllable is the vowel /æ/. In the second syllable of the word *button,* the heart can be a syllabic consonant /n̩/.

homonyms or homophones. Words that sound alike but are spelled differently, such as *meet* and *meat* or *write, right,* and *rite.*

hypercorrection. An error that happens when someone is being very careful to avoid a different error, or when they make a false analogy with a correct form. For example, if someone usually has trouble pronouncing /v/ and says /b/ instead, they might try so hard to say /v/ that sometimes they say /v/ even when /b/ is correct. (They might say /voy/ for *boy.*)

in contrast (two sounds are in contrast). Sounds that are heard by native speakers to be separate sounds are said to be *in contrast.* They are separate phonemes. For example, /b/ and /v/ are in contrast in English. They are considered to be separate sounds. In Spanish, /b/ and /v/ are not in contrast. Changing from one to the other does not make a different word in Spanish, but it does in English.

individual repetition. Pronunciation practice in which individual students repeat after a model (the teacher or a recording), one at a time.

inductive teaching. A teaching approach in which the teacher presents many examples of a rule, pattern, or generalization and leads students to figure out the pattern.

Examples → Rules

The opposite approach is called **deductive teaching**.

inflections. Forms of words that change to show a grammatical category, such as tense or number. In English, these are inflectional suffixes, or endings that have some grammatical meaning (as in *want/wanted, cat/cats, eat/eating,* or *hot/hotter*).

information questions. See **WH-questions**.

instrumental motivation. See **motivation**.

integrative motivation. See **motivation**.

intelligibility or comprehensibility. Both of these terms describe whether it is easy for listeners to understand what a speaker is saying. They both imply that the speaker's accent does not distract or cause problems for listeners. (We ask, "Can people understand this person?")

interdental. See **dental**.

interference. See **language transfer**.

International Phonetic Alphabet (IPA). A system of symbols developed in the late 1800s to represent all the sounds that are used in human languages. Variations of IPA are used in many dictionaries and textbooks, although most of them are not exactly like "real" IPA.

intonation. The **pitch** pattern of a sentence—the up-and-down "melody" of your voice as you speak.

intonation unit. A group of spoken words that has its own **intonation** contour. Because these usually also form a grammatical and semantic unit, such as a sentence, a clause, or a phrase, and usually express a small unit of thought, they are also called **thought groups**.

invisible /y/. When the letters *u, ue, eu, ew,* or *ui* represent the sound sequence /yuw/, as in *cube* or *music,* we say there's an invisible /y/. We hear the sound /y/, even though there's no separate letter that represents it.

kinesthetic learning modality. See **learning modalities**.

L1 (first language). The learner's first language or native language; the language that the learner feels most comfortable speaking.

L2 (second language). The learner's second language; the foreign language that is being learned.

labiodental. A **place of articulation** that describes a sound in which the upper teeth touch the lower lip. The sounds in this group in English are /f/ and /v/.

language transfer. The influence of the learner's native language on the way a new language is learned. The influence of the system of L1 affects the way the learner speaks L2. Also called **interference** or **native language interference**.

lateral. A description of a sound that is produced with the sides of the tongue open, such as /l/.

learning modalities. Different ways that people learn and understand new information:

auditory: Learning through hearing.

visual: Learning through seeing.

tactile: Learning through touching.

kinesthetic: Learning through doing—through body movements and manipulating objects and tools.

lexical meaning. A word with lexical meaning has meaning in itself. It refers to objects, actions, or ideas in the real world rather than showing grammatical relationships between other words in the sentence.

lingua franca core. Those aspects of pronunciation that are most necessary in producing speech that is intelligible to the widest range of native and nonnative speakers of English; the features that research has shown help most in increasing intelligibility when nonnative speakers communicate with each other.

linguistics, **linguists**. Linguistics is the systematic study of language and how it works. Linguists are people who study linguistics. (They're not necessarily people who speak a lot of languages. Those are *polyglots*.)

linking. In normal speech, the last sound of one word is often linked or blended with the first sound of the next word so that the two words sound like one unit.

lip rounding. A description of whether the lips are rounded, relaxed, or stretched a bit wide when a sound is pronounced.

liquid. A sound that is pronounced very smoothly, like water flowing in a river. The airstream moves around the tongue in a relatively unobstructed manner. The liquid sounds in English are /l/ and /r/. Liquid is one of the **manners of articulation**.

logographic or ideographic writing system. A writing system in which symbols represent whole words or parts of words, without referring to sound.

long vowels and short vowels (in phonics). In phonics, each vowel letter is said to represent two main sounds, a "long" sound and a "short" sound. In English these sounds are

long A	/ey/	short A	/æ/
long E	/iy/	short E	/ɛ/
long I	/ay/	short I	/ɪ/
long O	/ow/	short O	/ɑ/
long U	/yuw/ or /uw/	short U	/ʌ/ or /ə/

lungs. Two bag-like organs in the chest that allow us to breathe and talk. When we talk, we pull air into our lungs and then push it back out through the **vocal tract**.

main stress or primary stress. One syllable in every **polysyllabic word** is pronounced with more emphasis than the others. This syllable has the main stress or primary stress. It can be longer, higher, louder, and clearer than the other syllables. For example, the word *con•gra•tu•'la•tions* has five syllables, with the primary stress on the fourth syllable.

manner of articulation. A description of how we produce a particular consonant sound:

stop (or plosive). The airstream is blocked completely before it is released, like a tiny explosion.

fricative. The airstream is compressed and passes through a small opening, creating friction—a hissing sound.

affricate. A stop followed by a fricative—an explosion with a slower release.

nasal. The air passes through the nose instead of the mouth.

liquid. The airstream moves around or over the tongue in a relatively unobstructed manner.

glide or semivowel. The sound is like a very quick vowel.

merging. This term is used in two ways:

1. When a learner can't hear or pronounce the difference between two similar sounds in a new language, he or she may pronounce both sounds in the same way, so that both of them sound like the same familiar sound in his or her first language.
2. When a language originally has two separate sounds, but native speakers of the language gradually start pronouncing the two sounds in the same way, the difference between them can be lost. For example, the /w/ and /hw/ sounds in English have merged for most speakers, and only /w/ is left.

minimal pair. Two words that differ by just one sound, for example, *late* and *rate, beat* and *bit, sat* and *sap*.

mirroring or shadowing. Pronunciation practice techniques in which students mimic a video or audio recording, trying to speak in exactly the same way as the actors. In shadowing, students imitate only the words of the recording. In mirroring, they also imitate the gestures and facial expressions of the recording.

modal. An auxiliary verb that expresses ideas like necessity, ability, or possibility. The modal verbs in English include *can, could, will, would, may, might, shall, should,* and *must.*

morphemes. Words or parts of words that have their own unit of meaning. In English, these parts are *prefixes, suffixes,* and *word roots.*

motivation. A desire or willingness to do something, such as to change the way one uses language. These are three types of motivation in language learning:

> **integrative motivation**. The learner wants to be accepted into a group that uses the language. The group might still recognize the learner as an outsider, but he or she can function well in the group.

> **assimilative motivation**. The learner wants to be accepted as a real member of a group that uses the language—to fit in and not be thought of as an "outsider."

> **instrumental motivation**. The learner wants to be able to use the language to reach a goal: to get a job, to conduct business, to pass a test, or to travel easily in a foreign country.

muscle memory. An increased ability to do a particular physical activity more easily after practicing many times. The muscles "remember" how to do something because they've done it so often.

nasal. A sound in which the tongue or lips block off the vocal tract so air can't go out through the mouth. Instead, the passage leading up into the nose opens so that the airstream can go out through the nose. The English sounds in the nasal group are /m/, /n/, and /ŋ/.

nasal cavity or nasal passage. The space inside the nose where air passes in and out when we breathe through our nose. Part of the **articulatory system**.

native language interference. See **interference**.

new information. Information, facts, or opinions that the speaker assumes the listener doesn't know and wants to tell the listener for the first time.

obstruent. A sound that is made with some obstruction in the mouth. Stops, fricatives, and affricates are all types of obstruents. Sounds that are not obstruents are called **sonorants**.

old information. Something that has already been mentioned in the conversation, or something that the speaker assumes the listener knows about already.

omission. A sound change in normal **connected speech** in which a sound may disappear or not be clearly pronounced in certain contexts. Omission is also called *deletion, elision,* or *ellipsis.*

onset. In a written word, the beginning letter or letters that come before the vowel. In the word *cat,* the onset is *c.* In the word *street,* the onset is *str.* A word that begins with a vowel has no onset. See also **rime**.

open syllable. A syllable that ends in a vowel sound, like *go, see, eye, through,* or the last syllable in *party.*

palatal or alveopalatal. A **place of articulation** that describes sounds in which the blade of the tongue touches or almost touches the hard palate. The sounds in this group in English are /ʃ/, /ʒ/, /ʧ/, /ʤ/, /r/, and /y/.

palatalization. A type of **assimilation** in which an **alveolar** sound (/t/, /d/, /s/, or /z/) becomes a **palatal** sound (/ʃ/, / ʒ/, /ʧ/, or /ʤ/) when /y/ comes after it. Here are the combinations of sounds that can cause this change:

/t/+/y/ → /ʧ/ Is tha**t y**our dog?
/d/+/y/ → /ʤ/ It ma**de y**ou angry.
/s/+/y/ → /ʃ/ I'll mi**ss y**ou.
/z/+/y/ → /ʒ/ I**s y**our brother here?

part of speech. A grammatical category that describes words based on their form and function. In English, there are nouns, verbs, adjectives, adverbs, pronouns, prepositions, conjunctions, articles, and interjections.

phonemes. The distinctive sounds of a language—the sounds that native speakers of the language consider to be separate sounds. Changing from one phoneme to another changes the meaning of a word, or sometimes it makes a word meaningless.

phonemic alphabet. A set of symbols representing the **phonemes** (sounds) of a language, with one symbol representing exactly one phoneme. A phonemic alphabet is different from the ordinary spelling system. Many textbooks and dictionaries use phonemic alphabets to represent the pronunciation of words.

phonemic awareness. The understanding that words are made up of individual sounds that can be separated, counted and rearranged.

phonetic alphabet. A set of symbols, such as the *International Phonetic Alphabet,* that is intended to represent all the possible sounds of human languages, not just the sounds of one language. A full phonetic alphabet would be too complex to use in language textbooks and dictionaries.

phonics. The study of the systematic relationship between written letters and spoken sounds. Also, a way of teaching people to read that emphasizes the systematic relationship between written letters and spoken sounds of the language.

phonological filter. The way our brains let us hear the sounds of our own language very efficiently, but ignore or "filter out" unfamiliar, unnecessary sounds.

phonological processes. Sound changes that happen naturally to make combinations of sounds easier to pronounce. The following are the most common phonological processes in English:

> **linking.** A sound change in which the last sound of one word is linked or blended with the first sound of the next word so that the two words sound like one unit.

> **assimilation.** A sound change in which one sound becomes more similar to a sound that comes before or after it.

> **deletion.** A sound change in which a sound disappears or is not clearly pronounced in certain contexts.

phonology, phonologist. The study of speech sounds in language—the sounds themselves, how they are produced, and how they work together as a system in a particular language. A person who studies phonology is called a *phonologist.*

phrasal verb or two-word verb. A verb with two or more parts that work together to form a compound verb, such as *put on, get up, turn off,* and *take over.*

pitch. A measure of how high or low the voice is at a particular point in time. (This means high or low in the sense that a musical note is high or low; it doesn't mean high or low volume or loudness.)

pitch accent. In some languages, such as Japanese, a **polysyllabic** word may have one syllable that is higher in **pitch** than the rest, and this can change the meaning of the word. This syllable does not become louder, longer, or more emphasized than the others, as in English word stress. Only the pitch changes.

place of articulation. A description of which parts of the vocal apparatus are working when we produce a particular consonant sound.

> **bilabial.** Both lips touch or almost touch.

> **labiodental.** The upper teeth touch the lower lip.

> **dental or interdental.** The tip of the tongue touches the top teeth or between the teeth.

> **alveolar.** The tip of the tongue touches or almost touches the alveolar ridge (tooth ridge).

> **palatal or alveopalatal.** The body of the tongue touches or almost touches the hard palate.

velar. The back of the tongue touches the soft palate.

glottal. There is friction in the **glottis** (the space between the vocal cords).

plosive. See **stop**.

polysyllabic word. A word with more than one syllable, like *paper* or *dictionary*. (Words with one syllable are called *monosyllabic words*.)

popcorn reading. See **round robin reading**.

prefix. A word part that is placed before a word root to change its meaning, as in *happy/unhappy* or *port/transport*.

prescriptive rules. Rules that are written to try to tell people how they should talk or how language should work. These rules are not always based on a clear understanding of language and how it got to be the way it is.

primary stress. See **main stress**.

proclaiming tone. A pitch pattern used to mark new information in a thought group. New information, which most often comes near the end of a thought group, has a "bump up" in pitch on the prominent syllable, followed by falling intonation. Some authors refer to this pitch pattern as a *proclaiming tone;* the speaker is proclaiming, or announcing some new and important information.

prominence or prominent word. The word or syllable in each thought group that receives more stress than the others is called the *prominent word*, the *focus*, or the word with *sentence stress*. It is often the stressed syllable of the last content word in the sentence or thought group. It can also be the stressed syllable of a word that is being emphasized or contrasted with another word.

received pronunciation (RP). The standard form of British English pronunciation, based on educated speech in southern England. It is also called *the Queen's English, the King's English,* or *BBC English.* (Actually, relatively few people in the UK speak real RP.)

reduced form of a word. The pronunciation of a word when it is said in normal speech at a normal speed, and it is not being stressed. For example, the reduced form of *and* is /ən/ or /n̩/, and the reduced form of *to* is /tə/. In contrast, the pronunciation of a word when it is said carefully, and usually alone, is called its **citation form**. For example, the citation form of *to* is /tuw/, and the citation form of *and* is /ænd/.

reduced syllable. Vowels in unstressed syllables can become weaker, quicker, and less clear. They often (but not always) become /ə/ (schwa). These weaker syllables are called *reduced syllables.*

referring tone. A **pitch pattern** used to mark a **thought group** that gives **old information**. Thought groups that give old, shared information are often spoken with rising **intonation** or with a partial fall. The speaker isn't telling something new; he or she is simply referring to something that is already known.

resyllabification. A way of making consonant clusters easier to pronounce by splitting up a consonant cluster so that the last consonant is pronounced with the syllable after it.

retroflex. A description of a sound that is made with the tongue curled slightly backward, as in some pronunciations of /r/.

rhythm. The characteristic pattern of **stressed** and **unstressed syllables** when people speak a language, made up of syllables that are longer or shorter, faster or slower, and more or less emphasized.

rime. In a written word, the vowel and any consonants that come after it. In the word *cat,* the rime is *at*. In the word *street,* the rime is *eet*. If a word begins with a vowel, it has only a rime. See also **onset**.

round robin reading. A teaching technique in which the teacher calls on students, in seating order or at random, to take turns reading aloud from a textbook. Sometimes each student reads a sentence, or sometimes a paragraph. Also called **popcorn reading**.

sagittal section diagram. A picture of a cross-section of the vocal tract showing the positions of the tongue, teeth, and lips in pronouncing sounds, sometimes called a *Sammy diagram*.

schwa. A mid-central, lax **vowel** represented by the symbol /ə/. In English, the vowel sounds in many **unstressed syllables** change to /ə/.

secondary stress. In words of four or more syllables, there is often a syllable that receives a little stress, but not as much as the **primary-stress** syllable. We say this syllable has *secondary stress.* For example, the word *con•gra•tu•'la•tions* has five syllables, with the primary stress on the fourth syllable and secondary stress on the second syllable.

segmental features of pronunciation. The individual sounds (phonemes) of a language—the **vowels** and **consonants**.

segmentation. Breaking up a stream of sounds so that we can understand the words that are being said. For example, when we hear /ə'tæks/, we might interpret it as *attacks* or *a tax,* depending on the context.

semivowels. See **glides**.

sentence stress. See **prominence**.

shadowing. See **mirroring**.

short vowels. See **long vowels and short vowels**.

sibilant. A type of **fricative** or **affricate** produced with the tongue near the **alveolar ridge** or **hard palate**: /s/, /z/, /ʃ/, /ʒ/, /tʃ/, and /dʒ/ are the sibilants in English. This group of sounds may seem louder and harsher than other fricatives like /θ/ or /f/.

sight words. Words with spellings that do not follow predictable patterns and therefore have to be memorized individually, like *eye, eight,* or *would.*

silent letter. A letter that appears in the spelling of a word but does not represent a sound, such as *k* and *e* in the word *knife* or *gh* in the word *night.*

simple vowels. A category of vowel sounds in which the tongue stays in one position throughout the vowel.

soft palate. The softer part of the roof of the mouth, farther back than the hard palate. It is also called the *velum.* Part of the **articulatory system**.

sonorant. A sound that comes out of the mouth smoothly, with no obstruction or friction. **Nasals, liquids, glides,** and vowels are all kinds of sonorants. Sounds that are not sonorants are called **obstruents.**

standard American English or North American English. The standard form of English spoken in the United States and Canada. (There are slight differences between standard U.S. and Canadian English, but overall they are very similar.) It is often called simply *American English,* although in reality many varieties of English are spoken in North America.

stop. A sound in which the airstream is blocked completely somewhere in the mouth, air pressure builds up behind it, and then it's released, like a tiny explosion. There are six stop sounds in English: /p/, /t/, /k/, /b/, /d/, and /g/. Stops are sometimes called *plosives.*

stressed syllable. One syllable in a word that is emphasized more than the others. It can be longer, louder, and higher in pitch than the others and have a clearer vowel sound. In English, the syllables of a word may have one of three degrees of stress: strongly stressed (**primary stress**), lightly stressed (**secondary stress**), **unstressed** (tertiary stress).

stress-timed language. A language in which the time between **stressed syllables** remains fairly steady, and the **unstressed syllables** are shorter and crowd in between them. English is considered to be a stress-timed language. Stress-timed languages are sometimes called *stress-based languages.*

substitution. When a learner can't pronounce an unfamiliar sound in a new language, he or she may substitute a similar sound from his or her first language. This sometimes leads to misunderstanding by listeners.

suffix. A word part that is placed after a **word root** to change its meaning or grammatical category, as in *open/opened* or *nation/national.*

suprasegmental features of pronunciation. Aspects of pronunciation that affect more than just one sound segment, such as **stress, rhythm, linking,** and **intonation**—the musical aspects of pronunciation.

syllabic consonant. A consonant that is lengthened so that it becomes a whole syllable, even without a vowel. The consonants /n/, /l/, and /r/ can sometimes be a full syllable by themselves. This most often happens after a stressed syllable that ends in an **alveolar** consonant.

syllabic writing system. A writing system in which each symbol represents a whole syllable, either a vowel alone or a vowel plus one or more consonants. The symbols can't be separated into parts representing individual sounds.

syllable. A rhythmic unit in speech—a unit of sound that gets one "beat" in a word. A syllable must have a vowel (or a syllabic consonant). It might also have one or more consonants before the vowel and one or more consonants after it. For example, the word *banana* has three syllables: *ba•na•na.* The word *strong* has one syllable: *strong.*

syllable-timed language. A language that gives each syllable about the same amount of time. Japanese, Korean, Chinese, French, and Spanish are considered to be syllable-timed languages. Syllable-timed languages are sometimes called *syllable-based languages.*

tactile. See **learning modalities**.

tag question. A question that begins with a statement followed by a short question part at the end, like these: *Our test is today, isn't it? You called me, didn't you?*

tapped /t/ or flapped /t/. A sound made when the tongue taps the **alveolar ridge** very quickly, so that it sounds like a quick /d/. This is called an **alveolar flap or tap**, and it is represented by this symbol: [ɾ]. It's a **voiced** sound.

teaching English as a foreign language (TEFL). Teaching English or training teachers to teach English in areas where English is not the primary language. It's similar to **teaching English as a second language (TESL),** except that TESL concentrates on teaching in areas where English is the primary language in the community.

tense and lax vowels. A description of whether the muscles of the tongue and mouth are relatively tense or more relaxed when we say a vowel sound. It distinguishes pairs of vowels like /iy/ (tense) and /ɪ/ (lax) or /uw/ (tense) and /ʊ/ (lax). Although this is not an entirely accurate physical description, it can be a useful way of thinking about these sounds.

thought group. A group of spoken words that form a grammatical and semantic unit. It is often a sentence, a clause, or a phrase—a chunk of language that feels like a logical unit. Because each thought group has its own intonation contour, a thought group can also be called an **intonation unit**.

tongue position. A description of where the highest, tensest, or most active part of the tongue is when we pronounce a vowel sound. Description includes *vertical position* (high, mid, or low) and *horizontal position* (front, central, or back).

transliterate. To change words from one writing system to another by substituting the closest possible symbols in the other language. For example, the name of the country of Japan is written "日本" in Japanese, and transliterated as "nihon" or "nippon" in English.

trigraphs. Combinations of three letters that together spell one sound, such as *tch*, which represents /ʧ/ in words like *match*, or *igh*, which represents /ay/ in words like *high*.

trill. A consonant sound that is produced with rapid vibration of the tongue against some part of the mouth, often the **alveolar ridge**. In some languages, a sound represented by the letter *r* is an alveolar trill.

two-word verb, three-word verb, phrasal verb. A verb with two or more parts that work together to form a compound verb, such as *put on, get up, turn off, take over,* or *put up with.*

unaspirated. Pronounced without an extra puff of air. In English, **voiceless stops** are unaspirated when they come after /s/ at the beginnings of words (e.g. *store*)

unreleased stop. When we start to say a **stop** by blocking off the flow of air in our mouth, but we don't release the air, it's called an *unreleased stop*. Stops are often pronounced this way at the ends of words in English.

unstressed syllable. A syllable in a **polysyllabic word** that does not receive stress. In English, vowels in unstressed syllables become weaker, quicker, and less clear than vowels in stressed syllables. For example, in the word *'elephant,* the first syllable is stressed, and the last two syllables are unstressed.

variable word stress. In some cases, the position of stress in a word can change if this maintains a more comfortable overall rhythm. Having two stressed syllables together makes an awkward rhythm, so the stress sometimes moves to create an alternation of **stressed** and **unstressed syllables**. For example, when we say a *-teen* number alone, we stress it on the last syllable: *seven'teen*. When we say the same number with a noun after it, we often stress it on the first syllable: *'seventeen 'years*.

velar. A sound pronounced with the back of the tongue touching the **soft palate**. The English sounds in this group are /k/, /g/, and /ŋ/.

velarized. Pronounced with the tongue raised toward the **velum**, or **soft palate**.

velum. The softer part of the roof of the mouth, farther back than the **hard palate**. The velum is also called the **soft palate**.

visual. See **learning modalities**.

vocal cords or vocal folds. Two small membranes in the throat that vibrate together to produce the sound of the voice. Part of the **articulatory system**.

vocal tract. The space in the throat, mouth, and nose where sounds are produced.

voiced sound. A sound that is produced with vibration of the **vocal cords**. In English, some consonants are voiced, and all vowels are voiced.

voiceless sound. A sound that is produced without vibration of the vocal cords. In English, some consonants are voiceless, but no vowels are voiceless.

voicing. A quality of a sound that depends on whether the vocal cords are vibrating when it is pronounced.

vowel. A sound in which the airstream moves out though the vocal tract very smoothly. Words like *apple, east, over,* and *out* begin with vowels.

vowel quadrant. A diagram showing the approximate tongue positions for the vowels of a language. A vowel quadrant for English can be found in Chapter 5, "The Vowels of American English."

WH-question. A question that begins with a question word such as *who, what, where, when, why* or *how,* like these: *What time is it? When will you finish your homework?* Sometimes called an *information question.*

word families. Groups of words that have the same **rime** with the same pronunciation, and therefore are often taught together when children are learning to read.

word root. A part of a word that carries its basic meaning. It might occur alone (as in *dog, care,* or *cover*) or with one or more prefixes or suffixes (as in *dogs, careful, carefully, uncover,* or *discoverer*).

word stress. When a word has more than one **syllable**, one of the syllables is emphasized. It can be longer, louder, clearer, and higher in pitch than the others. In English, the syllables of a word may have one of three degrees of stress: strongly stressed (**primary stress**), lightly stressed (**secondary stress**), **unstressed** (**tertiary stress**).

yes/no question. A question that can be answered by "yes" or "no," like these: *Is today Thursday? Did you do your homework?*

References

Árva, P., & Medgyes, P. (1999). Native and non-native teachers in the classroom. *System, 28*, 355–372.

Avery, P., & Ehrlich, S. (1992). *Teaching American English pronunciation.* Oxford, UK: Oxford University Press.

Brazil, D. (1997). *The communicative value of intonation in English.* Cambridge, UK: Cambridge University Press.

Canagarajah, A. S. (1999). Interrogating the "native speaker fallacy": non-linguistic roots, non-pedagogical results. In G. Braine (Ed.), *Non-Native educators in English language teaching* (pp. 77–92). Mahwah, NJ: Lawrence Erlbaum Associates, Publishers.

Celce-Murcia, M., Brinton, D., & Goodwin, J., with Griner, B. (2010). *Teaching pronunciation: a course book and reference guide* (2nd ed.). New York, NY: Cambridge University Press.

Dryer, Matthew S. & Haspelmath, M. (Eds.) (2013). *The world atlas of language structures online.* Leipzig: Max Planck Institute for Evolutionary Anthropology. Retrieved from http://wals.info.

Gilbert, J. (2008). *Teaching pronunciation using the prosody pyramid.* Cambridge UK: Cambridge University Press.

Goodwin, J. (2001). Teaching pronunciation. In M. Celce-Murcia (Ed.), *Teaching English as a second or foreign language* (3rd ed.), pp. 117–133. Boston, MA: Heinle & Heinle.

Goodwin, J. (2005). The power of context in teaching pronunciation. In J. Frodesen & C. Holten (Eds.), *The power of context in language teaching and learning, pp. 225–233.* Boston, MA: Thomson Heinle.

Graham, C. (2006). *Creating chants and songs.* Oxford, UK: Oxford University Press.

Grant, L. (2010). *Well said* (3rd ed.). Boston, MA: Heinle Cengage Learning.

Hewings, M. (2004). *Pronunciation practice activities.* Cambridge, UK: Cambridge University Press.

Kelly, G. (2000). *How to teach pronunciation.* Harlow, UK: Pearson Longman.

Kenworthy, J. (1987). *Teaching English pronunciation,* London, UK: Longman.

Krashen, S. (2003). *Explorations in language acquisition and use.* Portsmouth, NH: Heinemann.

Ladefoged, P. (2005). *Vowels and consonants* (2nd ed.). Malden, MA: Blackwell Publishing.

Ladefoged, P. (2006). *A course in phonetics* (5th ed.). Boston, MA: Thomson Wadsworth.

Lane, L. (2010). *Tips for teaching pronunciation: a practical approach.* White Plains, NY: Pearson Longman.

Mahboob, A. (2004). Native or nonnative: what do students enrolled in an intensive English program think? In *learning and teaching from experience: perspectives on nonnative English-speaking professionals,* pp. 121–147. L. Kamhi-Stein (Ed.). Ann Arbor, MI: University of Michigan Press.

Medgyes, P. (1992). Native or non-native: who's worth more? *ELT Journal 46*(4), pp. 340–349.

Medgyes, P. (2001). When the teacher is a non-native speaker. In *Teaching English as a second or foreign language* (3rd ed.), pp. 429–442. M. Celce-Murcia (Ed.). Boston, MA: Heinle & Heinle.

Miller, S. (2007). *Targeting pronunciation: communicating clearly in English.* Boston, MA: Thomson Heinle.

Mullock, B. (2010). Does a good language teacher have to be a native speaker? In *The NNEST lens: non-native English speakers in TESOL,* pp. 87–113. Newcastle upon Tyne, UK: Cambridge Scholars Publishing.

Murphy, J. (2013). *Teaching pronunciation.* Alexandria, VA: TESOL.

Murphey, T. (1992). *Music and song.* Oxford, UK: Oxford University Press.

Redpath, P. (2011). Reading aloud allowed? Oxford University Press English Language Teaching Global Blog. Retrieved from http://oupeltglobalblog.com/2011/06/28/reading-aloud-allowed/

Roach, P. (1982). On the distinction between "stress-timed" and "syllable-timed" languages. In D. Crystal (Ed.), *Linguistic controversies,* pp. 73–79, London, UK: Hodder Arnold.

Sander, E. K. (1972). When are speech sounds learned? *Journal of Speech and Hearing Disorders,* Vol. 37, pp. 55–63.

Shockey, L. (2003). *Sound patterns of spoken English.* Malden, MA: Blackwell Publishing.

Swan, M., & Smith, B. (2001). *Learner English.* Cambridge, UK: Cambridge University Press.

Szpyra-Kozłowska, J. (2015). *Pronunciation in EFL instruction: A research-based approach* (2nd ed.). Bristol, UK: Multilingual Matters.

Tatar, S. & Yildiz, S. (2010). Empowering nonnative-English speaking teachers in the classroom. In *The NNEST lens: Non-native English speakers in TESOL,* pp. 114–128. Newcastle upon Tyne, UK: Cambridge Scholars Publishing.

Walker, R. (2010). *Teaching the pronunciation of English as a lingua franca.* Oxford, UK: Oxford University Press.

Wilson, K. (2010). Reading aloud in class is a complete waste of Time—Discuss. Ken Wilson's Blog. Retrieved from http://kenwilsonelt.wordpress.com/2010/10/14/reading-aloud-in-class-is-a-complete-waste-of-time-discuss/